GUANXI: HOW CHINA WORKS

China Today series

GUANXI: HOW CHINA WORKS

Yanjie Bian

polity

The right of Yanjie Bian to be identified as Author of this Work has been asserted in accordance with the UK Copyright, Designs and Patents Act 1988.

First published in 2019 by Polity Press

Polity Press
65 Bridge Street
Cambridge CB2 1UR, UK

Polity Press
101 Station Landing
Suite 300
Medford, MA 02155, USA

ISBN-13: 978-1-5095-0038-3
ISBN-13: 978-1-5095-0039-0 (pb)

A catalogue record for this book is available from the British Library.

Typeset in 11.5 on 15 pt Adobe Jenson Pro by Toppan Best-set Premedia Limited
Printed and bound in Great Britain by CPI Group (UK) Ltd, Croydon

The publisher has used its best endeavours to ensure that the URLs for external websites referred to in this book are correct and active at the time of going to press. However, the publisher has no responsibility for the websites and can make no guarantee that a site will remain live or that the content is or will remain appropriate.

Every effort has been made to trace all copyright holders, but if any have been overlooked the publisher will be pleased to include any necessary credits in any subsequent reprint or edition.

For further information on Polity, visit our website: politybooks.com

To Nan Lin
My Teacher, Doctoral Advisor, and Lifelong Mentor

Contents

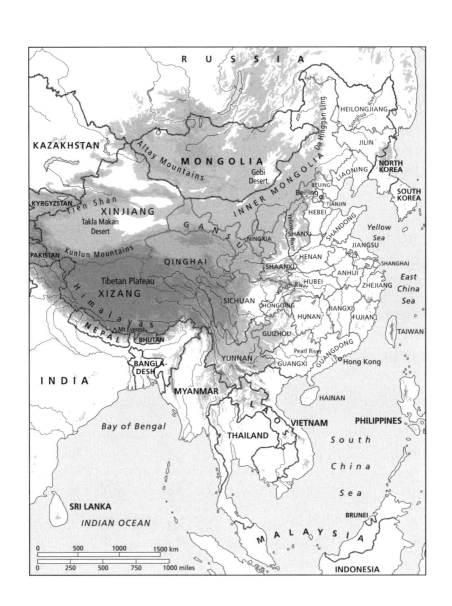

Chronology

1894-5	First Sino-Japanese War
1911	Fall of the Qing dynasty
1912	Republic of China established under Sun Yat-sen
1927	Split between Nationalists (KMT) and Communists (CCP); civil war begins
1934–5	CCP under Mao Zedong evades KMT in Long March
December 1937	Nanjing Massacre
1937–45	Second Sino-Japanese War
1944	Publication of "The Chinese Concepts of 'Face'" by Hsien Chin Hu, with first appearance of notion of *guanxi* in an English-language publication
1945–9	Civil war between KMT and CCP resumes
1947	Publication of 《乡土中国》 (*xiangtu zhongguo*, whose English translation *From the Soil: The Foundations of Chinese Society* was published in 1992) by Fei Xiaotong, with his theory of the mode of differential associations (差序格局, *chaxu geju*), a social network approach to Chinese social structure
1949	Publication of 《中国文化要义》 (*zhongguo wenhua yaoyi*, *The Essential Meanings of Chinese Culture*) by Liang Shuming, theorizing centrality of *guanxi* in Chinese culture and society
October 1949	KMT retreats to Taiwan; Mao founds People's Republic of China (PRC)
1950–3	Korean War
1952	Abolition of sociology as an academic discipline
1953–7	First Five-Year Plan; PRC adopts Soviet-style economic planning

1953	Publication of *Fabric of Chinese Society* by Morton Fried, first social science monograph on observational research of *guanxi* by a social scientist of non-Chinese origin
1954	First constitution of the PRC and first meeting of the National People's Congress
1956–7	Hundred Flowers Movement, a brief period of open political debate
1957	Anti-Rightist Movement
1958–60	Great Leap Forward, an effort to transform China through rapid industrialization and collectivization
March 1959	Tibetan Uprising in Lhasa; Dalai Lama flees to India
1959–61	Three Hard Years, widespread famine with tens of millions of deaths
1960	Sino-Soviet split
1962	Sino-Indian War
October 1964	First PRC atomic bomb detonation
1966–76	Great Proletarian Cultural Revolution; Mao reasserts power
February 1972	President Richard Nixon visits China; "Shanghai Communiqué" pledges to normalize US–China relations
September 1976	Death of Mao Zedong
October 1976	Ultra-leftist Gang of Four arrested and sentenced
December 1978	Deng Xiaoping assumes power; launches Four Modernizations and economic reforms
1978	One-child family planning policy introduced
1979	US and China establish formal diplomatic ties; Deng Xiaoping visits Washington
1979	PRC sends troops to Vietnam
March 1979	Restoration of sociology as an academic discipline; reestablishment of Chinese Sociological Association
February 1981	Nankai University Class of Sociology opened as year-long course in sociology, with Peter Blau, Fei Xiaotong, and Nan Lin, among others, teaching sociology and social network analysis for first time since restoration of sociology in China

1982	Census reports PRC population at more than one billion
December 1984	Margaret Thatcher co-signs Sino-British Joint Declaration agreeing to return Hong Kong to China in 1997
1989	Tiananmen Square protests culminate in June 4 military crackdown
1992	Deng Xiaoping's Southern Inspection Tour reenergizes economic reforms
1993–2002	Jiang Zemin becomes president of PRC; continues economic growth agenda
1999	First wave of Job-Search Networks Survey (JSNET Project) conducted to collect data on *guanxi* and occupational attainment
November 2001	World Trade Organization (WTO) accepts China as member
2002–12	Hu Jintao, General-Secretary CCP (and President of PRC 2003–13)
2002–3	SARS outbreak concentrated in PRC and Hong Kong
2003	Chinese General Social Survey series began
2006	PRC supplants US as largest CO_2 emitter
August 2008	Summer Olympic Games in Beijing
2009	Second wave of JSNET Project conducted
2010	Shanghai World Exposition
2012	Xi Jinping appointed General-Secretary of the CCP (and President of PRC from 2013)
2014–16	Third wave of JSNET Project conducted as a two-year panel study
2015	China abolishes one child policy
2017	Xi Jinping reappointed General-Secretary of the CCP's Central Committee (and President of PRC from 2018)
2018	National People's Congress removes two-term limit on China's Presidency

Preface

This book is about the social logic of how China works. The focus of analysis is on *guanxi*, the Chinese expression of personalized social relations. Personal and social relations are important in every culture and society because people live and work in the contexts of these relations. In Western countries, for example, it is common for people to have close personal relations while keeping social relations at a certain distance. In China, however, social relations may not matter much unless and until they are personalized to become part of a focal individual's *guanxi* network. You get a good job through your *guanxi* contacts. You start a new business with the money borrowed from and the business contract extended by your *guanxi* contacts. You manage an organization and sustain it through your *guanxi* networks of diverse ties. You are both ambitious and competent, and you are a big achiever in the job you do. But you may not get promoted to positions of higher rank or elected into prestigious societies of national honor without mobilizing your *guanxi* ties to help. Even filing a lawsuit or doing a legal job cannot be free of the underlying social logic of *guanxi* favoritism.

This book has grown out of my long interest in *guanxi* scholarship. Growing up in China, I lived in a *guanxi* culture. But this does not mean I automatically understood the nature of *guanxi* favoritism, or that I could uncover the internal and external logics of prevalent *guanxi* influence without adequate academic training. This training started with my reading of Fei Xiaotong's pre-1949 works when I was a college student in China in 1978–81. I gained a more systematic training in social network analysis (SNA) when I engaged in doctoral and post-doctoral research in the United States from 1985 to 1991. A SNA seminar with Nan Lin in my second year of doctoral study enlightened me, planting the scholarly seed of my research interest in *guanxi* as social exchange networks. Nan's teaching, his one-on-one coaching, his supervising of my dissertation, and his continuous mentoring during my postdoctoral career have been instrumental to my growth from a young student to a learned scholar about *guanxi* and social networks. This book is dedicated to Nan, my lifelong mentor.

A few other great scholars have each made a unique impact on my *guanxi* research. At Nankai University in 1981, Fei Xiaotong taught me and my classmates in a sociology class that marked the restoration of sociology to the Chinese college curriculum after its elimination in 1952. Fei's theory of the "mode of differential associations" gave me my first ever view of the centrality of *guanxi* in Chinese social structure. Andrew Walder, a senior colleague of mine when we both taught at the Hong Kong University of Science and Technology during 1997–2001, showed me how to study China in sociological perspective; his concept of "instrumental particular ties" uncovered the theoretical nature of *guanxi* practices in Mao's and the post-Mao era. The works of Mayfair Yang and Yunxiang Yan, two influential social anthropologists on *guanxi* scholarship, have directed my attention to both the complex cultural meanings of *guanxi* and the resilience of *guanxi* norms in China under reform; I benefited from their comments on my work, and I enjoyed our personal conversations as well as scholarly exchanges at and outside of academic conferences. Finally, Ron Burt, a SNA authority, and Nancy DiTomaso, a well-known sociologist of racial stratification, have each made a remarkable contribution to my rethinking of *guanxi*. Ron's definition of *guanxi* as a network structure and his original research on "event contacts" are a showcase of how the study of *guanxi* networks can enrich the SNA knowledge system. Nancy has urged me to compare *guanxi* in China to social capital in the US, and her insistence that "these are essentially the same thing" has left a deep mark in my mind when conceptualizing *guanxi* and social capital. I've enjoyed and will continue to enjoy my collaboration with each of them.

Jonathan Skerrett at Polity Press has been a strong force and support behind this book. He approached me for this book project and waited, long before I was convinced and available to write it for Polity's China Today series. Like other books in the series, this one is intended as a small text for college and postgraduate courses on China. For me, this book is actually a half-and-half product: one half of the book is on my original research and the other half a summary of theoretical and empirical materials from other *guanxi* researchers. Given the limited space, I have chosen to discuss the prevalence and the increasing significance of *guanxi* favoritism in the social, economic, political, and legal spheres in China under reform, leaving other topics unattended to. I've made an effort to present quantitative materials in a way that can be understood and appreciated by readers without much quantitative training. A number of more detailed statistical tables can be found online at the book's webpage on www.politybooks.com/guanxi. I'm grateful for Jonathan's patience as well as for the useful comments of two anonymous reviewers he invited on my behalf to evaluate an earlier draft.

I'm grateful also for many collaborators and participants in the survey projects I've conducted since 1997, and a good deal of data from these projects is presented in this book. Deborah Davis and Shaoguang Wang were my collaborators on a 1997–2000 project, sponsored by the Henry Luce Foundation, on urban consumers and material culture in Chinese cities; this project was the first opportunity to measure Chinese New Year visitor networks and social eating networks, which are discussed in chapter 2. The main participants in this project included Wang Hui (who passed away in 2017 at the age of 87) and Guan Ying in Tianjin, Lu Hanlong and Li Yu in Shanghai, Liu Xin and Wang Tie in Wuhan, and Song Ding, Xu Daowen, and Yi Songguo in Shenzhen. A grant from the Hong Kong Research Grants Council (HKUST6052/98H) funded my first Job-Search Network (JSNET) survey project in 1998–9, and a number of grants from China (11AZD022, 13&ZD177) financed subsequent data collections of the JSNET project in 2009, 2014, and 2016. The JSNET project is heavily used in this book, especially in chapter 3; the key collaborators in the project were Liu Shaojie and Wang Wenbin in Changchun, Zhang Wenhong in Tianjin and Shanghai, Bai Hongguang, Guan Xinping, and Mi Shu in Tianjin, Lin Juren and Wu Yuxiao in Jinan, Li Yu in Shanghai, Qiu Haixiong and Liang Yucheng in Guangzhou, Hu Rong and Gong Wenjuan in Xiamen, Feng Shiping and Li Huai in Lanzhou, and Li Liming, Yang Jianke, Zhang Shun, and Zhao Wenlong in Xi'an. My formal and current doctoral advisees Cheng Cheng, Guo Xiaoxian, Hao Mingsong, Huang Xianbi, Li Yinghui, Lu Qiang, Quan Xiaojuan, Sun Yu, Xiao Yang, Yang Yang, and Zhang Lei prepared datasets and many statistical tables and figures presented in this book and on the webpage, and Zhang Yixue provided technical assistance with the bibliography.

My special thanks are due to my wife Qinghong for her love and companionship. As always, she is the first listener to my "presentation" of ideas in rough form at home. Her reactions are as important as her personal reflections on Chinese life. I'm also grateful to my sons Peter and John, as well as their significant others Linda and Kayoko, respectively, for their emotional support. To them, Dad is always working and not making much time for the family. After this book, is a change expected? They may still wonder.

I thank Polity Press editors for their professional assistance. Jonathan Skerrett, once again, worked with me on my first drafts, offering highly useful comments on the narratives of each chapter as well as specific suggestions on the presentation of quantitative materials. Fiona Sewell provided thorough and diligent copyediting, and her effort has improved the exposition of this book. And others at Polity Press have been a source of advice and help at various stages of this book's production.

The main contents of this book were written and revised while I was taking my sabbatical leave from the University of Minnesota and residing at Xi'an Jiaotong University during the academic year of 2017–18. I'm grateful to both institutions for their support in many different ways.

Yanjie Bian
Minneapolis, Minnesota, USA
November 10, 2018
bianx001@umn.edu

1 | What is *Guanxi*?

What is *guanxi*? A British social scientist said the following: "Chinese *guanxi* is not a term which can adequately be expressed by an English-language equivalent of one word, the concept is too culture specific" (Parnell 2005: 35). "How much cultural specificity is there in the term *guanxi*?" one may ask. Well, it is complicated. This answer, believe it or not, can apply to almost all the questions we have about China. Chinese politics is complicated. Chinese history is complicated. China's market economy is one with Chinese characteristics, so it is complicated, too. What about Chinese culture and society? That is not just complicated, it is a big puzzle that no one really understands! This last statement represents the judgment we frequently hear from classroom instructors teaching about Chinese culture and society.

So, let us start our examination of *guanxi* with something simple. A simple understanding of Chinese *guanxi* reduces its cultural specificities and prepares readers for more complicated meanings of the term while reading through the text. In this spirit, I share my 1+3 points about what *guanxi* is: *Guanxi* is simply a connection between two individuals, but importantly it is a personalized connection, a subjectively close connection, and a potentially resourceful connection. Let us apply this 1+3 scheme to everyday Chinese life for further elaboration.

GUANXI IN EVERYDAY CHINESE LIFE

In a Personal Context

Guanxi is a connection between two individuals. This involves a dichotomy: kin and non-kin (Lin 2001a). Kin connections include ties of immediate family, extended family, close kin, and distant kin. Built upon blood and marriage lineages, kinship networks define structural boundaries for one's kin ties. Non-kin ties, on the other hand, are much broader than kin ties, and their structural boundaries are multidimensional. Any geographic place and social institution to which an individual has ever been attached during his or her lifetime establishes a structural boundary within which to develop non-kin ties. Hometown folks, classmates, comrades-in-arms, work colleagues, and neighbors are a few examples for illustration. But none of these can become or sustain *guanxi* ties if they fail to meet the following three qualifications: personal, close, resourceful.

Guanxi is a personalized tie. What makes a tie personal? A one-on-one conversation that shares secrets and gossips makes a tie personal. Expressing sympathy or offering care to a hospitalized friend makes a tie personal. Providing help as a favor to a neighbor who desperately needs it makes a tie personal. Saving a colleague from trouble even at one's own risk makes a tie personal. These kinds of scenarios do not occur randomly; only a proportion of kin and non-kin contacts are elevated to the level of personalized ties through events of personal significance. These events include, as we shall see throughout this book, life-cycle events of local significance (Yan 1996) and family emergencies (Chang 2010), events of cultural significance (Bian 2001), career promotion (Wang 2016), and business founding and development (Burt and Burzynska 2017).

Guanxi is a subjectively close tie. Personalized ties are personal, subject to the involved parties' perceptions of sentimental attachment and obligation fulfillment to each other. Even among kin, biological or role relationships do not automatically generate *guanxi* between people unless such relationships result in active and intimate interactions in the personal worlds (Kipnis 1997: 7). In this sense, Sahlins's (1965/1972) notion of "social distance" applies to both kin and non-kin ties in how they perceive each other. When these perceptions are mutually high, a *guanxi* tie is sustained; otherwise the accumulated problems may lead to the dissolution of a *guanxi* tie. The highest point of *guanxi* is when the two parties maintain mutual perceptions of *familial* sentiments and obligations to each other (Fei 1947/1992; Liang 1949/1986). That "master–apprentice relations are equivalence to father–son relations" (师徒如父子, *shitu ru fuzi*) is a well-known example of the point.

Finally, *guanxi* is a potentially resourceful tie. Personalized ties are expected by the parties involved to facilitate exchanges of favors for expressive and instrumental purposes. While expressive purposes are interactions intended for the emotional and psychological gains of the parties involved, instrumental purposes are the exchanges of tangible and intangible resources that benefit one or both parties in social interaction (Lin 2001b). In a *guanxi* tie, one is able to prevail upon another to perform a favor, and vice versa. The two parties need not be of equal social status (Yan 2006), but they must have access to non-redundant resources to satisfy the exchange of favors (Bian 2010). Failure to reciprocate a favor is a violation of mutual obligation and hurts sentimental feelings. Therefore, a close personal tie may quickly lose its instrumental value when the two parties are completely redundant to each other. This is especially so for career-driven people (Feng 2010). Among retirees and the elderly, close personal ties keep together resource-redundant people for expressive favor exchanges.

In a Business Context

Economic actors are socially embedded (Granovetter 1985). In Chinese *guanxi* culture, this has two important implications. First, it is the well connected who do business with each other and do it well. That is, entrepreneurs who have *guanxi* ties to resourceful others are likely to start a business and operate it to a respectable level (Bian and Zhang 2014). Second, poorly connected entrepreneurs who have bright business ideas must cultivate *guanxi* ties to resourceful others in order to convert and capitalize their ideas into profitable business operations (Zhang 2016).

Prior *guanxi* ties before business are of fundamental importance for new ventures to emerge. They are the support networks to obtain business opportunity, mobilize financial capital, and recruit core members of the business team (Bian 2008a). Lacking prior ties of this nature can be frustrating for foreign businesspeople investing in China, especially when they try to use Western values to make ethical judgments about developing and utilizing social relationships for economic activities (Lovett, Simmons, and Kali 1999; Nolan 2011). To Chinese businesspeople, "the social relationship is a prerequisite to get involved in a business relationship" (Gomez-Arias 1998: 150). Among 700 randomly selected businesses in the Yangtze River Delta, every one of them was assisted by at least one *guanxi* contact at founding (Burt and Burzynska 2017).

Guanxi networks are mechanisms of continuous business success. Kinship networks are at the core of the governance structure in township and village enterprises (Lin 1995) and function well as a substitute of property rights laws (Peng 2004). Barriers to entry motivate Chinese entrepreneurs to build their own networks of suppliers and distributors, and to develop competitive advantage in self-organized industrial clusters in which close-knit groups of like-minded people establish reliable business norms for the emerging private economy (Nee and Opper 2012). Ties to government officials, on the other hand, are the key channels through which to acquire economic resources (Li et al. 2011) and develop local firms (Wank 1999), govern relational contracts (Zhou et al. 2003), operate business groups (Keister 2001), and

systematically increase the economic performance of all types of enterprises (Chen, Chen, and Huang 2013), including publicly listed enterprises (Haveman et al. 2017).

In a Political Context

When resources and opportunities are vertically allocated in organizational hierarchy, *guanxi* ties operate in a political context, which involves
the distribution of power, the range of stakeholders involved and their
interests, and the interplay of formal and informal rules that govern
the interactions among different stakeholders. *Guanxi* ties to the stakeholders are especially important when informal rules are ......e practical
and effective than formal rules in a centralized power structure.

In a top national university, a great research project of international
significance cannot be founded unless it wins the favor of at least three
stakeholders. The first is the university lead scientist in the area who
has the professional authority as well as within- and between-university networks to ascertain the value of the project. The second is the
director of the functional office having operational authority to select
one project over others. The third and most important stakeholder is
the number one decision-maker of the university, whether the Party
secretary or the president. To win over severe competition for vertically
allocated major projects, *guanxi* ties must be used to persuade and
influence these stakeholders not just in public deliberations but more
importantly in private. Beyond the university boundary, *guanxi* ties to
key government officials are decisive because they wield the authority
to approve projects.

The importance of *guanxi* ties to stakeholders is widespread and
normalized. You frequently exchange text messages of no specific
purpose with your boss in order to gain intimacy and trust. You invite
significant others around you to banquets of social significance to
strengthen brotherly sentiments. You make sure to attend all events

of personal significance to your business partners so that they value your friendship and extend their contacts with you. More illicitly, you contact reviewers to ask for a favorable evaluation of an application for a grant, a book award, or a talent outline of nationally endowed professorships on behalf of your colleagues or former students. The last of these actions is unethical, for it violates the formal rules about the conflict of interest and personal interference. In China, these rules are documented but not implemented forcefully. When an overseas returnee professor failed to get his grant application awarded, he was informally told by one of the reviewers, a former classmate of his, that "we all *saw* [but did not read] your application, it was good, but you didn't call [to contact us], so we were not sure how serious you were!"

A Working Definition of Guanxi

At its basic level, *guanxi* refers to a dyadic, particular, and sentimental tie that has the potential for facilitating the exchange of favors between the two parties connected by the tie. To Chinese people inside or outside mainland China, any blood or marital relationship qualifies for this definition; hence, kin ties are highly likely to be *guanxi* ties of varying degrees of closeness. Persons linked by a non-kin tie, on the other hand, can develop *guanxi* between them if the parties repeatedly invest sentiments in the tie and at the same time build up mutual obligations to each other, making the tie special to both parties. The word "special" here means personal and personalized, or what sociologists term "particular" (Parsons 1937/1949).

When *guanxi* goes beyond the dyadic basis to connect more than two persons, a *guanxi* network emerges. In conventional social network analysis (SNA) terms, a *guanxi* network is an egocentric network in which a focal actor (ego) is connected to two or more other actors (alters) who are connected to still others. Before taking a SNA approach to conceptualizing *guanxi* into generalizable social science variables, let us first explore the culture-specific meanings of *guanxi*.

GUANXI AS LOCAL KNOWLEDGE

A colloquial term, *guanxi* is what Geertz (1983) calls "local knowledge." For Geertz, local knowledge is confined to people within a specific culture, and is embedded in the spoken and unspoken symbols and meanings as well as explicit and implicit codes of behavior of the local people.

Guanxi-*Relevant Colloquial Terms*

Two parties connected by a mutually recognized *guanxi* tie tend to have at least three interrelated feelings toward each other: (1) *ganqing* (affection), or feelings of affection one has toward the other party; (2) *renqing* (favor), or feelings of reciprocal obligation one owes to the other party; and (3) *mianzi* (face), or feelings of respect one gains from the other party when affections are rewarded and expected obligations fulfilled. Inversely, *ganqing* is hurt when affections go in one direction, *renqing* is considered nonexistent when expected obligations are never recognized or favors never returned, and *mianzi* is lost when attitudes and actions of ignorance or rejection are signaled or implied by the other party. These negative relational processes ultimately lead to the dissolution of a *guanxi* tie. Thus, *guanxi* is dynamic rather than static, and its effectiveness and duration depend on sentimental and behavioral exchanges between the parties involved.

Guanxi building is the process of developing mutual affection, strengthening reciprocal obligation, and increasing mutual respect between the parties that are connected by a tie. During one's life course, new members may be added to and old members eliminated from one's *guanxi* networks. For example, *guanxi* ties can be developed from among classmates (同学*tong xue*), comrades-in-arms (战友*zhan you*), work colleagues (同事*tong shi*), and countrymen (同乡*tong xiang*). In rural villages, the exchange of gifts has become a way of life in maintaining social relationships with kin and neighbors (Yan 1996; Kipnis 1997), and the persistence of this lifestyle follows the norm of mutual reciprocity through frequent inter-household interactions at life-cycle events of local significance, which has been characterized by the colloquial term 礼尚往来 "*lishang wanglai*" (Chang 2010: 226–7 for table V-1). In Mao's urban society, in which redistributive resources were allocated through the work-unit system (Bian 1994a), work colleagues were a greater source of perceived support than the family or kinship (Ruan 1998). In both rural and urban societies, friends are a broad category of multiple cultural meanings and behavioral implications (Smart 1993), but very close friends are likely to become pseudo-kin by addressing each other as brothers or sisters, especially among northerners (Bian 2010). To be sure, *guanxi* building is a behavioral art, requiring interpersonally justified strategies in such social interactions as conversations, banquets, and gift exchanges. The so-called "art of *guanxixue*" (关系学, Yang 1994) is about these strategies of *guanxi* cultivation, maintenance, and utilization at interpersonal levels.

One colloquial term is hard to translate into an understandable English word. This is *gan qin* (干亲), which may mean "nominal kin" or "ritualized kin" to the best of my English understanding. It refers to the conversion of a non-kin tie into a kin tie through a ritualized ceremony either in private or in public. One example is the conversion of a master–apprentice relation into a ritualized father–son relation, in which the apprentice begins calling the master 干爸爸 (*gan pa-pa*) or 干爹 (*gan die*) and behaves as an adopted son of the master. Another example is the conversion of close friends into "sworn brothers" (把兄弟, *ba xiongdi*), in which friends recognize each other as brothers and treat each other accordingly. While ritualized kin relations prevailed in official and underground societies before the 1949 Communist revolution, they were nearly eliminated under Mao's regime (1949–76) in which the term "comrade" was used to address each other in social relationships (Vogel 1965). Reform-era China has observed the replacement of "comrades" with "friends" in formal and informal appellations (Gold 1985) and the revival of ritualized kin relations in official and unofficial societies at local levels (Feng 2010).

Three relational manifestations can characterize *guanxi* ties (Bian 2010). First, *guanxi* ties connect people of a high level of acquaintance or familiarity (*shu*); these are the people who know each other very well. Second, *guanxi* ties connect people of high intimacy (*qin*), whether they are close kin or, if not, treat each other as pseudo-kin. Intimacy in Chinese *guanxi* culture is equivalent to family, as evidenced by the popular slang phrase "亲如一家" (*qinru yijia*, felt like one family). A similar phrase was used for the Beijing Olympic Games in 2008, "One World, One Family" (世界一家亲 *shijie yijia qin*). Third, *guanxi* ties connect people of high trust (*xin*); in other words, these are the people who are accountable for each other. Each of these relational manifestations is measurable in terms of both subjective evaluation and objective behavior. In this sense, *guanxi* as a particular tie is a combination of high acquaintance, high intimacy, and high trust, and this combination redefines *guanxi* as a standard SNA concept that minimizes cultural specificities (Wellman, Chen, and Dong 2002).

Cardinal Relations and Confucian Roots of Relational Ethics

Many of the codes of *guanxi*-relevant behavior just discussed are deeply rooted in Confucianism, the dominant ancient Chinese philosophy. Unlike the Greek philosophical tradition, which is centered on ontological and epistemological questions, the Confucian philosophical school is centrally concerned with ideal-typical human relations through which to maintain social harmony in official and unofficial societies (Tu 1993). To Confucius, human beings are good in nature, but individuals are teachable and improvable through the cultivation of virtue and the maintenance of ethics. Social roles are fundamentally unequal in social status, and a harmonious social order is established and maintained when human actors of different social roles and unequal social status interact with one another according to the Confucian ethical codes of behavior. Five pairs of social roles are considered by Confucian scholars to be the most important in a family-centered society, resulting in "five cardinal relations" (五伦) as presented in table 1.1.

The first pair of roles consists of the ruler and the ruled. Key to this pairwise relation is the upholding of righteousness and the moral disposition to be good. That is, the ruler is benevolent to the ruled, who in turn will be loyal to the ruler. The second pair of roles consists of father and son. When father and son are bound by familial love, a loving father will be loved by his faithful son. The third pair of roles consists of husband and wife. Distinctive in their duties, the husband needs to show benevolence toward his wife and the wife needs to respect the husband with thorough obedience. The fourth pair of roles consists of brother and brother. In this pair, the elder brother is

Table 1.1: Confucian Concepts of Relational Ethics, Virtues, and Characters

Concept	Chinese	Elaboration	Three obediences
Ruler and ruled	君臣	Righteousness (or duty)	The ruled must obey the ruler
Father and son	父子	Love (or affection)	Son must obey his father
Husband and wife	夫妻	Distinction	Wife must obey her husband
Brother and brother	兄弟	Precedence	
Friend and friend	朋友	Sincerity (or trust)	

expected to love the younger brother, who in return pays respect to the elder. Finally, the fifth pair of roles consists of friend and friend. Trustworthiness or accountability is to be expected between friends.

Hierarchical ties are clearly characteristic of the first four cardinal relations. Although the friend-to-friend relation is not prescribed as hierarchical, it is implicitly not a relation for people of equal social status either. In Confucian thought on social order, the family is the center of social structure, and social relations beyond the family mimic and are modeled after family relations. While the ruler–ruled relation mimics the father–son relation, the friend–friend relation is modeled after the brother–brother relation, in which the elder brother is of higher status than the younger. Under this Confucian code of conduct, male friends in close relationships address each other as elder/younger brothers and behave accordingly, not just among gentlemen in imperial China but also among Chinese Communist revolutionaries such as Mao Zedong, Zhang Guotao, Zhou Enlai, and Zhu De (Zhang 1980). This influence of Confucianism has gone beyond China, as hierarchical social relations are characteristic of other East Asian cultures (Bian and Ikeda 2014/2016).

Connections of Unequals and the Ideal of Social Harmony

The Confucian-prescribed relations are essentially relations of unequal social status (Yan 2006). This is clearly evidenced by the three-obediences principle, presented in table 1.1. Here, three of the five cardinal relations are redefined in a superior–subordinate relationship: The ruled must obey the ruler, the son must obey his father, and the wife must obey her husband. These three cardinal relations in fact are of a higher order than the other two cardinal relations, which can transform into a superior–subordinate relationship as well: The younger brother must obey his elder brother, and junior friends, by age or social status, must obey senior friends. Therefore, although the Confucian "five constant virtues" appear to apply to all people in society, these virtues (be nice, good, obligated, proper, and accountable to others) are more expected of lower-status people when interacting with higher-status others. Finally, the Confucian code's "eight moral characters" include explicit or implicit emphasis on the hierarchical ordering of kinship, political, and social relationships (e.g. filial piety, sibling piety, loyalty (to ruler)).

The hierarchical structure of Confucian social relations is not meant to break up relational harmony. Relational harmony is a state of equilibrium that is necessary and must be maintained within networks of social relations as well as in society at large (Fei 1947/1992). However, the Confucian framing of relational harmony is the harmony of unequals (和而不同, *he er butong*), in which social harmony is maintained by heterogeneous egos and alters within a network of particular ties (Pan 1993).

THEORETICAL MODELS OF *GUANXI* IN THE SOCIAL SCIENCES

In comparison to Confucian philosophy, contemporary social science research on *guanxi* is rather a new tradition. Chinese-language publications of theoretical significance to *guanxi* scholarship began to emerge in the late 1940s and unfortunately stopped during the Maoist era (1949–76), in which not only was China's social science research taken over by political ideology and orthodox Marxism-Leninism, but many subjects of study, including sociology, were terminated. Only after 1978 did we see the rebirth of sociology and *guanxi* research in China (Bian and Zhang 2008; Bian 2009). Empirical studies have since been conducted, diverse perspectives offered, and research literature accumulated quickly (Zhang 2011a, 2011b; Feizhou Zhou 2017).

This section is not designed to survey the large body of *guanxi* literature. My goal here is to summarize diverse perspectives on *guanxi* into distinctive theoretical models. These models are designed to minimize cultural specificities and focus on the theoretical properties of *guanxi* that are generalizable across cultural systems. This intention is inspired by an increasing number of social science researchers of non-Chinese origin who study *guanxi* (Kipnis 1997; Guthrie 1998; Keister 2001; Gold, Guthrie, and Wank 2002; Wellman, Chen, and Dong 2002; Burt and Burzynska 2017; Burt and Opper 2017), but it is also rooted in my belief that social science models can upgrade culture-specific knowledge to a higher level of scientific inquiry into social phenomena. The three theoretical properties we will explore represent *guanxi* as: the social extension of familial ties; instrumental particular ties; and asymmetric social exchange. In doing so, I shall make use of the term "*guanxi* capital." Following the new research tradition on social capital (Lin 2001b), I define *guanxi* capital as the social resources that are mobilized by actors from their *guanxi* networks to help achieve expressive and instrumental goals (Bian 2001).

Guanxi *as the Social Extension of Familial Ties*

This school of thought argues that the family is the core of social structure and the original source of social relations in Chinese society. Consequently, *guanxi* is understood as the web of extended familial sentiments and obligations. Proponents of this conception include, in the Chinese-language literature, Fei Xiaotong (1947/1992, translated into English) and Liang Shumin (1949/1986), and in English, Morton H. Fried (1953/1969), C. K. Yang (1959/1965), and Ambrose King (1985, 1991).

Liang (1949) began by recognizing that each person is born into a complex set of relations with parents and other family members. He argued that in China these relations are ethical in nature, combining both sentiment (*qing*) and obligation (*yi*). In interaction among family members, sentiments and obligations complement and reinforce each other, creating a harmonious structure that resists confrontation and encourages cooperation within the family. Because group life based on individual interests never became a mode of social organization in China, argued Liang, the ethical relations of familial sentiments and obligations were extended from the family into larger society, becoming characteristic of Chinese culture. Liang thus termed Chinese culture and society ethics-centered (伦理本位 *lunli benwei*).

Fei (1947/1992) emphasized that the ethical relations of familial sentiments and obligations are egocentric. Therefore, the farther an alter is from an ego's family, the wider the range of the ego's tie to the alter, and the lower the degree of the ego's sentiments and obligations to the alter. Fei called this tendency "the mode of differential associations" (差序格局 *chaxu geju*). Fried's (1953/1969) study of a county seat in Anhui province before 1949 confirmed that the web of familial and kinship obligations indeed extended into and became the "fabric" of the economic, political, and social organizations of the county seat before the Communist revolution. C. K. Yang's (1959/1965) research on post-revolution Chinese families in Guangdong indicated that agricultural collectivization did not greatly alter this structure, because the unofficial, informal networks of familial and kinship sentiments and obligations provided the social support mechanisms through which peasant families survived in the economy of transition and hardships in the 1950s. King (1985, 1991) argued that the relational ethics of *guanxi* can explain behavioral patterns of Chinese individuals in post-World War II Hong Kong, Taiwan, and Mao's mainland China, pointing to the persistence of *guanxi* in shaping social life among the Chinese across political regimes.

Because familial obligations and sentiments shape the communities extended from the family and kinship, Lin (2001a) has conceptualized these communities as "pseudo-families." According to Lin, pseudo-family ties refer to intimate friendships. These ties come about in different ways in rural and urban Chinese societies. In

Yang's village and Fried's county seat, intimate social and economic relations were normatively restricted to the family, and the pseudo-family ties were a "social fiction" to widen the boundaries. In broader and more complex urban societies, Lin argues, pseudo-family ties develop from diverse social and patron–client relations. While frequent interactions and mutual exchanges are objective conditions under which these social relations may transform into ties of high intimacy, key to a pseudo-family tie is the intimate friend's subjective recognition of such a tie. One general indication is that the pseudo-family ties link persons who normally call each other brothers or sisters and whose children normatively call their parents' friends aunts or uncles.

The scholars I have just reviewed have implied that the capacity to mobilize social resources from *guanxi* networks lies in a focal individual's fulfilling moral and ethical obligations to his or her family and pseudo-families. For example, in Yang's village or Fried's county seat, the men who fulfilled these obligations earned respect (or *face*) from villagers and neighbors, and this moral fulfillment was important for carrying out one's duties in public domains.

Face is relational because it lies in how a focal actor is evaluated by the members of one's *guanxi* networks (Hu 1944). In his theory of the mode of differential associations, Fei maintained that face is based on sentiments and closeness between face givers and face receivers: face is largely ensured from social circles close to the ego's family, but less so from the circles that are farther away. Therefore, the facework that everyone must do is to strengthen social relations in the farther and wider circles by the standards of familial sentiments and obligations. Liang believed that the web of extended familial sentiments and obligations reflected the nature of the classless social structure of China. In this structure, rational persons must extend ties of familial sentiments and obligations to as many people around them as possible, thereby accumulating *guanxi* capital.

Guanxi *as Instrumental Particular Ties*

Unlike early writers on *guanxi*, researchers into contemporary urban Chinese society have suggested that *guanxi* refers to exchange networks of "instrumental particular ties" (Jacobs 1979; Chiao 1982; Walder 1986; Hwang 1987; Yang 1994). While particular ties of a personal nature are often associated with expressive purposes (Parsons 1937/1949), Walder (1986) argues that Chinese *guanxi* ties are particular ties that are in fact intended to obtain instrumental benefits, and thus calls them "instrumental particular ties. This view does not automatically reject the idea that *guanxi* is a web of extended familial sentiments and obligations; here, instead, the defining character of *guanxi* is the instrumentality of particular ties (familial ties included) that facilitate favor exchanges. The shift in emphasis to instrumental particular ties points to a different set of implications for the relational bases of *guanxi*, sources and bases of *guanxi* capital, and strategies of *guanxi* capital accumulation in Chinese society.

When *guanxi* is defined as instrumental particular ties, the relational bases of *guanxi* are no longer limited to family and pseudo-families, but also include a broad range of social and work-related connections. Walder (1986) found that in Mao's China three kinds of instrumental particular ties shaped work life. The first was ties between state planners and factory directors. In a socialist redistributive economy, annual budgets are "soft" because state-owned enterprises can fix deficits in the accounting books with the permission of state planners. Under this soft budget constraint (Kornai 1986), all factory directors demanded economic resources from state planners, but those who established particular ties with state planners were better able to extract government resources. The second was ties between Party officials and political activists in the workplace. In the political culture of Party clientelism, the best strategy for getting ahead was to show personal loyalty to the Party secretary who controlled career mobility opportunities. The third was ties between shop-floor supervisors and subordinary workers. In this relationship, shop-floor supervisors operated day-to-day management through networks of loyal workers, who received favorable work assignments, performance evaluations, and bonuses and prizes from their supervisors. The defining character of these various particular ties was instrumental, argued Walder, because favor exchange was both the motivation and the anticipated outcome of the particular ties.

In the exchange networks of instrumental particular ties, the key source of *guanxi* capital lies in one's reputation for keeping promises to provide and return favors to the members of one's *guanxi* networks. In other words, the rule of the game is reciprocity. Yang (1994) observed that in post-Mao China, indebtedness and the obligation to reciprocate are the binding power of social relations. In this context, face is a mixture of sentiment, mutual trust, and loyalty between the parties engaged in favor exchanges (Hwang 1987). Facework of this kind was found to operate in business circles nowadays (Cheng and Rosett 1991; Chen, Chen, and Huang 2013) and has been linked to the notion of tie strength in the study of job searches in China (Bian 1997; Bian and Huang 2015a) and Singapore (Bian and Ang 1997). Consequently, the goals of social networking have shifted from extending ties of familial sentiments and obligations to cultivating ties of diverse resources for mutual favor exchanges (Barbalet 2018).

Guanxi *as Ties of Asymmetric Social Exchange*

Nan Lin (2001a) has provided both a critical review of the *guanxi* literature and a new conceptual model of the nature and operating mechanisms of *guanxi* networks. Recognizing the different emphases on the sentimental basis and on the instrumental uses of *guanxi* by previous researchers of China, he argues that both of these characterize *guanxi* when it is defined in the broad context of social exchange networks of asymmetric transaction.

Lin distinguishes between economic exchanges of symmetric transaction and social exchanges of asymmetric transaction. The rationale of economic exchanges is to focus on short-term transactions of valued resources and the gain relative to loss in the resources transacted between the parties involved. In contrast, the rationale of social exchanges shifts the focus to a long-term commitment to maintaining relationships in which resources are embedded. In social exchanges, transactions of resources are asymmetric in that resources flow from favor giver to favor receiver, and this is also true when the resource flow in social networks is access to other ties (in this case, the favor giver acts as a network bridge). But the favor giver does gain – by being recognized as resourceful. The spread of recognition in social networks enhances the reputation of the favor giver, thus helping the favor giver maintain and strengthen his or her network centrality.

Lin classifies *guanxi* as a type of social exchange, permitting instrumental uses and favor-seeking purposes to characterize *guanxi* networks. However, he argues that "it is the relationship that is valued and must be maintained, not the value of the favor transacted per se"; thus, "instrumental action becomes the means and *guanxi* [building] becomes the end" (Lin 2001a: 22). It is in this sense that Lin also emphasizes the sentimental basis of *guanxi*.

In Lin's conceptualization, the relational bases of *guanxi* become very broad, including all kinds of kin and non-kin relations. The key source of *guanxi* capital is neither the reputation for fulfilling moral obligations to family and pseudo-families, nor the reputation for keeping promises in favor exchanges; after all, resource transactions in social exchanges are asymmetric. Instead, *guanxi* capital lies in one's reputation as a generous favor giver and a network bridge to resourceful ties. In this context, face – the Chinese version of social capital – can be reinterpreted: Face giving means lending access to connections, and face receiving means getting access to connections. Expectedly, granting favors (access to connections) is the best strategy to maintain one's networks and enhance one's capacity of accumulating *guanxi* capital.

Summary

Table 1.2 displays the key points of the three theoretical models just reviewed. From the model of social extension of familial ties to the model of instrumental particular ties and on to the model of networks of asymmetric transaction, we see systematic change in the essence and core components of *guanxi* networks: from an ascribed kinship core to an achieved reciprocal core and to a network-diversity core. Sources and mechanisms of *guanxi* capital – the processes in which to mobilize social resources from *guanxi* networks – as well as strategies of *guanxi* capital accumulation change accordingly. Whether this change reflects a historical shift that corresponds to China's social-structural and institutional transformations in the past two centuries is a question open for empirical research. This research agenda should include questions of the relative efficacies of these models, along with emerging new models, in the *guanxi* networks of Chinese individuals in the twenty-first century. To advance this research agenda, a SNA approach is needed in conceptualizing *guanxi* in generalizable social science variables.

A SNA APPROACH TOWARD *GUANXI*

SNA is a multi- and inter-disciplinary field of study of social networks. It has developed standard analytic tools for the field, and the comparative significance of *guanxi* research will be strengthened if these tools are used to study *guanxi* networks (Wellman, Chen, and Dong 2002). The key task here is to identify and measure the *core* relational forms

Table 1.2: Three Social Science Models of *Guanxi*

	Model I	Model II	Model III
Focus of analysis	Social extension of familial ties model	Instrumental particular ties model	Networks of asymmetric transaction model
Definition of *guanxi*	Web of extended familial sentiments and obligations	Exchange networks of instrumental particular ties	Social exchange networks of asymmetric transaction
Relational bases	Family, kinship, community	Family, kinship, community, work	Family, kinship, community, work, all significant others
Sources of *guanxi* capital	Reputation for fulfilling moral obligations to family and pseudo-families	Reputation for keeping promises of providing and returning favors	Reputation for being network bridges to resourceful ties
Mechanisms of *guanxi* capital	Face based on sentiment and closeness	Face based on mutual trust and loyalty	Face based on repeated asymmetric transaction
Strategies of *guanxi* capital accumulation	To extend ties of familial sentiments and obligations	To cultivate ties of diverse resources for favor exchanges	To increase network centrality for more network ties

of *guanxi* that are likely to generate predictable patterns of social behavior in a fast-changing China. I identify several important, though not exclusive, core relational forms of *guanxi*: role type, tie strength, tie multiplexity, route of connectivity, and embedded resources. Each is elaborated in turn.

Role Type

The three theoretical models just reviewed point to a tripartite role-type measure of *guanxi*. The first is kin ties, including parents, spouses, children, extended family ties, close kin ties, and distant kin ties. The second is pseudo-kin ties, including dyads of teachers and students, masters and apprentices, supervisors and subordinates, colleagues, classmates, comrades-in-arms, neighbors, hometown folks, and close friends. One test of whether or not non-kin ties are close enough to have become pseudo-kin ties is whether the parties in the ties have developed a good deal of family-like sentiment, so much so that they address each other in kinship terms, such as brothers, sisters, aunts, and uncles. The third and last role type is other non-kin ties, through which people recognize each other as acquaintances (熟人 *shuren*).

The three role types are theoretically informed (Granovetter 1973) and empirically rooted in Chinese culture and society (Lin and Bian 1991; Bian 1997). But they continue to be open for empirical confirmation and justification to reflect local specificities, as China is ethnically diverse, geographically large, and institutionally dynamic.

Tie Strength

Tie strength is a theory-informed and empirically quantifiable concept of interpersonal connections. It refers to the totality of several dimensions of social interactions between an ego and his or her alters: frequency of interaction, degree of intimacy, degree of emotional attachment, and extensity of resource exchanges (Granovetter 1973). While each dimension can be quantified without measurement ambiguity, the four dimensions are empirically correlated with one another (Marsden and Campbell 1984) to allow for a single, composite variable of tie strength to be used in empirical studies in and beyond Western contexts (Granovetter 1995; Lin 1999; Bian 1997, 1999, 2008b; Tian and Lin 2016).

How are the culture-specific meanings of *guanxi* reflected in the social science concept of tie strength? One of the central cultural meanings of *guanxi* is relational particularism. This notion refers to the extent of personalization in a social relation between the involved parties, and it points to a social world of what Fei (1947/1992) describes as "the mode of differential associations," or in SNA terminality "the overlapping of egocentric networks." In this mode, Fei elaborates, a person builds his/ or her egocentric network of close and distant alters through repeated sentimental and instrumental exchanges. Strategic efforts of network building are made by the ego to increase the degree of particularism (shortening social distances) with resourceful alters and decrease the degree of particularism (lengthening social distances) with less-resourceful alters. These elaborations of *guanxi* are consistent with what social network analysts call "strong ties" (Bian 1997) rather than weak ties.

Lo and Otis (2003) observe an emerging form of "generalized particularism" in transitional China. This term is defined as the tendency for *guanxi* to be increasingly applied beyond the confines of primordial relationships. The driving force for this tendency, these authors argue, is the quiet and speedy expansion of civil society in which networks of autonomous associations emerge and grow beyond the state and the family. In this view, tie strength in the Chinese context reflects a full continuum of particularism, and one's *core guanxi* ties are strong ties, distributed toward the right side of the weak–strong continuum.

Tie Multiplexity

Tie multiplexity refers to multiple functions and channels which a tie provides to connected parties. Substantively it is "the overlap of roles, exchanges, or affiliations in a social relationship" (Verbrugge 1979: 1286), and structurally it is a "multi-stranded tie" that connects two actors in multiple, however redundant, channels from which to rise fell-back opportunities as in "old boy networks" (Mitchell 1969).

Chinese *guanxi* ties are characteristically multiplex ties, which mix qualitatively different norms of exchange, namely expressive with instrumental, social with economic, symbolic with material, personal with public, friendship with businesslike, familial with collegial. The habitus of norm mixing is exemplified in the Chinese notion of face, a term whose very meaning is against differentiation of exchange logics (King 1991). *Guanxi* operates by the relational logic of asymmetrical exchange, because each time there is an exchange the receiver gains a substantial favor and the granter increases prominence, network centrality, and the power for future favor returns (Lin 2001a). No wonder many Chinese entrepreneurs conduct businesses with friends, comrades-in-arms, former classmates, hometown folks, or relatives.

Route of Connectivity

A fundamental value of social networks is the transmission and diffusion of social ties across structural boundaries. Social network analysts have thus studied not only direct ties but also indirect ties. The theory of six degrees of separation predicts that anyone is connected to any other person around the world through six or fewer relationships; the theory's mathematical proof and empirical findings from "small world" studies have entered standard texts of social network analysis (Newman, Barabási, and Watts 2006).

In the Chinese context, an individual's web of *guanxi* is a mixture of direct and indirect ties. This is reflected in both the theory of the mode of differential associations (Fei 1947/1992) and the notion of generalized particularism (Lo and Otis 2003). In the pre-reform era, for example, "wait-for-assignment" youths had to reach out to job-assigning officials through direct and indirect ties, and strong-tie inter-mediaries were mobilized to link the job seeker as the favor receiver with the respective helper as the favor grantor (Bian 1994a). In the post-reform era, this scenario has been reexamined and the same pattern revealed (Bian and Huang 2015a). Yang (2002) observes many new forms of *guanxi* practice in business circles, and the great majority of these new forms involve the simultaneous presence and working of direct and indirect ties.

Embedded Resources

Network-embedded resources are the social capital with which to enhance expressive and instrumental actions (Portes 1998; Burt 2000). These are the resources that can be accessed and mobilized through networks of ongoing social relationships (Lin 2001b), and tangible and intangible resources are in numerous forms. All these forms can be conceptualized into two kinds of network-embedded resources: infor-mation and influence of power.

However defined, *guanxi* is commonly understood to facilitate favoritism. In a granter–receiver dyad, the former grants a favor to the latter, and the latter repays in a different form of favor either imme-diately or later. The first part of this favor exchange is fundamental because without it the exchange would not have started. What is the main form of favor involved in this first part of the exchange? It is the influence of power, not merely information, that is possessed and exercised by the favor granter. The sources of this power are associated with the granter's position, status, wealth, and network centrality, and the influence of power is felt and in effect when it is used to help the favor receiver.

Information is another resource that is widely available in social networks. Unlike *guanxi* favoritism in China and the "old boy networks" in the United States (Rees 1966; Mitchell 1969) or elsewhere, getting and spreading information through social networks is considered to be ethical, and social contacts relaying job ads, writing letters of recommendation, and voluntarily offering referrals to prospective employers are socially acceptable and institutionally legitimized in many advanced countries. The social network studies in Western market societies are mainly about the extent to which network-transmitted information reduces market deficiencies (Granovetter 1995). The situation for reform-era China will be examined in later chapters.

GUANXI AS RESOURCE MOBILIZER: A CONCLUDING NOTE

But why should we pay attention to *guanxi*? What is the result, the outcome or fruit of *guanxi* capital? One consensus that is widely shared by both SNA and *guanxi* researchers is that social resources are embedded in and can be mobilized from networks of ongoing social relations (Lin 2001b). Social networks matter and have real effects in social outcomes. Here I identify five different relational forms of *guanxi* in which certain kinds of social resources are embedded and from which they can be mobilized.

The first and most basic relational form of *guanxi* is a tie of connectivity (versus dis-connectivity) between two parties, and its embedded resources are mutual recognition and communication between members of a shared community. To measure this level of *guanxi*, one asks: "Are you connected to him or her?" In other words, "Do you know each other well?" *Guanxi* as a tie of connectivity is not unique to China; it is culturally constant.

The second relational form of *guanxi* is a sentimental tie; its embedded resources are human affections, including sympathy, care, love, and a sense of altruistic, not reciprocal, help to others with whom we are associated. This level of *guanxi* requires a great amount of everyday interaction among people, but its cross-cultural, cross-national, and cross-regime variations need to be empirically studied. The greater the amount of this level of *guanxi* in everyday life, the nicer our social worlds will be. Is reform-era China moving toward abandoning this nice aspect of *guanxi* in favor of the rise of a rationalized and yet uncertain and sometime disastrous market economy?

The third level of *guanxi* is a sentiment-derived instrumental tie; its embedded resources are substantial help with reciprocal implications and expectations for the parties linked by a *guanxi* tie. This level of *guanxi* is highly available from kin and pseudo-kin ties (Lin 2001a). Here, the embedded resources are the unintended consequences of good relations (Arrow 1998), and its very logic is against the deliberate *guanxi* building aimed at instrumental values and outcomes. Is the rise of the market economy with Chinese characteristics creating external conditions that oppose the development of this level of *guanxi* in favor of overt favoritism and naked favor exchange?

The fourth relational form of *guanxi* is an instrumental particular tie; its embedded resources vary hugely in type but the norms of reciprocity, face, and favor are primary. This is the widely understood meaning of *guanxi* in the scholarship on the subject. The relational bases of this level of *guanxi* vary, but the degree of particularism is a positive signal for the start of a possible favor exchange between *guanxi* parties. Nevertheless the norms of reciprocity, besides anything else, are deterministic for the continuation or termination of a *guanxi* tie. To what extent do these kinds of *guanxi* ties grow or decline in proportion to the rise of the market economy in China, and under what conditions?

The fifth and last level of *guanxi* is an obligational tie or a well-understood informal contract. Its embedded resources are specific, the generated behaviors are highly patterned, but the relational origins, bases, or forms vary randomly. These kinds of obligational ties have grown tremendously in business circles and political spheres, facilitating land allocations and real-estate developments; lubricating construction projects; and contributing to illicit services and dealings, official corruption, and money-for-power-influence exchanges. These are the ugly face of *guanxi* and the dark side of *guanxi* capital. Have these kinds of *guanxi* practices and *guanxi* influences stayed within business circles and political confines? Or are they spreading to all economic and social spheres in an increasingly marketized China?

Using these principles for analysis, let's now explore the role that *guanxi* plays in different domains of Chinese society.

2 | *Guanxi* and Network Building _____

This chapter will describe the ways in which *guanxi* networks are developed and maintained through everyday interactions and social interactions at events of personal significance. Much of the empirical data to be presented has been collected by using SNA approaches to network measurement, and the three instances that we will be examining are: networks of daily contacts and *guanxi* as an everyday phenomenon (Fu 2005); networks of social eating partners and the importance of banqueting in China (Bian 2001); and networks of visitors during the New Year celebrations (Bian 2008b). Built into each of these examinations is a "position generator" (Lin and Dumin 1986), which measures hierarchical dimensions of *guanxi* networks. This data allows for an exploration of how *guanxi* networks vary within and between social classes. I will use the personal stories of my informants as well as my own experiences and observations to illustrate the *guanxi* logics of network building in Chinese society today.

GUANXI INTERACTION AS AN EVERYDAY PHENOMENON

What Is an Ordinary Day?

It is Thursday in China. This is an ordinary day for E ("ego"), a college professor and the chair of a social science department. E gets up early and carpools with a friend, A1 ("alter" #1) to go to work. E attends a dean-chair joint meeting in the morning, and afterwards catches up with the dean, A2, getting his advice on an issue about his research project. E has a working lunch with two junior colleagues from his research team, A3 and A4, to lay out a plan for solving the issue. E makes sure to pay the lunch bills for all three of them. Returning to his office, E finds an email message from a former student, A5, asking for a letter of recommendation in support of his application to doctoral programs. Late afternoon, E is at an oral defense by a doctoral advisee of A1's, his carpool friend, and he ends up going to dinner with four other colleagues serving on the advisory committee, A6 to A9, along with A1, his doctoral advisee B1 (so labeled to denote a secondary alter or an indirect tie to E), and three other graduate students B1a to B1c, or B1's close friends. E returns home late. His wife, A10, reminds him that they are going to their son's graduation concert tomorrow evening. She has invited all her close friends, B10a to B10f, to go to the concert because their son will be the concert leader. Well, that will please E for sure. Figure 2.1 displays a diagram for this ego–alter network.

Guanxi interaction is an everyday phenomenon. But what does it mean to *guanxi*-network building for every one of us on an ordinary day? On an "ordinary" day, E has contact with some people, like A1 to A5 and A10, whom E usually sees and interacts with almost every day. On that particular day, E also has contact with some other people, A6 to A9 and the B's, whom he sees and interacts with less frequently. Focusing on "an ordinary day" in which two different kinds of alters are "daily contacts" for any ego, sociologists have developed a scholarly device to collect information about "networks of daily contacts" (Fu 2005). In this section, with the assistance of the Chinese General Social Survey (CGSS), I examine the networks of daily contacts for adult Chinese individuals, paying attention to how network building is related to the *guanxi* logics in urban China today. The CGSSs are national probability samples and thus give us strong confidence that the findings here are generalizable to all urbanites in Chinese cities

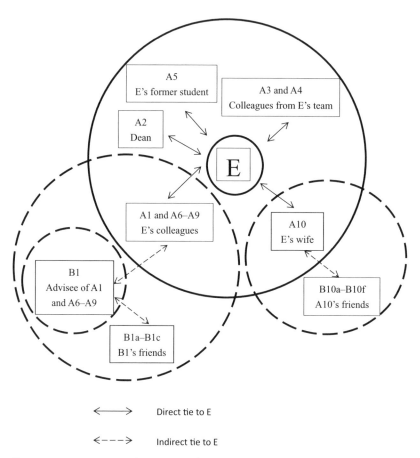

Figure 2.1: An Ego–Alter Network

without any dispute (consult Bian and Li 2012 for details of the CGSS designs).

The CGSS in 2012 collected information on networks of daily contacts from a probability national sample of 5,819 adults aged 18 and above. The CGSS battery of daily contacts is composed of six questions and a total of seventeen items. A key feature of this battery is the differentiation between kin contacts and non-kin contacts. This dichotomy allows for a kin/non-kin comparison with attention to *guanxi* as the social extension of familial sentiments and obligations. Another feature of the battery is the application of a ten-job "position generator" (Lin and Dumin 1986) to daily contacts. This part of the data is useful for measuring the potential of hierarchical resources that are embedded in and can be mobilized from the networks of daily contacts. The summary results are presented in table 2.1. What lessons do we learn about *guanxi* in Chinese people's everyday lives? In this section, we will explore class variations in kin and non-kin contacts, the heterogeneity of daily contact networks, and the international reach of *guanxi*.

Kin Daily Contacts and Interclass Similarity

The CGSS used the following question to collect information on kin contacts. "On an ordinary day, with how many family members or relatives, *excluding those who live with you*, do you have contact through telephone, mails, internet, or face-to-face?" Looking at the emphasized phrase, we understand that members of the immediate family living under the same roof are not counted as a contact in the CGSS measure of daily kin contacts. A member of our immediate family is assumed to be a "constant" contact for us, and the CGSS is aimed at "variation" in daily kin contacts beyond the respondent's household.

The CGSS respondents in 2012 had no problem in picking an imaginary "ordinary day" and counting their kin contacts. As shown in panel A of table 2.1, 20.1 percent of the respondents admit that they make no contact with any relatives outside the home on an ordinary day. We do not know whether these people have any relatives outside the home or not, and if they do what the reasons for making no contact are. Lacking this kind of detail is a drawback of large-scale surveys. Nevertheless, it is shown that about 80 percent of the CGSS respondents all make daily contact with at least one relative. Predominantly,

Table 2.1: Daily Contact Networks (CGSS 2012, N = 5,819)

Network	Category	N	%
A. Kin daily contacts			
On an ordinary day, with how many family members or relatives, excluding those who live with you, do you have contact through telephone, mails, internet, or face-to-face? Your best estimate is: [**mean = 3.25**]	0 persons	1169	20.1%
	1–5 persons	4147	71.3%
	6–10 persons	326	5.6%
	> 10 persons	177	3.0%
B. Non-kin daily contacts			
On an ordinary day, with how many people other than family members or relatives do you have contact through telephone, mails, internet, or face-to-face? Your best estimate is: [**mean = 6.91**]	0 persons	1012	17.4%
	1–5 persons	3163	54.4%
	6–10 persons	761	13.1%
	> 10 persons	883	15.2%
C. Relative status of non-kin daily contacts			
Among non-kin contacts with whom you frequently socialize, which of the following best describes social characteristics of these people? Circle one.	Higher	519	9.2%
	Lower	87	1.6%
	Equivalent	5019	89.2%
D. Contacts of foreign residence			
Do you have relatives, friends, or acquaintances in a foreign country?	Yes	723	12.4%
	No	5094	87.6%

Table 2.1: Daily Contact Networks (CGSS 2012, N = 5,819)—cont'd

Network	Category	N	%
E. Contacts of foreign origin			
Do you have acquaintances of foreign origin?	Yes	400	6.9%
	No	5412	93.1%
F. Contacts of international reach			
	Yes	869	15.0%
	No	4952	85.0%

G. Daily contact networks by class	Job holders N	Kin contacts Mean	Non-kin contacts Mean	Job diversity 1–10
Total	2108	2.52	5.88	3.09
Managerial	62	2.90	6.92	5.10
Professional/ technical	187	2.99	9.21	5.33
Clerical	49	3.06	7.57	4.51
Manual workers	1208	2.30	4.84	2.46
Small business owners	537	2.98	8.85	3.72
Private firm owners	65	3.23	15.61	5.37
F-test score		4.6	15.1	88.4

For simplicity of presentation, categories in A and B are merged from the original categories: 0, 1–2, 3–4, 5–9, 10–19, 20–49, 50–99, 100 or more. Means are calculated by using midpoint values of these original categories.

people make contact with up to five relatives (71.3 percent), a small minority make contact with six to ten relatives (5.6 percent), and the upper 3 percent in the "kin networking hierarchy" make contact with more than ten relatives a day.

These figures indicate a dense kinship network of daily contacts. Counting all responses from the CGSS respondents, we envision an imaginary average Chinese urbanite who makes daily contact with 3.25 relatives outside the home. To someone this figure may mean a phone call to her aging father at home, a visit to her hospitalized mother far from home, and a chat with her sister on the WeChat (微信 *wei xin*) network. Broadening our view, this average daily contact number of 3.25 translates into 23 occasions of contact with relatives per week and 1,200 occasions of contact with relatives on a yearly basis. These are a lot of contacts among relatives living away from each other.

While the CGSS dataset does not offer information about what people do with the relatives contacted, there is little interclass variation in kinship networks of daily contacts (as shown by the low 'F value' (4.6) in panel G). The column indicates that manual workers have a substantially lower number of kin contacts (2.3) but the other occupational classes are close to each other and all have above-average numbers of kin contacts. Note that panel G is confined to paid-job holders, who have a lower average number of daily kin contacts than that of the total sample; about two-thirds of the total sample did not have a paid job at the time of the survey and they were expected to have more time and greater personal need to contact relatives on any ordinary day. Little interclass variation in networks of daily contacts among relatives implies that kinship networks are universally important to the Chinese.

Non-Kin Daily Contacts and Interclass Variation

For measuring non-kin daily contacts, the CGSS used a similar question. "On an ordinary day, with how many people other than family members or relatives do you have *contact* through telephone, mails, internet, or face-to-face?" I emphasize the word "contact" for readers' attention. In the survey "contact" was defined as an interaction of personal significance. Say you are a school teacher and give lectures to fifty students a day. This counts as no contact for you on any chosen workday because you do not involve yourself in personal interaction with any of your students. But you meet two of your colleagues at lunch to talk about a number of topics, personal or work-related. This counts two contacts. These kinds of examples were used during CGSS interviewer training. Most importantly, all CGSS interviewers were briefed to let the respondent decide whether or not someone met on an ordinary day was counted as a contact, simply because personal contacts are personal.

Panel B in table 2.1 shows a large interpersonal variation in non-kin networks of daily contacts. More than 17 percent of the respondents make no contact beyond kinship, but 54.4 percent have one to five non-kin contacts, 13.1 percent have six to ten, and 15.2 percent more than ten. These figures translate into a mean of 6.91 non-kin contacts for an imaginary average Chinese urbanite. For this imaginary person, the figure translates into more than 48 instances of contact with non-kin alters per week, or more than 2,500 instances of contact with non-kin alters on a yearly basis. As compared to kin networks of daily contacts, there is a relatively larger and statistically significant interclass variation in non-kin networks of daily contacts.

In the subsample of 2,108 job holders (panel G), the mean number of non-kin contacts decreases to 5.88, which indicates that job holders have fewer chances to socialize with non-kin contacts than non-working adults. Nonetheless, private firm owners take the lead by having 15.61 non-kin contacts on an ordinary day. This is followed by professionals (9.21 contacts), small business owners (8.85), clerical workers (7.57), and managers (6.92). Manual workers are the only occupational class having a substantially lower number of non-kin contacts (4.84) than the imaginary average job-holder.

Network Heterogeneity in Daily Contacts

We explore two aspects of network heterogeneity in daily contacts. The first is status heterogeneity between the respondent and his or her non-kin daily contacts. Panel C shows that the CGSS respondents were asked the following question: "Among non-kin contacts with whom you frequently socialize, which of the following *best* describes social characteristics of these people?" Less than 10 percent (9.2 percent) of the respondents chose the response "you have contact more with people who are socially higher than those who are lower"; a tiny minority (1.6 percent) chose the response "you have contact more with people who are socially lower than those who are higher"; and 89.2 percent chose the response "the majority of people with whom you have contact are socially equivalent to you." This most populated third category indicates a high degree of ego–alter equality in status perception in the networks' non-kin daily contacts.

The tendency toward ego–alter equality in perceived status, however, does not tell the full story of network heterogeneity in China. Panel G, again confined to job holders, examines job diversity among all daily contacts, kin and non-kin. A ten-job battery was presented to CGSS respondents, asking them to identify whether their daily contacts work in any of these jobs. In theoretical abstraction, a job title translates into one degree of job diversity. Therefore, a higher degree of job diversity implies greater reachability across the socioeconomic hierarchy in Chinese society (Lin 2001b; Bian 2008b). The results show an average of 3.09 degrees of job diversity for an imaginary average job holder in urban China. But interclass variation is huge (as evidenced by 88.4 F-values among six occupational classes). Specifically, private firm owners once again take the lead by having 5.37 degrees of job diversity, followed by professionals (5.33), managers (5.10), clerical workers (4.51), and small business owners (3.72), leaving manual workers (2.46) the only occupational class having a substantially lower degree of job diversity than the imaginary average job holder in China.

The International Reach of Chinese *Guanxi* Networks

In the global age (Albrow 1996, 2017) many of us are globally connected. You live in China but perhaps some of your relatives and friends live in other parts of the world. You may not contact them frequently but still can maintain a certain level of intimacy and thus retain the capacity of *guanxi* mobilization when needed. Perhaps you operate a kitchen-utensils business in China, but some of your supplies and technology are from foreign countries and your products are sold in many other countries. For this business, you work regularly with partners and acquaintances in foreign countries and some of them become your close friends. How do we assess the international reach of Chinese *guanxi* networks?

The CGSS 2012 had two items about this. The first item is about contacts of foreign residence. One-eighth (12.4 percent) of the respondents had contacts of foreign residence. The second item is about contacts of foreign origin. Close to 7 percent (6.9 percent to be exact) of the respondents were positive. Combining these two indicators creates a composite variable showing that 15 percent of the respondents have established contact ties of international reach. This level of network international reach is much lower than in Japan (34 percent), Korea (50 percent), and Taiwan (63 percent).

Summary

On a daily basis, the imaginary average urban adult in China makes contact with more than ten significant others on a personal level. About one-third are kin contacts and more than two-thirds non-kin contacts. On a scale from one to ten degrees of job diversity, daily contacts on average cover 31 percent of a full range of job diversity. Because the job diversity scale is hierarchical, this number implies a considerable capacity of *direct reachability* of the *guanxi* network for an average Chinese urbanite. Two illustrations suffice here. On an occupational hierarchy of 100 ranking positions, the average Chinese can reach out to thirty-one near positions. On China's administrative hierarchy of twenty-four ranks, a middle-ranking cadre of rank 12 can reach out to four ranks in each direction up and down the hierarchy.

At aggregate level, networks of daily contacts inform us of several features of Chinese *guanxi* networks. Chinese kinship networks are dense and homogenous, with a high frequency of everyday interaction and an extremely low degree of interclass variation. These findings imply the universal value of kinship networks to Chinese individuals and families across levels of the socioeconomic hierarchy. Non-kin networks, on the other hand, are more likely to connect people of perceived equal status than people of perceived different status. At the same time, however, networks of daily contacts, kin and non-kin combined, have a considerable degree of structural diversity, giving advantaged classes greater potential than disadvantaged classes to exchange favors across levels of the socioeconomic hierarchy. This potential is enlarged and elevated to a higher level for the more than one-seventh of Chinese adult individuals who have established network ties of international reach.

GUANXI CULTIVATION AND EXPANSION THROUGH BANQUETS

Banqueting plays a big part in *guanxi* networks in China. In the West, the term "banquet" generally connotes a large, elegant, and elaborate party on a formal occasion, such as a state dinner, a wedding banquet, or a retirement party. In the Chinese context, however, I follow Yang (1994) by using it to refer to a wider range of gatherings of relatives, friends, and acquaintances that involve "social eating" – eating a meal with significant others for social purposes (Bian 2001). Among our daily contacts just analyzed, some are the people with whom we have consumed social meals, for example E sharing a working lunch with two junior colleagues, and later dinner with colleagues serving on the same doctoral advisory committee. Therefore, we ask: To what extent do banquets help build *guanxi* networks? Is there any way to measure "social eating networks?" How are people's *guanxi* networks cultivated and expanded through social eating? I begin with my personal experiences.

Three Social Eating Encounters

I was sent down to the countryside upon graduation from middle school in Tianjin in 1973. I was 17 years and 8 months old, to be exact, and I was the leader of twenty former classmates of similar age sent together to a poor village of about 200 households. Most households in the village lived in hardship. On a cold winter evening in my second year in the village, I was invited to a dinner at the home of Mr. K, the head of my production team. At the dinner were Mr. K (45 years old), his wife (similar age), and me: just three of us. It was a private, warm, and pleasant atmosphere, and the very first time I was invited to a villager's home for rather a formal dinner. I do not recall what we ate, but I cannot forget one thing the couple showed me after dinner. At his wife's suggestion, Mr. K made sure the doors were closed tight, the curtains were drawn together, and no one was outside the house. Then, from deep within a big wooden chest, the only furniture they had in the house, he took out a package wrapped in old newspapers. The package was laid on the dinner table, and Mr. K carefully unpacked it by opening the paper wrappers one layer at a time. I watched closely, paying attention to the inside of the package: something like a piece of paper which was still wrapped in a handkerchief. It was the deed of the lands Mr. K's family owned before!

The couple then took turns to tell me their stories. They told me where "our" lands were located in the village, how fertile the lands were when "his family" owned them, what a glorious time it was before the collectivization of the late 1950s, and how terrible life had been thereafter. Growing up an urban kid under Communism, I did not have a rural relative, nor had I learned anything like this from books or classroom lectures. I took a huge lesson from the couple about life in the "socialist" countryside. That was the starting point when I began establishing a real sense of the positive meaning of privatization. As might be expected, I became a close friend of the couple.

Many years later, I taught at Hong Kong University of Science and Technology (HKUST). I was 42 and had been in the United States for twelve years, first in graduate school for my doctoral degree and then for my research and teaching jobs at Duke and Minnesota universities, respectively. Living in the United States for a long time, I had gotten used to the culture of Dutch treat when colleagues got together for lunch or dinner and split the bills. At HKUST, I was surprised by the difference in lunch arrangements between my colleagues of Western origin and those of Chinese origin: The former were normalized by Dutch treat to settle the charge, but the latter frequently had someone voluntarily taking care of the bills out of their personal pocket. Both lunches were occasions to learn the new information, opinions, ideas, values, beliefs, and personalities that were usually not visible at faculty meetings.

Now, I've worked with many collaborators from the Chinese mainland over the past three decades. They are "true" Chinese because they understand the "social order" of banquets. The host takes the head chair, speaks first, and sets the tone and selects the topics of conversation. The guest of honor is seated on the right of the host and is expected to talk to the host more frequently than to anyone else around the table. The rest of the people attending the dinner are all seated in an "orderly" way: Senior colleagues are seated closer to the host, less senior colleagues next, and junior colleagues at the opposite side of the table far from the head chair. If a senior colleague comes late, the less senior colleagues already seated all stand up and switch seats to make sure that the senior colleague gets the "right" spot to be seated. When the host is a junior colleague offering a "thank-you" banquet to his or her superiors, the most respected person among the invitees is offered the head chair to play the symbolic role of the host. At these "social-orderly" banquets, current relationships are strengthened and future collaborative opportunities are created.

The three social eating encounters just described inform us of several important features of a banquet as the venue of *guanxi* networking. Trusted persons are invited to a private banquet where secrets of personal importance are shared. A *guanxi* tie is either in the making or elevated to a new level of trust, intimacy, and mutual reciprocity. A small-group banquet in a restaurant is expected to be paid for by a host, even if it is a lunch attended by colleagues with close relationships in the workplace. A feeling of brotherhood or sisterhood usually emerges to define the atmosphere of small-scale gatherings. Many banquets are hierarchical even if the attendees are close colleagues or longtime friends. Both expressive and instrumental goals are served by these banquets. Banquets may appear to be less deliberate and more informal and spontaneous. But many of these banquets do involve considerable planning of whom to invite, who should pay, and what to talk about throughout the banqueting process. Network building through social banquets in the *guanxi* culture is more deliberate than spontaneous.

Consumption of Social Meals

In May of 1998, 356 urban households in Shanghai, Tianjin, Wuhan, and Shenzhen agreed to participate in a week-long study on eating arrangements the household heads had for each lunch, dinner, and nighttime snack consumed within the week (Bian, Davis, and Wang 2007). As shown in table 2.2, a total of 5,054 meals were recorded, of which 19 percent eaten alone by the respondents, 60 percent with the family, and 21 percent with "others." This last category meets our definition of social eating. This figure indicates that about one-fifth of meals are of social and relational nature in urban China. For simplicity, a "social meal" is defined here as the meal eaten by an ego (the respondent in the study) and one or more alters of non-immediate family tie.

Of the 1,086 social meals recorded, 53 percent were paid for by either ego or alter, which compares favorably with 20 percent of the meals paid for as a Dutch treat. The remaining 27 percent of meals were paid for through "other arrangement." This was a pre-designed response category on the questionnaire with the intention of avoiding the language of "paid for by employer" or "paid for by public funds," which would give respondents an impression of corruption and thus possibly distort the reliability of their answers. As for the purposes of social meals, 63 percent were expressive ("just for a conversation") and 28 percent instrumental ("talk about a business"). The intended purpose of social eating does matter for who pays the bills: An expressive purpose decreases the one-person payment arrangement to 45 percent and maintains the Dutch treat arrangement at 19 percent, but an instrumental purpose increases the one-person payment arrangement to 85 percent while substantially reducing the Dutch treat arrangement to 9 percent. These figures indicate that social eating is a mixed arrangement in China.

The 356 respondents were also requested to record information about the partners with whom they consumed a social meal during the week that was studied. Kin (19 percent) and pseudo-family (45 percent) contacts together accounted for a strong majority of social eating partners, but "other" alters, at 36 percent, were substantial. Social meals were more likely to occur between people of the same occupational class (60 percent), but still 40 percent was a large quantity to

Table 2.2: Measures and Descriptive Statistics for Networks of Social Eating

Variables	(N) %	Variables	%
Total meals eaten	(5054)	Relational composition	
% eat alone	19	Kin ties	19
% eat with family	60	Pseudo-family ties[a]	45
% eat with others	21	Other ties[b]	36
Eating with others	(1086)	Class composition[c]	
Who pays?		Same as ego's	60
% ego or alter pays	53	Different than ego's	40
% ego and alter jointly pay	20		
% other arrangement	27	Network diversity (Mean)	
What's it for?		Average # ties (1–14)	5.86
% just for a conversation	63	Average # job positions (1–20)	5.17
% talk about a business	28	Average # types (1–12)	3.68
% for other purposes	9		
Just for a conversation	(608)	Talk about a business	(274)
% ego or alter pays	45	% ego or alter pays	85
% ego and alter jointly pay	19	% ego and alter jointly pay	9
% other arrangement	37	% other arrangement	6

[a] These include guests of the family, villagers, classmates, army comrades, teachers, students or apprentices, neighbors, and friends.

[b] These include superiors and subordinates at work, work colleagues of the same rank, other work-related contacts, and business partners and contacts.

[c] A three-class scheme is used here, including cadre class, professional-technical class, and working class.

characterize the many social meals consumed by people of different class categories. The respondents who were involved in social meals with others were well connected, as evidenced by a large average number of 5.86 types of *guanxi* contacts (out of the maximum of fourteen types), 5.17 different job titles for the contacts (out of the maximum of twenty job titles), and 3.68 types of employers for these contacts (out of the maximum of twelve types of employers). On a standard scale from 1 to 100, these figures translate into forty-two degrees of tie diversity, twenty-six degrees of job diversity, and thirty-one degrees of employer diversity. By the criterion of job diversity, social eating networks are more homogenous than networks of daily contacts (thirty-one degrees of job diversity). But to a considerable degree, social eating networks are quite diverse in terms of tie diversity and employer diversity.

Banquet Guest, Banquet Host, and Banquet Attendee

Three roles can be identified to differentiate social eating participants: (1) a banquet guest, (2) a banquet host, and (3) a banquet attendee (in China, this role is often informally known as "escort eater" (陪吃, *pei chi*)). Receiving and accepting a banquet invitation is considered as having received face from the host, indicating the invitee's and the host's potential to mobilize *guanxi* resources from each other. Inversely, failure to invite someone of high status or strong influence signals the path of resource mobilization ineffective. If the invitee accepts the invitation and attends the banquet, this points to two capacities: the capacity of the banquet host to maintain *guanxi* and to commend *guanxi* resources from the invitee later, and the capacity of the invitee to maintain and extend *guanxi* networks (getting the opportunity to develop potential *guanxi* connections through banqueting). Therefore, the frequency of being a banquet guest, host, or attendee is a sensible measure of social capital in the Chinese context. Results show that income increases the frequency of one's being a banquet guest, host, and attendee (an additional data table is available from this book's webpage online*). So, economic power makes a difference in social eating participation, not just for inviting others but also for being invited as guests and escort eaters. In contrast, Chinese Communist Party (CCP) members are more likely than non-members to be banquet guests and attendees but not banquet hosts. Note that a banquet host is defined in the present analysis as someone who pays the bill. If CCP membership is an indicator of political power, the finding here implies the rent-seeking capacity of the politically powerful.

Network variables help explain a great deal of the extent to which one participates in social eating and in what roles. Network sizes do not have a direct impact, but all other network variables do. Network composition matters. People with close network ties to kin, pseudo-kin, and other contacts are more likely to be involved in social eating in all three roles. Network diversity also matters. People with more diverse networks are more likely to participate in social eating in all three roles than those with less diverse networks. But the class heterogeneity of a personal network does not matter much. It plays a small part in increasing one's likelihood of becoming a banquet guest, but not for the roles of banquet host and banquet attendee.

Findings from a National Sample Survey

While the findings just described are from a small study in the late 1990s, the CGSS 2012 collected information about social eating from the probability national sample of adults aged 18 and above. The CGSS approach toward social eating was focused on social meals consumed among non-kin contacts ("How often do you go out to eat or drink with three or more non-kin others?") and the results allow for an analysis of several issues with social eating networks.

---

* www.politybooks.com/guanxi

First, there is a fairly large variation in social eating participation – of the 5,819 respondents, 42 percent admitted that they did not participate in social eating at all (additional data table available online). This is followed by 28.7 percent of the respondents who attended "a few" social eating events, 20.1 percent "sometimes," and only 9.2 percent "often" consumed social meals with others. This variation is by class. Private firm owners have the highest average rate of participation (5.29), followed by professionals (4.07), clerks (4.06), managers (3.89), and small business owners (3.16), leaving manual workers (1.88) as the only class lower in participation than the national average (2.34).

Second, the context of social meal consumption is hierarchical. Respondents admit that "someone with special status often speaks first" (38.6 percent), "someone often dominates the conversation" (42.1 percent), and "seating is arranged even on informal occasions" (23.8 percent). Taking these responses seriously, we can construct a Likert scale measuring the extent to which a social eating context follows a hierarchical order. It turns out that 43.3 percent are free of hierarchical order, 23.1 percent in low hierarchical order, 20 percent in medium hierarchical order, and 13.5 percent in strong hierarchical order.

Third, social eating occasions generate opportunities of *guanxi* expansion. Of the 3,368 respondents who stated that they participated in social eating, 87.9 percent made new friends. Their opportunities of meeting new friends varied, and this variation is largely explained by the class categories to which participants belong. Once again, private firm entrepreneurs take the lead by having the highest probability of meeting new friends through social eating (5.08), followed by managers (4.02), clerks (4.09), small business owners (3.99), professionals (3.55), and finally manual workers (3.15). The results also show that through new friends met, social eating participation significantly increases one's network diversity and upper reachability, and that participants in social eating are happier when they have a higher rather than lower degree of participation.

Finally, social eating networks have a consistent impact on institutional trust. This impact is corrosive: higher participation in social eating networks reduces people's trust in political institutions simply because social eating networks are likely to flow politically sensitive information about the dark side of agents of political institutions. More specifically, increased participation in social eating networks significantly reduces trust in government (−.431), the police (−.096), the court (−.056), and local cadres in the residential community (−.115).

Summary

Social eating is a *guanxi* occasion. The imaginary average Chinese urbanite consumes more than one-fifth of lunches, dinners, and night-time snacks with significant others on social eating occasions. More than likely, the cost of the meals on these occasions is not split but covered by one party to signify the spirit of brotherhood or sisterhood shared by social eating parties of close *guanxi*. This spirit is mixed with the norm of reciprocity when the social purpose of the meals gives way to instrumental purposes, in which case the one-party-payment arrangement becomes predominant. Social eating banquets are likely to follow a hierarchical order, but very frequently new friends are met at social eating, enlarging network diversity as well as increasing network upper reachability.

GUANXI EXCHANGES AT EVENTS OF CULTURAL SIGNIFICANCE

Guanxi building is cumulative and through events of personal significance. By events, I mean events bigger than the social meal that an average Chinese individual attends for one in five meals. Consider three friends, A, B, and C. A is invited to B's wedding banquet and C is not. This means a lot both to the close A–B relationship and relatively a more distant A–C relationship. D receives a memorable gift from his former doctoral advisee E when D turns 60, the age that Confucian scholars consider a critical point of transition in the life course. But his other former doctoral advisees, F's, do not even send an email message to wish him well on his sixtieth birthday. This signifies that the D–E relationship has elevated to a personal level whereas the E–F's relationships stay at teacher–student formality. *Guanxi* is a personalized relationship, and there is nothing to do with *guanxi* going on if a relationship is confined to formality. The point to be conveyed here is not so much about who is related to whom at what levels. Rather, events of personal significance are opportunities to assess the nature and quality of *guanxi* networks of ongoing social relations.

My focus in this section is on events of cultural significance. Unlike events of personal significance such as weddings and birthdays, events of cultural significance occur for all members of a given society at the same point in time. This allows for a general population survey to collect information about social interactions in which people engage with each other at certain events of cultural significance. In Chinese *guanxi* culture, events of cultural significance are occasions for ritualized social exchanges among people of personal significance to each other. For example, during the Spring Festival, the New Year celebration on the lunar calendar, the Chinese people are culturally expected to socialize with one another if they are in the core networks of their significant others. Thus, we can use a "New Year exchange network" generator to measure and assess the forms and structural variations of an individual's *guanxi* networks.

New Year Celebration as a Cultural Tradition

The lunar New Year celebration has both sacred and secular traditions in China. The sacred tradition dates back more than 4,000 years to when Shun (舜), one of the five legendary emperors of ancient China long before Emperor Qin Shi-huang (259–210 BC), ascended the throne. On that day, Shun was acclaimed as the Son of Heaven and led his subjects to worship heaven and earth. Since then, Chinese people have regarded this day as the first day of the year. It is said that this is the origin of the lunar New Year, later called 春节 (*chun jie*) in Chinese or Spring Festival in English translation. It usually falls on a day in January or February on the Western calendar.

The sacred tradition of Spring Festival has continued in forms of folk religion, superstition, and other cultural rituals into the modern era. I remember my grandma, an illiterate woman without her own name, worshiping heaven and earth before the portrait of the god of the kitchen (灶王爷 *zao wang ye*) while she began preparing food for the family's New Year celebration. This celebration is a long period, extending from the eve to the fifteenth day of the New Year, when no family would really cook; therefore, food preparation can be a substantial amount of work before the celebration begins. I was growing up in my grandma's house before moving back to live with my parents to go to a public kindergarten affiliated with my father's factory when I turned six in 1961. Before then, each year before the New Year's eve I watched my grandma sticking new portraits of the god of fortune (财神 *cai shen*), the god of doors (门神 *men shen*), and Lord Guan (关帝 *guan di*), along with colorful paper-cut artworks, to the walls, doors, windows, and even some furniture in her house. These rituals, among others, were regarded as part of "Four Olds" (四旧 *si jiu*) and were all stopped by Mao's Red Guards during the Cultural Revolution (1966–76). Ironically, some of these rituals along with new cultural forms of holiday celebration have since come back in to family life in urban and especially rural China (Davis and Friedman 2014).

The English translation "Spring Festival" vividly and accurately brings out the character of the secularized New Year celebration. It is the first day of the spring term and should be celebrated with joy and happiness because the cold winter is about over and warm spring days are coming. So, before the spring farming that kicks off a year-long schedule of continuous hard work in agricultural society, people take the opportunity to celebrate the glories of the past year and wish each other well for the new fortunes of the coming year. While the celebration centers on family reunions, it also involves people paying home visits to senior relatives and respected superiors (i.e., teachers, masters, supervisors, etc.), exchanging holiday greetings and wishes with close friends and nice neighbors, and in contemporary times socializing with colleagues and business partners as well. Indeed, the celebration of the Chinese New Year is a big social event of tremendous significance, personal and cultural.

Ritualized Social Exchanges at the New Year Celebration

Family reunion is the dominant theme of the New Year celebration among Han Chinese and it starts with the evening banquet on New Year's Eve. A married son, if not living with his parents, will rush back with his wife and children to his parents' house before dinner time and stay through New Year's Day. A married daughter must be with her husband and stay in her mother-in-law's house on New Year's Eve and New Year's Day. She will "return to mother's house" (回娘家 *hui niangjia*) with her husband and children on the second day of the New Year. On the fifth day, married sons and their families go back to their parents' home to symbolically welcome the god of fortune. And the fifteenth evening sees their final visit to their parents' home to celebrate the Lantern Festival (元宵节 *yuanxiao jie*), the last event of the New Year celebration.

Family celebrations require ritualized exchanges of greetings, gifts, and banquets. At the turn of the New Year, family members are expected to greet one another personally. Traditionally, small children present their greetings to the elderly with a formal obeisance and press their heads to the floor (磕头 *ke tou*). Nowadays this ritual continues in some families, but in others it is replaced by bowing to the elderly. In return, the elderly give "growing-safe money" (压岁钱) in a red envelope (红包) to each child. In recent years the amount of cash has become substantial, and the total spending in this category can be a big figure when a married couple give this money to their unmarried nephews and nieces on both sides, as well as to the small children of their other relatives and close non-kin friends. When the total amount of this money is calculated as a proportion of total household monthly income, a 1998 study (described in greater detail shortly) shows that it was 24 percent in Shanghai, 29 percent in Tianjin, 38 percent in Wuhan, and 52 percent in Shenzhen (Bian, Davis, and Wang 2007).

Married sons and daughters are also expected to present both greetings and gifts to their parents and grandparents as an act and symbol of filial piety. While these usually do not involve cash, married children give substantial gifts of food, clothing, or home furnishing to their aging parents. On all occasions when families meet during the New Year's celebration, evening banquets in restaurants or at home are the high points of feeling the spirit of familial togetherness. During multiple courses, people take turns to offer toasts to each other for good health and longevity, thank each other for support during the past year, and exchange wishes for the bright future of the children. Married siblings may take turns to host banquets for each other's families. When the husband and wife are both from a single-child family, their parents invite each other's families to banquets held in the name of their married children.

Beyond the family and kinship, the New Year's celebration is also the time for social networking with friends, colleagues, and neighbors. The rules for home visiting, gift giving, or feast exchanging with non-kin contacts are not as clearly prescribed as for the family, but the New Year is the time to socialize with *guanxi* contacts that are perceived to be important on personal levels. If the relationship is thought to be close by one party but the other party fails to even make a greeting contact during the New Year celebration, it is a signal to the parties that this relationship is no longer important. Conversely, the New Year's celebration can be a one-time opportunity to revitalize a deteriorated relationship or transform a weak relationship into a stronger one.

Findings from an In-Depth Study

Bian, Davis, and Wang (2007) conducted a study of 401 households in Shanghai, Tianjin, Wuhan, and Shenzhen. About 100 families with diverse backgrounds were selected through a social-class-adjusted probability sampling strategy in each chosen city. These cities are all on the east coast, but in four disparate geographical areas whose distinctive dialects and local cultural practices allow for analyzing interregional variation, while the study results are still generalizable to urban China. During the study period, each selected household was asked to complete a daily log of activities during New Year's Eve and the first five days of the New Year, the period concentrated on social networking.

Figure 2.2 provides summary results on New Year exchanges among kin, friends, colleagues, and neighbors. The high bars close to the top to the left of the chart indicate a fully engaged kinship network in the New Year celebration. Of the 386 families studied, 98.7 percent had face-to-face greeting exchanges with their families and relatives and only five families were unable to do so, due to traveling during the period studied. When the relatives got together, nearly all of them had gift exchanges with each other (93.8 percent) and most of them invited each other to banquets together (86.8 percent). Those families who were unable to give gifts (including cash gifts) or host banquets were constrained by their poor economic conditions, in which case they were usually asked not to offer gifts or banquets. Kinship networks of sentiments and obligations transcend class boundaries.

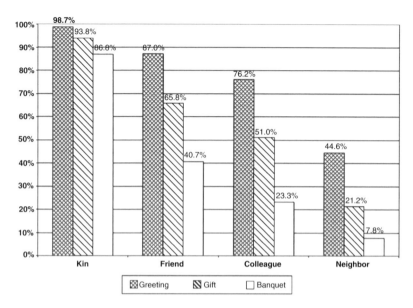

Figure 2.2: Percent Distribution of Households in New Year Social Exchanges

The extent of social exchanges among non-kin contacts is much smaller than in kinship networks. As can be seen, greeting exchanges decrease from 87 percent for friendship networks to (in rounded figures) 76 percent for colleague networks and to 45 percent for neighbor networks. This implies that on average 13 percent of urban families lack close friends, 24 percent lack close colleagues, and 55 percent lack close neighbors. Neighbors are close by and it costs little to pay a visit in leisure time. So why do so many neighbors not even come out to greet each other during the New Year celebration?

First, neighborhood age matters for all social exchanges. The data shows that a one-year increase in neighborhood age will generate a 43 percent greater probability of having neighbors engage in greeting exchanges, and this effect is even stronger for gift exchanges (by 54 percent) and banquet exchanges (by 137 percent). It takes time for neighbors to accumulate familial sentiments and obligations to do something special at an event of cultural significance. Regional differences are also important (additional data table available online). Shanghai residents are significantly more likely to engage with relatives than are residents in Tianjin, Wuhan, and Shenzhen, but they are significantly less likely to engage in exchanges with friends and colleagues. In terms of neighbor networks, residents in Tianjin have the greatest extent of greeting exchanges, but residents in Wuhan and Shenzhen are more likely to engage in gift and banquet exchanges.

GUANXI NETWORKS AND SOCIAL CLASS

Increasing class inequality has characterized reform-era China. This has been evidenced by the increase in the Gini index of income inequality from 0.24 in the late 1970s to about 0.50 in the second decade of the twenty-first century (Li and Luo 2012); the rise of "the new rich" property class (Goodman 2014); the re-empowered political, managerial, and professional elite (So 2003); the emergence and expansion of the "middle class" (Li 2005); and Mao's largely differentiated and marginalized working class (Bian et al. 2018). Our question in this section is not about class inequality in material rewards but about class variation in social relationships. We ask: Are advantaged social classes well connected? Are disadvantaged classes socially marginalized and separated from the rest of Chinese society?

Guanxi *Network Ties by Social Class*

A socially isolated class has its members connected within class but disconnected between class categories. In contrast, a socially integrated class has its members not only connected within class but also well connected with members of other class categories, especially advantageous social classes. Based on Bourdieu's (1986) notion of "position of social distinction," for China we can identify three socially distinctive class categories: (1) officials who exercise political and administrative power at various levels of a durable party-state, (2) mangers and entrepreneurs who exercise economic power over resource and reward allocations, and (3) professionals who exercise knowledge and skill power over the allocation of human capital. Which social classes have greater connections to these three positions of high social distinction in China?

Table 2.3 provides a tentative answer. Based on a large-scale survey of job holders in Chinese cities (Bian 2008a), seven occupational class categories are identified, from officials to non-skilled workers. The survey respondents were asked to identify whether their New Year visitors worked in jobs classified into three positions of high social distinction, namely, officials, managers, and professionals. The bottom of table 2.3 shows that 61 percent of the respondents had ties to officials, 45 percent had ties to managers, and 56 percent had ties to professionals. These three figures indicate that some individuals are well connected to high social positions, but others are not. Are the latter from disadvantaged classes?

The main body of the table offers a definite response. When the non-skilled workers are treated as a reference class category, for which the class-average probability of connecting to officials, managers, and professionals is set at a level of 1, the class-average probabilities are calculated to show whether the class-average probability of having certain ties is greater or lower than 1. As can be seen, the non-skilled workers are least likely to have ties to officials; business owners and the self-employed are equally unlikely to develop ties to managers; and the self-employed are least likely to have ties to professionals. It is worth noting that ties of the three positions of high social distinction are based on home visits during the New Year celebration, and therefore these ties are not business or collegial but are the ties of

Table 2.3: Class Variation in Ties to Positions of High Social Distinction and Network Composition (N = 4213)

Class category (% of total)	Ties to officials (0, 1)	Ties to managers (0, 1)	Ties to professionals (0, 1)	Network size (1–300)	Network ceiling (6–95)	Network diversity (1–20)
Official (8.3%)	2.14	1.10	1.45	1.17	1.20	1.15
Manager (10.4%)	1.79	1.44	1.57	1.15	1.15	1.14
Professional (13.1%)	1.42	1.38	3.16	1.21	1.21	1.32
Clerical worker (9.1%)	1.44	1.23	1.28	1.05	1.13	1.12
Skilled worker (20.5%)	1.18	1.10	1.36	1.06	1.08	1.06
Business owner (0.8%)	1.17	0.74	1.09	1.32	0.96	1.12
Self-employed (10.6%)	1.08	0.76	0.85	1.06	0.99	0.91
Non-skilled worker (27.1%)	1.00	1.00	1.00	1.00	1.00	1.00
Average	61%	45%	56%	28.7	75.8	6.3

Figures in the last six columns are exponential coefficients obtained from logistic models on class differences in ties to the identified categories. In each model, "non-skilled worker" is the reference category, whose average probability of having ties to each identified position of social distinction is statistically set at 1.00. Each model includes the following variables to control for individual differences: gender, age, age square, CCP membership, college education, work sector, household income, residence status, and work relations on the job.
Source: Adapted from Bian (2008a: tables 5.1 and 5.3)

personal significance. In a sense, these are *guanxi* ties among Chinese individuals and households. From this perspective, we can draw a few tentative conclusions from the overall pattern of the findings presented here. First, officials, managers, and professionals are the well-connected occupational classes in China. Second, clerical workers and skilled workers are less well-connected. Third, despite their class variations in material outcomes, the self-employed and non-skilled workers are equally poorly connected to positions of high social distinction.

Guanxi *Network Structure by Social Class*

Table 2.3 continues to examine the question of class variation in social connectiveness but from the angle of network structure. Here, New Year visitors are analyzed to measure network size (number of visitors), network ceiling (the highest prestige of visitors), and network diversity (number of distinctive job positions among visitors). These measures show a very large interpersonal variation in network structures among the Chinese respondents: an average of 28.7 visitors with a range from 1 to 300 visitors, an average network ceiling of 75.8 prestige scores with a range from 6 to 95, and an average 6.3 occupations with a range from 1 to 20.

In comparison to non-skilled workers, whose average level of network size, network ceiling, and network diversion is set at 1, the class-average levels of network structure measures are calculated for other occupational-class categories. As for officials, their network sizes are 17 percent larger, 20 percent higher, and 15 percent more diverse. Managers and professionals show similar tendencies in the three network structures, but clerical workers and skilled workers have substantially lower strengths in terms of network size, ceiling, and diversity. Interestingly, business owners have the largest average network sizes among all class categories (32 percent larger), but their network ceilings are quite low (4 percent lower, $1.00 - 0.96 = 0.04$) while their network diversity is the same as that of clerical workers. The self-employed and non-skilled workers are truly the disadvantaged in *guanxi* networks: relatively smaller network sizes, substantially lower network ceilings, and narrower ranges of occupational positions from and to which they maintain *guanxi* contacts.

Guanxi *Network Capital by Social Class*

Network ties to positions of high social distinction and network structures are the relational mechanisms through which to accumulate social capital. Here, social capital refers to the social resources that are embedded in and can be mobilized from social networks (Lin 2001b). In the Chinese context, because our measures of network ties and network structures are based on New Year exchange networks, and since New Year exchange networks are *guanxi* networks, it is reasonable to term the social capital that is generated from New Year exchange networks *guanxi* network capital. Based on Chinese General Social Surveys in 2003, 2006, and 2008 with a total sample size of 6,465 respondents, table 2.4 presents interesting results on class variation in two measures of *guanxi* network capital.

The first measure of *guanxi* network capital is termed "resource volume." This refers to the total average resources that an individual can generate through his or her *guanxi* network. We can interpret the percentage points when talking about a *guanxi* network's resource volume in percentage variation away from the imaged average Chinese urbanite. The socially advantaged classes (officials/managers, professionals, and clerical workers) are much higher than the imaged average urbanite in resource volume, and the socially disadvantaged classes (manual workers and small business owners) are much lower than the imaged average urbanite on this measure, while private firm owners are moderately above the imaginary average urbanite.

Table 2.4: Class Variations in *Guanxi* Network Capital

Variables	N	Resource volume (standardized score)		Resource diversity (standardized score)	
		Mean	% change	Mean	% change
Total	6465	0.0	0.0	0.0	0.0
Officials/managers	159	0.74	27.0%	0.58	21.9%
Professionals	430	0.75	27.3%	0.28	11.0%
Clerical workers	258	0.66	24.5%	0.34	13.3%
Manual workers	3512	−0.16	−6.4%	−0.16	−6.4%
Small business owners (hire seven or fewer)	2007	−0.11	−4.4%	0.12	4.8%
Private firm owners (hire eight or more)	99	0.17	6.8%	0.51	19.5%
F-test score		117.9		47.8	

Source: CGSS 2003, 2006, 2008

The second measure is resource diversity: how diverse the resources a *guanxi* network can generate. This measure indeed gives us a different look at class variation in Chinese *guanxi* networks. As expected, officials/managers are most advantaged in having the highest resource diversity, enjoying a large margin of about 22 percent higher than the imaginary average urbanite. Professionals and clerical workers are also advantaged in resource diversity, as their *guanxi* network's abilities to generate diverse resources are 11.0 percent and 13.3 percent, respectively, higher than the imaginary average urbanite. Manual workers are extremely low in network resource diversity (6.4 percent lower) while small business owners are moderate (4.8 percent higher). Private firm owners are a big winner in network resource diversity:

they are about 20 percent higher on this measure than the imaginary average urbanite.

Interclass Connectedness in Guanxi Networks

Thus far, the research findings presented here are focused on class variation in *guanxi* networks. One important question about the class–*guanxi* relationship is the extent to which members of disadvantaged classes are disconnected from those of advantaged classes. This is the question about interclass connectedness, for which table 2.5 shows summary results from a loglinear analysis of New Year visits (Bian et al. 2005).

Table 2.5: Propensities for Connectivity Within and Between Classes

Line	Theoretical image	Model specification	d.f.	G^2	p
0	Harmonious society	*No class*: Equally and fully connected within and between classes	144	180	.020
1	Workers separated	*Two classes*: Manual and non-manual disconnected from one another	141	115	.946
2	Dual elite	*Three classes*: Administrative and professional elites vs. manual workers	137	105	.980
3	Multiple elite	*Four classes*: Political, managerial, and professional elites vs. manual workers	131	93	.995

The results are obtained from loglinear models. Line 0 model is rejected by the data (p =.020). Lines 1–3 models are each supported by the data.
Source: Adapted from Bian et al. (2005: tables 4 and 5)

Table 2.5 begins with a theoretical image of China as a harmonious society. This image is not so much about equality in material outcomes as about an equally and fully connected social world. For sources of this image, think of the traditional Chinese notion of 大同 (*datong*, societal harmony) or the most recent CCP ideology of building a harmonious society (和谐社会 *hexie shehui*). But this theoretical image is empirically rejected, as it is significantly different from reality (the very low p-value demonstrates its low probability in relation to the data). By this single criterion of social connectedness alone, China is in no ways a harmonious society, at least not yet.

The next three theoretical images are empirically supported by the data. The first image is that manual workers are significantly unlikely to be connected to non-manual workers; here p-value is .946 on line 1, which is quite close to a perfect fit (p-value ≈ 1) between theory and reality. The second image is that China is a dual-elite society: where the elite is split between those with political credentials who gain administrative positions of high prestige, authority and material benefits, and those without political credentials who gain professional positions of high prestige, but little authority and lower material benefits (Walder 1995). While Walder's original analysis was focused on distinctive paths to administrative and professional elite positions in the Communist regime, here we confirm this image with a relational analysis. Data results on line 2 show a p-value of .980, indicating that administrative elites and professional elites are somewhat connected with one another but the members of the two elite classes are significantly unlikely to be connected to manual workers. The third image adds a small complexity by separating political elite and managerial elite, while keeping professional elite as an integrated class category. The results on line 3 show support for this image: its p-value is .995, that is, only .005, or a probability of 0.5 percent, away from a perfect fit between theory and reality.

Summary

Guanxi exchange networks predominant at the New Year's celebration provide a scholarly measurement through which to examine interclass inequality in *guanxi* networks as well as interclass connectedness. Considerable amounts of interclass inequality are found in an analysis of several large-scale surveys. Officials, managers, professionals, clerical workers, and private firm owners are consistently found to have greater access to resourceful *guanxi* networks than the imaginary average urbanite; but small business owners and, especially, manual workers are socially marginalized. These patterns lead to an overall pattern of working-class separation from the rest of Chinese society, over which the well-connected administrative and professional elites exercise the power of control.

A CONCLUDING NOTE: RURAL– URBAN DIFFERENCES

The empirical findings presented in this chapter are from social surveys of urban households and individuals. An imaginary average Chinese urbanite has been used to characterize the *guanxi* network ties, *guanxi* network structures, and *guanxi* network capital of a "model" Chinese person living in the *guanxi* society. To satisfy our curiosity as to how different rural residents may be from this urban model, in this concluding note I compare the urban model with a rural model. This comparative analysis is made possible by the China Survey of Social Change (CSSC), in which rural and urban residents were selected from a probability sample of the adult populations in the twelve province-level administrative regions of Western China (Bian and Zong 2016). While the CSSC is not a national survey and does not include the more developed East and Middle, it offers large sample sizes (5,793 rural households and 5,153 urban households) and uses the same items to measure the personal networks of rural and urban residents. These merits of the CSSC dataset give us considerable confidence in obtaining a rural–urban comparison. Table 2.6 provides summary results.

A quick look at the table leaves us with the impression that the average rural resident is consistently different from the average urban resident. For the non-statistics lover, a t-score greater than 1.96 or a p-value lower than 0.05 is the sign of a statistically significant difference between two groups under study. Of the fifteen items used, only the first, network size of daily contacts, fails to satisfy this criterion. Here, the average urban resident has a slightly larger network size of daily contacts (18.4) than the average rural resident (17.5), but the difference is too small or the standard error is too large to make it statistically significant. Substantively, this means that on average rural residents socialize with about the same number of daily contacts as urban residents in Western China.

We now can put the remaining fourteen items into two sets for a simplified discussion. The first set includes items 2–4, where rural–urban differences are in a negative direction. This means that the average rural resident has higher values in the items than the average urban resident. More specifically, as compared to the average urban resident, the average rural resident has a higher kin density of daily contact network (38 percent vs. 31 percent), a larger holiday network size (35.96 holiday contacts vs. 31.97 holiday contacts), and a higher kin density of holiday networks (67 percent vs. 59 percent). If we are informed by these three items, rural networks are more concentrated in kinship ties than urban networks. This is completely understandable, for rural residents are significantly constrained by the geographic and kinship structures of village communities whereas urban residents are better able to socialize with others from society at large. Therefore, the three items that show negative signs speak against rural residents in building a socially diverse personal network.

Table 2.6: Rural–Urban Differences in Network Measures: Mean and Standard Deviation (in Parenthesis)

Variable and measure	Urban	Rural	t-score	p-value
1 Size of network, daily contacts	18.4 (28.3)	17.5 (22.9)	1.84	0.070
2 Kin density, proportion of kin contacts	0.31 (0.26)	0.38 (0.27)	−12.2	0.000
3 Size of holiday networks	31.97 (33.68)	35.96 (41.38)	−5.37	0.000
4 Kin density, holiday networks	0.59 (0.24)	0.67 (0.22)	−17.56	0.000
5 Cadre density, proportion of cadre contacts	0.36 (0.48)	0.29 (0.45)	7.88	0.000
6 Leadership density, proportion of leaders	0.26 (0.44)	0.19 (0.39)	8.89	0.000
7 Participation in social eating as hosts	80.02 (39.98)	73.07 (44.36)	8.57	0.000
8 Participation in social eating as guests	84.02 (36.65)	75.64 (42.91)	10.88	0.000
9 Meeting new friends via social eating	62.45 (48.43)	52.89 (49.92)	9.72	0.000
10 Job diversity, holiday networks	4.30 (2.84)	3.08 (2.57)	23.41	0.000
11 Prestige ceiling, holiday networks	61.82 (27.99)	43.27 (33.13)	31.26	0.000
12 Frequent online network size	21.35 (44.07)	9.47 (24.19)	35.52	0.000
13 Proportion of exchange using text messages	0.62 (0.48)	0.42 (0.49)	20.79	0.000
14 Total spending on holidays	1641.29 (3580.28)	946.81 (2178.78)	12.27	0.000
15 Proportion of spending on holiday social activities	0.41 (0.25)	0.38 (0.26)	6.44	0.000

Rural household N = 5,793. Urban household N = 5,153.
Source: CSSC 2010

The second set of items leads to the same conclusion. Eleven items (items 5–15) are included in this set and all show statistical significance in a positive direction. This means that the average urban resident enjoys higher values in the items than the rural average resident. Let us run through these items to characterize the rural–urban differences. As compared to the average urban resident, the average rural resident has a substantially lower proportion of cadres and leading cadres in their daily networks (items 5 and 6); is significantly less likely to engage in social eating with others (items 7–9); is significantly lower in job diversity and network ceiling (items 10 and 11); is falling significantly behind in online networks (items 12 and 13); and spends less money in holiday socialization in terms of both absolute and relative numbers (items 14 and 15).

Clearly, rural China and urban China differ in networks of social relations. Since the late 1970s, China has increased its urbanization tremendously, from 18 percent in 1978 to an estimated 60 percent by 2020 and to 70 percent by 2030 (Chinese Academy of Social Sciences 2017). More and more Chinese citizens will be living in towns and cities. Therefore, the features of the urbanite networks I've described and analyzed in this chapter can be used as a yardstick to characterize and assess those of the networks for the new urbanites. But an analysis of *guanxi* also tells a story about the shape of Chinese society and inequality within it.

3 | *Guanxi* and Jobs ────────────────

A longstanding controversy has focused on the influence of *guanxi* on job allocation. On the one hand, a stream of empirical evidence shows that *guanxi* has provided an informal channel through which Chinese individuals have obtained jobs both before and after the post-1978 market reforms (Bian 1994a, 1994b, 1997, 1999, 2002, 2008a; Bian and Huang 2009; Lin, Ao, and Song 2009; Tian and Lin 2016), and wage income at job entry and throughout the job career is significantly higher for the better connected (Bian, Zhang, and Cheng 2012; Bian and Huang 2015b; Bian, Huang, and Zhang 2015; Huang and Bian 2015; Zhao 2013). On the other hand, researchers have also found that *guanxi* had little effect on job searches in the 1990s and early 2000s, when labor markets began to operate effectively in the non-state sector (Hanser 2002; Huang 2008). When *guanxi* was found to matter, it had a reverse effect: the well-connected obtained bad rather than good jobs (Obukhova 2012; Obukhova and Lan 2013). Guthrie (1998, 2002) has argued that *guanxi* will decline in importance and play a minimal or no role in China's labor markets when hiring decisions in the state and especially the non-state sectors are rationalized by an increasingly efficient market economy.

This chapter addresses this controversy in several ways. First, I will begin with a review of how *guanxi* affected job allocation under the redistributive logic of the Maoist era. Next, I discuss mixed findings and competing views about the effect and non-effect of *guanxi* on occupational attainment in the post-Mao era. This will be followed by the presentation of a theoretical framework in which to examine the dynamics of *guanxi* in the economic transformation of changing degrees of institutional uncertainty and market competition. The next section is used to present a set of empirical evidence from large-scale surveys of job holders on the increasing usage of *guanxi* ties in job acquisition and the persistent influence of *guanxi* in getting good jobs throughout the reform era. The final part of this chapter will provide a summary of the main findings on *guanxi* and jobs in China under reform.

THE MAOIST ERA

Redistributive Logic and Job Assignment

The socialist transformation of the country's industry and commerce during the mid-1950s began a new era in which urban labor markets quickly gave way to state domination. China's National Statistical Bureau, the official source of national data, has made available urban labor force data for selected years (an additional data table is available from this book's webpage online*). In 1952, three years after the founding of the PRC in 1949, nearly half of the urban labor force was in the private sector, leaving slightly more than half in the state and collective sectors. By 1957, the private sector's share of urban labor force had dropped to less than 5 percent. It dropped further to almost nil in the late 1970s. Meanwhile, the state and collective sectors grew proportionally; by the end of 1978, which marked the beginning of market reforms under Deng Xiaoping's leadership, China's state (91.71 percent) and collective (8.29 percent) sectors totally dominated in urban labor force.

The Maoist ideology is that labor is not a commodity but a national resource. This means that every Chinese citizen should be granted

_____

* www.politybooks.com/guanxi

the constitutional right to work, but at the same time Maoist ideology virtually eliminates private labor rights. A 1988 study of Tianjin, China's third largest city, located in the north, shows what this state domination of urban jobs meant to local citizens during Mao's years. From 1949 to 1960, "direct individual application" for jobs, an important method for operating labor markets, was in sharp decline, from 64 percent to 21 percent. In the next sixteen years, from 1961 to 1976, the year of Mao's death and the end of the Cultural Revolution decade, the use of this method to get jobs dropped further, to 5 percent. It is during the 1977–88 period, in which market-oriented reforms were gradually introduced, that we see the relative level of direct individual application going back to 20 percent (Bian 1994b, table 1).

In place of direct individual application was state assignment, a dominant method through which Maoist China allocated urban jobs. Then, graduating seniors from middle- or higher-level schools were required to wait for and accept jobs assigned to them within their city of household registration (*hukou*). Likewise, retired military personnel were reallocated back to their *hukou* city and assigned jobs in the same way. Job transfers between work units (*danwei*, or employers) were organized to satisfy the needs of state planning, and career advancement was never a legitimate reason for workers to change jobs. Requests for job change due to personal or family reasons would not be accepted unless the requesters secured appropriate labor quotas from the government or found their counterparts in the prospective work units with whom to exchange jobs. It was not uncommon that couples worked in separate places, not to mention that a rural wife would have to stay in her home village when her husband got a job to work away in a distant town or city. On the whole, the system of job assignment was built without recognizing personal choices for jobs (Whyte and Parish 1984), resulted in an extremely low rate of job turnover (Walder 1986), and led to the widespread phenomenon of "the work unit ownership of labor" (Davis 1990). This was a redistributive system without labor markets; job assignments by the state and lifelong employment were the hallmarks of an otherwise inefficient labor control regime under state socialism.

Formal principles and regulations were laid down by the government to govern job assignments. These included the creation of annual labor quotas to sufficiently meet the demand for jobs, the specification of recruitment criteria for all job positions, the denouncement of discrimination against women or the disabled, and the use of labor contracts to discipline the work units and the newly hired (Bian 1994b: n. 6). Job-assigning officials in schools, work units, and government offices were supposed to follow the principles and regulations, but these were so general and abstract that they could not prevent informal processes from ruling specific job assignments behind the scenes. As a matter of fact, both job-assigning officials and wait-for-assignment urban youths actively pursued their personal agendas; while the former favored individuals directly or indirectly connected to them, the latter mobilized their *guanxi* contacts to obtain desirable assignments.

The state socialist regime was not without competition for jobs. Jobs varied in prestige (Lin and Xie 1988), in cash and non-cash incomes (Whyte and Parish 1984; Walder 1986), and in opportunities for career advancement (Lin and Bian 1991; Zhou, Tuma, and Moen 1996, 1997). These job variations were largely associated with the positions of work units in the state hierarchy (Bian 1994a); work units under a higher level of administrative jurisdiction were more likely to provide better working conditions, higher incomes, more redistributive benefits, and, in general, greater life chances (Walder 1992; Zhou, Tuma, and Moen 1996, 1997). Consequently, all youths waiting for state assignments wanted to work in the resource-rich state sector rather than the resource-poor collective sector (Lin and Bian 1991), in larger rather than smaller industrial enterprises (Logan and Bian 1993), and in higher-ranked rather than lower-ranked work units (Walder 1992; Bian 1994a).

The Role of Guanxi *in Job Allocation*

Bian's earlier works (1994a, 1994b, 1997, 1999) present a series of pieces of empirical evidence on the significance of *guanxi* ties for entering desirable work units before the emergence of labor markets around the late 1980s. Of 982 randomly sampled residents of Tianjin, more than 82 percent found their first urban jobs through state job assignments, but 42 percent admitted that they used *guanxi* ties to job-assigning officials to get into desirable work units. The use of *guanxi* to change jobs between work units, a difficult move to make then, increased to 52 percent. Note that these percentages may be underestimates of the real level of *guanxi* usage given the retrospective data collected in the Tianjin city: A good proportion of Tianjin respondents got their first jobs ten or twenty years before the 1988 survey, and both memory loss and a sense of illicitness in usage of *guanxi* during Mao's years may lead to an underestimate. Nevertheless, these percentages applied equally to men and women, but those job seekers whose fathers worked in the state sector or highly ranked work units were better able to get help from job-assigning officials in powerful positions. Bian's statistical models show that among otherwise equal workers, as compared to non-*guanxi* users who changed jobs, *guanxi* users increased their probability of job changes by 41 percent, but a higher level of education made no difference at all in job-change opportunity (Bian 1994b: table 5).

The underlying logic of *guanxi* influence in China's job assignment regime was favoritism: an individual actively performing a favor for someone in their social network. This qualitatively differs from the influence of social networks in market economies in a Western context, which predominantly rely on the sharing of information, rather than direct favors. In the United States, for example, networks of social contacts matter in job searches mainly because weak ties of infrequent interaction and low intimacy transmit non-redundant information about job openings; this was forcefully argued by and evidenced in Granovetter's (1973, 1974) seminal works about the strength of weak ties. While information about jobs in the socialist job-assignment regime was necessary for any "wait-for-assignment" youth to enter a desirable work unit, the information made no difference unless he or she also had a tie to a relevant job-assigning official, who would then secretly assign a job as a personal favor (Bian 1997, 1999).

One must understand that this kind of favoritism worked at multiple levels of the job assignment system. The following stories tell us how.

Story 1: A parent's friend was a personnel director whose help behind the scenes was decisive for a job assignment to a desirable work unit.

> It was harder to get a good work-unit assignment within the bureau [of railway administration to which I was assigned]. I got help from the chief of the bureau's labor office, who was a good friend of one of my mother's brothers. I was extremely happy to be assigned as a conductor in the Tianjin–Shanghai route; that was the best line managed by the bureau. (cited from Bian 1994b: 978)

Story 2: Changing jobs between work units in the case of Ms. Zhou required multiple *guanxi* ties in order to make the move. First, she had a baby and did not want to continue her railroad conductor job as it required frequent traveling. Facing resistance from her leader, who did not want her to leave, she had to ask a bureau official above the leader to accept her request. Next, she wanted to move to a profitable state-owned motorcycle repair shop close to her home. The shop director's daughter was a good friend of hers; "We were *guanxi* to each other." As a result, she received permission from the director, who promised that she could move in "as soon as she obtained a labor quota" from the labor bureau of the district in which his shop was located. It was extremely difficult to get a labor quota without the right *guanxi*. Well, the right *guanxi* was finally located through a series of search efforts: a relative of one of her former classmates was an associate director in the district labor bureau, who advised the motorcycle repair shop to prepare an application but sent it to his office by "following a normal procedure." It took a couple of months for his office to grant the requested labor quota to the motorcycle repair shop, and Ms. Zhou finally got the job there. (This account is summarized from a long description in Bian 1994b: 994–5.)

In pre-reform China, job-assigning officials at various levels were expected to follow formal procedures to conduct job assignments. But the stories just related make it explicit that at the same time these job-assigning officials also had considerable discretionary powers to assign people with or without the same qualifications to very different kinds of work units for very different kinds of job positions, creating the opportunity for favoritism to affect job-assignment outcomes. In the two stories, in each case strong ties of obligation and trust mattered rather than weak ties of non-redundancy; when people were not directly connected to relevant authorities, kin and close friends were mobilized to serve as intermediaries on behalf of youths waiting for employment, as in the case of Ms. Zhou moving from her train conductor job to a job in a motorcycle repair shop. More than 45 percent of Bian's Tianjin respondents relied on indirect *guanxi* ties to secure jobs (Bian 1997: 374). By either direct or indirect routes, one thing was clear and in common: *Guanxi* favoritism was behind the scenes and affected the results of job assignments for many individuals under the Maoist redistributive regime and its legacy.

THE POST-MAO ERA

Did the logic of *guanxi* favoritism give way to the logic of network information when China gradually dismantled the state job-assignment regime during the 1980s and 1990s?

Market Transition Theory

The theory of market transition seems to imply a positive answer. Nee (1989) argues that the transition from redistribution to market, regardless of how gradual or slow the process is, will necessarily transfer power and incentive from state redistributors to direct producers (i.e., entrepreneurs, professionals, skilled workers, and peasants), causing a fundamental change in stratification mechanisms, from which two predictable patterns emerge: the decreasing values of political power and political capital, and the increasing values of entrepreneurship and human capital. For Nee (1992), the market transition implies the rise of horizontal ties among direct producers and the decline of vertical ties that characterize the previous patron–client relationships of state distributors and work units under their jurisdiction.

The Declining Significance of Guanxi *Thesis*

In line with Nee's market transition theory, Guthrie (1998) learned from his Shanghai informants (managers and entrepreneurs) that after the post-1992 wave of market reforms (see a review by Naughton 2007), *guanxi* no longer counted in their hiring decisions or other decisions about partnerships, choice of suppliers and sellers, and allocation of incentives within the enterprises, state or non-state. The conditions under which such *guanxi*-free behaviors occurred, Guthrie assumed, were that state-owned enterprises, like private firms, had transformed from state-subsidized work units into independent economic entities; as a result, under the hard, rather than soft, budget constraints (Kornai 1986), both state and non-state employers with uncoverable deficits would all go bankrupt and be unable to get extra-budgetary subsidies from the government as they would have before reform, causing them to become profit driven, economically calculating, and, in general, rationalized. Guthrie summarizes these interpretations in his widely circulated hypothesis on the declining significance of *guanxi*: China's growing market economy would become increasingly rational, eliminating *guanxi* favoritism, an irrational behavior, from economic decision-making. Note that Guthrie considers information-rich social networks, not *guanxi* favoritism, to be important because these networks are believed to help economic actors reduce information asymmetries in the hybrid, fast-changing, and unsettled Chinese economy (Guthrie 2002).

Mixed Empirical Findings

Three studies of job searches during the 1990s and later years seem to lend partial support to Guthrie's hypothesis. Hanser (2002) finds that *guanxi* had little significance for first-time job seekers' employment opportunities in the 1990s, in both the rising market sector and the reformed state sector. Huang (2008) interviewed college-graduate job seekers in Shenzhen; her informants indicated that personal connections, especially strong ties, gave limited access to useful information, and they in fact needed to demonstrate ability rather than *guanxi* to favorably impress prospective employers. While these two studies are based on anecdotal evidence from small, non-probability samples, the third study should be taken more seriously since it was a questionnaire survey conducted with random samples of graduating seniors from several top-ranked universities in China. In this study Obukhova and Lan (2013) show that, although graduating college seniors made a good effort to search for jobs, using both formal and informal channels, those securing jobs through strong ties received bad rather than good jobs.

Representative household surveys, however, show a quite consistent pattern of the existence, persistence, and perhaps increasing significance of *guanxi* in China's labor markets after the post-1992 waves of market reforms. Results from three large sample surveys are briefly reviewed here.

First, a 1999 five-city survey of wage earners showed that it took a longer time to find a job through *guanxi* contacts than through formal channels, but the jobs found through these contacts, whether mobilized through stronger or weaker ties, were more likely to match the qualifications of the job seekers and thus result in better pay than those not found through *guanxi* contacts. These patterns did not vary between the 1980s and 1990s (Bian and Huang 2009, 2015b; Huang and Bian 2015).

Second, the 2003–8 Chinese General Social Surveys (CGSSs), based on a nationally representative sample of households in rural and urban China, showed that the number of people using *guanxi* contacts to find jobs in the cities increased by 20 percent in the first fifteen years of the reform era (1978–2002), with an equal increase in strong ties and weak ties observed (Bian 2008a; Tian and Lin 2016). These *guanxi* users were better able to get good jobs, move to higher positions when they changed jobs, and receive higher pay (Zhao 2013).

Finally, a 2006 national sample survey of China showed that diverse social contacts generated greater opportunities for job attainments in the first decade of the twenty-first century China (Lin, Ao, and Song 2009; Son and Lin 2012; Lin, Fu, and Chen 2014). In the 2006 survey study, "diverse social contacts" refer to contacts who vary in social status (education), political authority (CCP membership and office position), economic resources (wealth and income), and personal attributes (gender, age, marital status, self-evaluated health, etc.), and they are mobilized by job seekers through ties of varying strengths but favoring strong ties rather than weak ties.

The Resilience of Guanxi Thesis

Given all these observations, what can we say about the declining significance of *guanxi* thesis proposed by Guthrie? Anthropologist Mayfair Yang (2002), a pioneering and accomplished researcher on *guanxi*, has made a thorough assessment and a powerful critique of Guthrie's thesis. To her, Guthrie was narrowly focused on a small number of large state enterprises in Shanghai, took at face value the answers from managers interviewed, and oversimplified in drawing his conclusion about the decline of *guanxi*. Much of Yang's critique is also on the problematic methodology adopted by Guthrie: "If Guthrie was hoping to catch any act of *guanxi* practice that would check against what the managers were telling him about the decline of *guanxi*, it would hardly take place in public on the factory grounds, but at the managers' homes, at business banquets, or at nightclubs and scenes of evening business entertainment" (Yang 2002: 462). Although *guanxi* usage may decline in the pre-reform contexts of consumer goods that are now easily available from the market, Yang finds the rise of *guanxi* usage in obtaining new forms of scarce supplies, namely those due to market deficiencies, such as bank loans and long-term projects of strategic importance, and especially finds continued hierarchical controls by a durable party-state; these emerging forms of *guanxi* practice mostly occur in business circles, where Guthrie believes there had been the decline of *guanxi*. Restating her positions from *Gifts, Favors, and Banquets* (Yang 1994), a prize-winning book on the art of *guanxi*, and incorporating new findings from recent ethnographies and social surveys, Yang rejects Guthrie's approaches that "treat *guanxi* as a fixed essentialized phenomenon which can only wither away with the onslaught of new legal and commercial regimes," and forcefully argues that *guanxi* is "resilient as it is adapting to new institutional arrangements with the introduction of capitalism" (Yang 2002: 459).

Surfacing from the Yang–Guthrie debate are qualitatively different views of how *guanxi* practice and *guanxi* influence in the fast-changing Chinese economy should be understood and conceptualized. Guthrie (1998, 1999, 2002), influenced by neoclassical institutionalism, offers a market-as-rational-institution view, considering *guanxi* to be favoritism-laden relations, and believes that *guanxi* practice and *guanxi* influence will be reduced to a minimum when markets and legal systems develop to maturity. In sharp contrast, Yang (1994, 2002), coming from a long tradition of cultural anthropology, proposes a *guanxi*-as-cultural-repertoire view, considering "resilient" *guanxi* to be deeply rooted in Chinese culture, which is adaptive to institutional changes and constantly creates and recreates new forms of behavioral manifestations, and in such ways *guanxi* influence will persist, if not increase, during and after market reforms.

THE DYNAMICS OF *GUANXI*

A Theoretical Model

How can we digest the empirical controversies and theoretical debates just reviewed in a theoretically coherent way? In other words, how do we theorize about the dynamics of *guanxi* in China's transformation toward a market economy? Table 3.1 presents a typology summarized from Bian and Zhang (2014), in which economic transition from redistribution to market is considered to occur in a two-dimensional space of changing degrees of institutional uncertainty and market competition.

The *guanxi* influence figures in table 3.1 are logistic coefficients of whether or not jobs are obtained through the assistance of *guanxi* contacts (see p. 84). The models were estimated separately for the four sectors, and each model consists of a large number of control variables. Detailed results are available from the author upon request.

In neoclassic economic theory, uncertainty arises when economic actors lack sufficient knowledge and consequently anticipate unmeasurable, uncodifiable, or non-quantifiable risks about the future status of their economic actions (Knight 1921: 19). In an institutional perspective, North (1990) considers institutional uncertainty as a set of economic rules and operational regulations that are ambiguous,

Table 3.1: Typology of *Guanxi* Dynamism

	Market competition	
Institutional uncertainty	Low	High
High	**II**: Expanding space of *guanxi* Early reforms Post-1978 *Guanxi* influence = 1.87	**III**: Great space of *guanxi* Later reforms Post-1992 *Guanxi* influence = 3.61
Low	**I**: Limited space of *guanxi* State redistribution Pre-1978 *Guanxi* influence = 1.00	**IV**: Conditional space of *guanxi* Globalized economy Post-China's entry into World Trade Organization (2001) *Guanxi* influence = 1.87

Source: Adapted from Bian (2018: tables 1 and 2)

non-transparent, and incompatible with one another. Institutional uncertainty is low when economic rules and operational regulations are specific, transparent, and compatible with one another. Market competition, on the other hand, is low when entry to the market is monopolized by the state or nonstate oligarch, and market competition is high when entry is open to multiple competitors.

China's socialist redistributive economy from 1956 to 1978 operated at lower degrees of institutional uncertainty and market competition. Then, state planning was the single source of formal institutional arrangements through which to coordinate the allocation of material, financial, and labor resources for production, distribution, and consumption. This was made possible by one-for-all public ownership in which all enterprises and institutions were put under the jurisdiction of government, leaving little space for economic activities of a private nature. As transactions between economic entities were managed through administrative fiats, market competition was minimal. Labor allocation, a focal interest of analysis in this chapter, was controlled through state job assignments (Bian 1994b), and labor mobility was kept extremely low through the system of household registration and the work-unit ownership of workers (Davis 1992).

Increasing Institutional Uncertainty in China's Reform Era

Post-1978 reforms largely improved China's economic environment, but institutional uncertainty was increased by the reform strategies themselves. Three reform strategies are relevant here. The first is the strategy of "reform without design," which made market institution building lag behind emerging market activities, creating institutional non-transparency (Bian 2002). The second is the strategy of piecemeal, gradual reform, which allows for the coexistence of incompatible institutions, market and redistributive, for decades and even today, creating enormous opportunities for official corruption and illicit business operations (Shirk 2007). And the third is the strategy of trial-and-error reform experiments, which created room for local governments to act on their own powers and in their own interests, increasing institutional ambiguity and implementation variations across localities (Naughton 2007).

These reform strategies are all from central government, China's ultimate source of institutionalization. Every five years the Communist Party Congress is held to make regulative adjustments which minimize the institutional uncertainties generated by the reform measures that were experimented with in the previous five years. In the meantime, however, fast market growth generates new activities, to which the three reform strategies we have reviewed are to apply, and institutional uncertainty is therefore increased to a new level. This pattern of reform-generating uncertainties continued as market reforms deepened during the 1990s, even beyond China's entry into the World Trade Organization (WTO) in December 2001, a month after the WTO voted to approve China's proposal to enter. An international source of regulation and institutionalization, the WTO's reach and influence have been limited by China's large size and enormous inter-regional variations. At present, in localities and industries in which market activities have developed well and WTO influence has been felt, institutional uncertainty is expected to be decreasing; in other localities and industries in which new developments are concentrated under mixed institutional arrangements, institutional uncertainty is persistent or rising.

Increasing Market Competition in China's Reform Era

Since 1978, the degree of market competition in China has increased, mostly as a result of reforms. In the first decade, it mainly resulted from the decentralization of economic decision-making, experimenting with the household responsibility system in villages and manager responsibility system in factories (Naughton 2007). The product market emerged and state industrial quotas shrank in great numbers, ultimately to nil. In the second decade, the labor control policy was replaced by a two-way selection policy, in which employers and prospective employees chose each other at their own will (Davis 1992). Migrant peasant labor flooded into the cities, but a large number of state workers lost jobs, becoming unemployed or becoming unprotected wage labor in the non-state sector. In the third decade, property rights reforms finally were implemented, and a "grab the big and release the small" policy let many state factories be privatized, although the state retained the largest industrial and commercial companies under reformed state ownership (Naughton 2007). While the state has regained the monopoly in industries of strategic importance, the post-WTO Chinese economy raises the level of market competition on a global scale.

Propositions and Hypotheses on the Changing Significance of Guanxi

The increasing degrees of institutional uncertainty and market competition matter for the relevance and activeness of *guanxi*. An economy of increasing institutional uncertainty is one that is full of information asymmetries, lacking formal institutions to ensure trust between economic actors, and weak in legal enforcements to punish illicit behaviors. These institutional gaps or holes created space in which *guanxi* plays a large role (Bian 2002), and are the ultimate reasons for the rise of patron–client ties between state officials and entrepreneurs, which engineered China's economic takeoff under the models of local state corporatism (Walder and Oi 1999), Communist commercialism (Wank 1999), or network capitalism (Boisot and Child 1996; Tung and Worm 2001). On a micro-level, *guanxi* gives economic actors a competitive edge because of its bonding and bridging values within and between these actors, and such values are more needed and more appreciated when an economy becomes increasingly competitive (Nee and Opper 2012). For the Chinese transition economy, two propositions can be stated here. First, the higher the institutional uncertainty, the greater the roles that *guanxi* plays in maintaining economic actors' comparative advantage. Second, the higher the degree of market competition, the greater the propensity for *guanxi* to be used to strengthen economic actors' comparative advantage.

The interaction between these two propositions gives us the four empirical, testable hypotheses depicted in table 3.1. The lower left cell represents the pre-reform Chinese economy, whose institutional uncertainty and market competition both were at lower levels. This means that the pre-reform Chinese economy had a relatively smaller space for the roles of *guanxi* (hypothesis 1).

Moving up vertically, the upper left cell represents the initial reform period in which institutional uncertainty was rapidly increased by the three reform strategies we have reviewed. In this period, market competition began to increase, but on a small scale, in the form of small commodity markets, incentive wages in state factories, and household farming and family businesses. The roles of *guanxi* are expected to be more relevant, more active, and on the rise in the initial reform period (hypothesis 2).

Moving horizontally, the upper right cell represents the later reform period after Deng Xiaoping's Southern Inspection Tour in 1992. In this period, we observed the implementation of a thoroughgoing package of reform measures, which opened labor markets and financial markets, attracted foreign direct investment, and allowed private companies to grow on their own. This is a period when *guanxi* played the most significant roles in resource allocation and business operations (hypothesis 3).

Moving downward, the lower right cell represents the post-WTO era, in which the Chinese economy became more competitive on a global scale. Institutional uncertainty is expected to remain persistent and perhaps rising in localities and industries where the reach of WTO influence is limited, but in other localities and industries it becomes increasingly effective in reducing institutional uncertainty. Thus, the significance of *guanxi* is conditional upon the effectiveness and influence of post-WTO institutionalization in this period (hypothesis 4).

EMPIRICAL EVIDENCE FROM LARGE-SCALE SOCIAL SURVEYS

Are there systematic findings to confirm or disconfirm these hypotheses? For systematic findings, I value large-scale social surveys over case studies. Case studies are very useful for researchers exploring the underlying logic of *guanxi* dynamism under specific circumstances, but it is extremely risky to generalize the findings from case studies to a broader scope at a higher level of theoretical abstraction, as in the case for Guthrie's (1998, 2002) declining significance of *guanxi* thesis. Unlike case studies, large-scale social surveys, especially those based on probability sample designs, are representative of the population that is confined to a city, a region, or the nation, and therefore are helpful in examining *guanxi* usage and *guanxi* influence in a broad context of structural and institutional specifications. In my possession are the datasets from two large-scale household survey projects, JSNET and CGSS, for each of which a brief description is presented here.

JSNET and CGSS Surveys

JSNET is the acronym of the Job Search Networks survey project I conducted in multiple Chinese cities from 1988 to 2014. The project was focused on the measurement of *guanxi* and its influence on job search processes and job outcomes during China's reform era. It was started with a questionnaire survey in Tianjin in 1988. A decade later, the revised and enriched questionnaire was used in a survey of Hong Kong in 1998 and of five Chinese cities in 1999 (Changchun, Guangzhou, Shanghai, Tianjin, Xiamen). Another decade later, the 2009 survey was conducted, with a further revised and enriched questionnaire, in eight Chinese cities, namely those surveyed in 1999 plus Jinan, Lanzhou, and Xi'an. These eight cities were used again in the 2014 JSNET survey, for which most of the 2009 survey instruments were kept and new items were added. These eight cities cover a large regional variation from the most developed east (Shanghai, Tianjin, and Jinan) and southeast (Guangzhou, Xiamen) to the less developed northeast (Changchun) and northwest (Lanzhou and Xi'an). While each city's survey was independently administered, with a sample size of 700–1,000 households for each survey year, for purposes of comparability it was based on the same questionnaire and followed the same probability sampling design to randomly select households and respondents. From the 1999 survey onward, "migrant labor households" were selected, using a quota sampling method in 1999 and a street mapping method in 2009 and 2014.

CGSS is the acronym of the Chinese General Social Survey, a national representative sample survey of randomly selected households in China. It began in 2003 with a sample size of 6,000 households in urban areas only, but starting in 2004 it had a sample size of 10,000 households randomly selected in both rural and urban areas. The CGSS was by design an annual survey in the first ten years, 2003–13 (but missing 2007 and 2009 due to lack of financial support), and it changed to a biannual mode starting in 2015, skipping all even-numbered years. By 2013, data was collected through personal interviews with a structured questionnaire, and from 2015 computer-assisted personal interviewing (CAPI) was used. The relevant measures on job-search networks were included in 2003 and 2008 CGSSs. Details about the sample design and implementation of CGSSs can be found elsewhere (Bian and Li 2012).

Overall, JSNET and CGSS datasets are cross-sectional surveys based on probability city (JSNET) or national (CGSS) samples of given years, thus providing an excellent source of reliable information that allows for a trend analysis of *guanxi* dynamics in China's urban labor markets.

Table 3.1, as we have seen, includes summary results about the changing influence of *guanxi* on job acquisition in the four sectors of varying degrees of institutional uncertainty and market competition. For the lower left cell, representing low institutional uncertainty and low market competition, *guanxi* influence is set at 1.00. In reference to this sector, sector II, with an increased degree of institutional uncertainty, has *guanxi* influence increase to 1.87. This means that job seekers in this sector are 87 percent more likely to get jobs through *guanxi* than their counterparts in the reference sector. Sector III shows a much higher figure, 3.61, as the increases in both market competition and institutional uncertainty combine to greatly magnify *guanxi* influence on job acquisition. But the magnitude of *guanxi* influence decreases to a 1.87 level in sector IV, in which institutional uncertainty drops to a low level. Overall, the data presents strikingly impressive results of statistical analysis in support of hypotheses 1–4.

Evidence 1: The Increasing Usage of Guanxi *Contacts in Job Acquisition*

Putting this data to further use, our first question is about the trend of the usage of *guanxi* contacts in getting a job: Has *guanxi* usage been increasing, decreasing, or stabilizing along with market reforms? Figure 3.1, based on three JSNET and two CGSS surveys, depicts increasing trends of *guanxi* usage in job acquisition from 1978 to 2014.

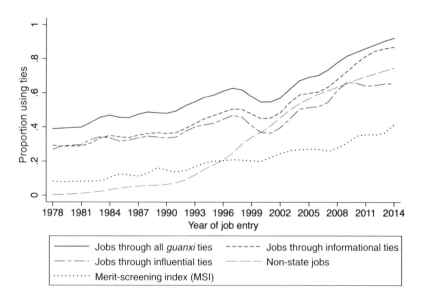

Figure 3.1: Trends of Job Acquisition through *Guanxi* Ties, 1978–2014 (N = 19,016)
Data compiled from CGSS 2003, 2008; JSNET 1999, 2009, 2014.

In the JSNET surveys, carried out in 1999, 2009 and 2014, respondents were asked about the year they obtained their current job and whether or not it was assisted by their *guanxi* contacts. Given the questions, the data presented in figure 3.1, and in all figures and tables in this chapter, is retrospective. *Guanxi* contacts were broadly defined in the surveys by any kin, friend, acquaintance, or an indirectly connected person who provided informational or more substantive assistance that was "helpful or useful for getting your job" (the language in the surveys).

The top curve in figure 3.1 shows that year-specific proportions of jobs found through *guanxi* contacts more than doubled over the thirty-seven years. In 1978, the year China's market reforms began, 39 percent of jobs were allocated through *guanxi* contacts, and in 2014 this had increased to 92 percent. This increasing trend remained rather steady from 1978 to 1995, in which Maoist lifelong employment and state job assignments gave way to the emergence and growth of term contracts and labor markets (Davis 1992). After a brief fall from 1999 to 2002 when the restructuring of state-owned enterprises resulted in a large number of layoffs, it picked up again in 2003 and rose to its highest level in 2014. The increase in the trend did not seem to stop during the second decade of the twenty-first century.

Evidence 2: Informational and Influential Contacts Both Increasing?

Guanxi contacts, displayed in the top curve in figure 3.1, include all kinds of social ties used by the survey respondents in getting jobs. A more strict and narrow definition of *guanxi* may exclude some of these ties from being counted in. To Guthrie (1998, 2002), for example, the rise of social ties in getting job information would not necessarily be in conflict with his argument about the declining significance of *guanxi*, which is understood as ties of favoritism and influence of power. Although an insider's information about a job opening would certainly be considered a favor to someone who badly needed it, a more substantive favor in the Chinese context would be the influence of power from *guanxi* contacts to press for a favorable decision to hire a particular candidate. How can we make the distinction between informational contacts and influential contacts?

The CGSS and JSNET surveys included a battery of items measuring the specific forms of assistance the respondents received from their *guanxi* contacts during the search for their current jobs. These forms of assistance are:

1 giving information about a job;
2 giving information about the employer;
3 providing advice on applying for the job;
4 helping to organize application materials;
5 helping to prepare the job application;
6 helping to submit the job application;
7 recommending the respondent to the employer;
8 approaching relevant parties on behalf of the respondent;
9 arranging for the respondent to meet relevant people;
10 accompanying the respondent to visit relevant people;
11 solving concrete problems for the respondent's job search;
12 making commitments or promises to the employer;
13 offering a job to the respondent directly;
14 other kinds of assistance;
15 unspecified assistance.

During the surveys, the respondents were presented with this battery of items and asked to "check all that applied" (additional data table available online). While 40 percent checked two or more responses, analytically a theoretical distinction can be made between the first five items and the rest of the battery. When assistance is directed at the job applicant (items 1–5), the *guanxi* contact's role is fundamentally informational. In sharp contrast, when assistance is directed at the prospective employer (items 6–15), it contains some degree of influence of power that the *guanxi* contact can exert on a hiring authority. We therefore can decompose *guanxi* contacts into two categories: informational contacts and influential contacts.

Figure 3.1 shows that informational and influential contacts both were on the rise across the thirty-seven years. Specifically, jobs found through the assistance of informational contacts increased from 29 percent in 1978 to 87 percent in 2014, and jobs found through influential contacts increased from 27 percent in 1978 to 66 percent in 2014. A great majority of Chinese respondents used multiple *guanxi* contacts (an average of three) for getting jobs, and this is why each year's sum of the percentages of users getting information and influence exceeds the overall percentages of *guanxi* contact users. While in each year more jobs were found through informational contacts than through influential contacts, these two categories of *guanxi* contacts experienced similar increasing trends across the years, with the years since 2009 showing influential contacts stabilizing around the level of 65 percent. Over the time, however, *guanxi* contacts became increasingly functional for channeling both information and influence with roughly equal effectiveness, a finding that supports Mayfair Yang's *guanxi* as cultural repertoire view and disproves Doug Guthrie's declining significance of *guanxi* thesis.

Evidence 3: The Pattern of Change in Guanxi *Usage*

The failure to find evidence for the declining significance of *guanxi* thesis leads us to pay attention to the process of China's marketization. One piece of wisdom from institutional economics is that markets do not always rationalize, since they also respond to political, social, and cultural forces in any given society (North 1990). This implies that formal institutionalization under a rational market image, such as the screening of job applicants through meritocratic rules, may not grow proportionally with marketization, leaving room for network informa-tion and network influence to affect labor market competition. Figure 3.1 presents initial evidence for this argument. Non-state jobs, a key indicator of China's marketization and labor market competition, increased from less than 1 percent in 1978 to about 75 percent in 2014. At the same time period, however, the merit-screening index (MSI), which measures the extent to which job applicants are screened by the formalized rules of meritocracy (Bian and Huang 2015b), slowly improved during the thirty-seven years, from a mere 4 percent of jobs that were screened under formal rules of meritocracy in 1978 to 41 percent in 2014, with the greatest growth of meritocracy rules occur-ring in the most recent years, since China's entry into the WTO in December 2001.

Evidence 4: Guanxi *Influence on Attained Jobs*

Table 3.2 presents a set of statistical results estimated from regression models on the extent of *guanxi* influence on attained jobs. For easy understanding, percentage-point differences are calculated from the regression coefficients. Model 1 is about *guanxi* influence on one's job-outcome satisfaction. This is measured by one's satisfaction or dissat-isfaction with five job outcomes: salary, promotion, occupational prestige, housing benefits, and other fringe benefits provided by the employer. The respondent rated each of these job outcomes on a five-point scale ranging from "very satisfied" to "very unsatisfied." The results in model 1 show that among otherwise equal workers, users of influ-ential *guanxi* contacts were 5 percent more satisfied with job outcomes than their counterparts among non-*guanxi* users with an average level of satisfaction, and users of informational *guanxi* contacts had an equal level of job-outcome satisfaction to that of their counterparts.

Model 2 comes from the respondents' evaluation of their relation-ships with supervisors, equal-level colleagues, and subordinates in the

Table 3.2: Network Effects on Job Qualities (JSNET1999, N = 4,350)

Explanatory variables	Model 1	Model 2	Model 3	Model 4	Model 5
	Job-outcome satisfaction	Work relations satisfaction	Job-worker matching	Hierarchical bridging	Market connectedness
	Mean = 14.9	Mean = 10.1	Match = 36.7% Mismatch = 63.3%	Mean = 15.0	Mean = 7.5
Informational contacts	0.0%	0.0%	25.1%	1.4%	0.0%
Influential contacts	5.0%	3.2%	22.3%	2.0%	3.0%

When a coefficient is statistically insignificant, its percentage-point difference is 0.0 percent. A fuller statistical data table is available from this book's webpage online.

Source: Percentage-point differences recalculated from Bian and Huang (2015a: table 3, panel C, models 1–2), and Bian, Huang, and Zhang (2015: table 4, models 3–5)

workplace, using a five-point scale similar to that for job-outcome satisfaction. As shown in model 2, among otherwise equal workers, users of influential *guanxi* contacts were 3.2 percent more satisfied with work relations than their counterparts among non-*guanxi* users with an average level of satisfaction, and users of informational *guanxi* contacts had an equal level of work relations satisfaction to that of their counterparts.

Next, we look at how *guanxi* contacts matter for job–worker matching, a critical measure of labor market efficiency (Jovanovic 1979; Granovetter 1981; Kalleberg 2007). While research efforts to measure job–worker matching have been rare in China, the 1999 JSNET survey respondents were asked the following question: "Upon entering the job, how were your prior work skills or trainings compared to the announced requirements of the job by the employer? Would you say, (1) the same, (2) similar, (3) different, or (4) no explicit requirement was announced." Based on responses to this question, our measure of job–worker matching is a dichotomy, being coded 1 for matched ("same" or "similar") and 0 for not-matched ("different" or "no explicit requirement") jobs. On the whole, 36.7 percent of the respondents had jobs to which their qualifications were knowingly matched to employer-announced requirements, but a great majority had unmatched jobs by 1999. While these figures tell us of Chinese labor markets far from an equilibrium image of efficiency, our interest here is in both the direction and extent of *guanxi* influence on job–worker matching. We receive good news from model 3: compared to non-*guanxi* users who otherwise have equal qualifications, both users of informational *guanxi* contacts (25.1 percent) and users of influential *guanxi* contacts (22.3 percent) are significantly more likely to have matched rather than mismatched jobs. This is an important piece of evidence that Chinese *guanxi* contacts increase rather than decrease labor market efficiency.

Models 4 and 5 present the results about the extent to which *guanxi* contacts matter for getting two different kinds of strategic positions at work. One position refers to "hierarchical bridging jobs," which give occupants the opportunities to connect to a wide range of organizational players within the workplace. The other position refers to "market-connected jobs," which give occupants the opportunities to connect to a wide range of economic players in the marketplace. While both strategic positions are of high earning potential (Bian and Logan 1996), our interest here is in the extent to which *guanxi* contacts matter for assignments to these positions. Table 3.2 shows very interesting results: Compared to otherwise equally qualified non-*guanxi* users, users of informational contacts have a higher probability of being assigned into hierarchical bridging jobs but an equal probability of being assigned to market-connected jobs, and yet users of influential contacts enjoy a greater probability of being assigned into both kinds of high-earning positions.

A summary of table 3.2 results suffices here. *Guanxi* contacts matter significantly for getting different kinds of "good" jobs. Between informational contacts and influential contacts, however, the former matters much less than the latter. Users of informational contacts do enjoy a probability of getting jobs that match their qualifications and jobs that give them the opportunity to connect to a wide range of organizational players within the workplace hierarchy. Nonetheless, users of influential contacts not only beat every otherwise equally qualified counterpart for getting matched jobs, jobs of hierarchical bridging, and jobs of high market connectiveness, which make them highly satisfied, but they also work in highly satisfying social environments (high satisfaction with work relations). *Guanxi* influence matters greatly and positively for both jobs and workers in China.

Evidence 5: Guanxi *Influence on Entry-Level Wage*

If *guanxi* contacts matter for getting good jobs, then they should matter for entry-level wage, for many reasons. In the United States, for example, it has been found that social contacts transmit information between job candidates and their prospective employers, leading to a higher wage offer (Granovetter 1974). Social contacts can also function as employee referrals, offering sufficient information about the qualifications of job seekers and thus reducing the costs of an otherwise more expensive, formal search, and making employers willing to throw the savings into attractive offers to secure the best-qualified candidates (Fernandez and Weinberg 1997). Some social contacts are insiders in the firm, and they disclose information about prior hires and help job seekers negotiate higher starting wages (Seidel, Polzer, and Stewart 2000).

These informational mechanisms are believed to be true in China, especially when labor markets grew in their own rights during the reform era. Market reforms have granted hiring organizations the right to screen and hire, thus making network-transmitted information relevant and important for both job seekers and prospective employers in the Chinese context. At the same time, there are good reasons to believe that *guanxi* ties of favoritism and influence increase the entry-level wage in the Chinese context. First, job seekers indeed mobilize powerful *guanxi* contacts to influence prospective employers for a good job and a higher wage. Second, oftentimes job offers and entry-level wages can be flexible; this is the case especially in emerging labor markets and smaller workplaces with low institutionalization. Third, the influence of *guanxi* favoritism is expected when meritocracy is not forcefully exercised in job markets with low skill specificity. For these various reasons, we expect that the usage of informational and influential *guanxi* contacts will significantly increase one's entry-level wage.

The JSNET 2009 survey collected data on the entry-level wage. This is the monthly wage on entry into the current/last job reported by the respondent. As shown in table 3.3, *guanxi* users enjoy an average advantage of 23.7 percent higher entry-level wage than otherwise-equal non-users, an impressively large wage differential. When *guanxi* users are decomposed into four groups, the average advantage is 40.1 percent for users of informational contacts, 23.5 percent for users of influential contacts, and 24.4 percent for users of mixed contacts. While the average advantage is impressive for each type of *guanxi* users, the advantage for users of informational contacts is relatively the highest.

Does *guanxi* influence on entry-level wage vary across work sectors, job types, and reform periods? Table 3.3 indicates that *guanxi* ties increase entry-level wages more significantly in the less-institutional-ized state competitive sector and non-state sector than in the more-institutionalized state sector.

The *guanxi* effect is greater for professionals than for administrators, and it is greater for non-skilled laborers than for skilled workers. The combination of informational and influential contacts has a significant effect on entry-level wage in all job types, and for non-skilled workers all three types of *guanxi* contacts have consistently significant effects on the entry-level wage. Overall, these results do not significantly vary across periods and point to the tendency for *guanxi* influence on entry-level wage to be more consistent for jobs of lower skill specificities across reform periods.

Evidence 6: Greater Guanxi-Wage *Influence for Job Changers*

The JSNET 2009 survey had 2,851 non-changers (or first-job holders, 55.3 percent of the sample) and 2,303 job changers (44.7 percent of the sample). Table 3.4 compares *guanxi* influence on the entry-level wage between first-job seekers and job changers. As compared to otherwise equally qualified first-time job holders, users of *guanxi* contacts earn an average 14.9 percent higher entry-level wage. For job changers, on the other hand, compared to otherwise equally qualified job changers, users of *guanxi* contacts earn an average 30.1 percent higher entry-level wage.

Table 3.3: *Guanxi* Effect on (ln) Entry-Level Wage (JSNET 2009 Survey, N = 5,154)

	Total	State monopoly	State competitive	Non-state	Professional	Administrative	Skilled	Non-skilled
Model 1								
Use of *guanxi* contacts	23.7%	0.0%	24.9%	40.6%	26.2%	18.6%	14.2%	25.9%
Model 2								
Informational contacts	40.1%	97.8%	49.0%	0.0%	34.3%	0.0%	0.0%	50.1%
Influential contacts	23.5%	0.0%	25.1%	27.9%	0.0%	0.0%	31.1%	24.5%
Mixed contacts	24.4%	0.0%	26.0%	59.0%	30.6%	27.8%	15.3%	24.1%

Entry-level wage has been transformed into a natural logarithm (ln) form. Entries are percentage-point differences calculated from the coefficients of regressions on the log-transformed wage. When a coefficient does not satisfy the two-tail significance test (p < .05), its percentage point difference is 0.0 percent. Fuller statistical data tables are available from this book's webpage online.

Table 3.4: *Guanxi* Effects on (ln)Wage (JSNET 2009 Survey)

	First-job seekers				Job changers			
	Total	State monopoly	State competitive	Non-state	Total	State monopoly	State competitive	Non-state
Model 1								
Use of contacts (total)	14.9%	0.0%	38.0%	0.0%	30.1%	39.0%	27.4%	123.4%
Model 2								
Informational contacts	25.9%	0.0%	107.3%	34.3%	48.1%	48.0%	0.0%	0.0%
Influential contacts	20.1%	0.0%	0.0%	0.0%	22.0%	56.4%	0.0%	41.9%
Mixed contacts	17.0%	0.0%	0.0%	0.0%	28.8%	35.0%	40.2%	133.7%

Entry-level wage has been transformed into a natural logarithm (ln) form. Entries are percentage-point differences calculated from the coefficients of regressions on the log-transformed wage. When a coefficient does not satisfy the two-tail significance test (p < .05), its percentage point difference is 0.0 percent. Fuller statistical data tables are available from this book's webpage online.

Further analysis shows that among first-job seekers, as compared to otherwise equally qualified non-*guanxi* users, users of informational contacts increase their entry-level wage by 25.9 percent, users of influential contacts by 20.1 percent, and users of mixed contacts by 17.0 percent, but users of unspecified contacts have no advantage. Among job changers, however, these relative advantages are respectively much bigger: 48.1 percent for users of informational contacts, 22.0 percent for users of influential contacts, 28.8 percent for users of mixed contacts, and 32.4 percent for users of unspecified contacts.

This *guanxi* influence on the entry-level wage of first-job seekers and job changers can be considered across three economic sectors. In the state monopoly and state competitive sectors, *guanxi* matters for the entry-level wage of job changers but not for first-job seekers, but *guanxi* influence on the entry-level wage exists for both first-job seekers and job changers in the non-state sector. *Guanxi* influence on the entry-level wage is more consistent in the state competitive sector and the non-state sector, where there is a much greater effect of influential *guanxi* contacts and mixed-resources contacts than that of informational contacts, and these effects are much stronger for job changers than for first-job seekers.

Evidence 7: Guanxi *Influence on the Wage in the Current Job Career*

Do *guanxi* contacts used during job searches have lasting effects on the wage in one's current job career? Table 3.5 presents four regression models estimated in response to this question. Model 1 shows that among otherwise equal wage earners, users of informational contacts during job searches do not have a net earning advantage (an insignificant coefficient of −.005), but users of influential contacts do, by an impressive margin of 8.5 percent.

Model 2 treats a post-15-year job career as a point of reference. It shows that the effect of influential contacts is greatest in the mid-career

Table 3.5: *Guanxi* Effects on (ln) Current Wage (JSNET 2009 Survey, N = 4,350)

	Model 1	Model 2	Model 3	Model 4
Informational ties	0.0%		0.0%	0.0%
Influential ties	8.5%		8.1%	7.9%
Job matching			8.2%	7.0%
Job's hierarchical bridging				1.1%
Job's market connectedness				1.9%
Job tenure for:				
1–5 years		12.9%		
6–10 years		22.6%		
11–15 years		10.2%		

Entry-level wage has been transformed into a natural logarithm (ln) form. Entries are percentage-point differences calculated from the coefficients of regressions on the log-transformed wage. When a coefficient does not satisfy the two-tail significance test (p < .05), its percentage point difference is 0.0 percent. A fuller statistical data table is available from this book's webpage online.

of 6–10 years (22.6 percent) and is also present and significant in the first five years of a job career (12.9 percent). These findings make it explicit that the influence of power, rather than the information flowed through *guanxi* contacts, has lasting effects on wage income in China.

Model 3 is an extension of model 1 by incorporating informational contacts, influential contacts, and job matching as the additional predictors of wage income. It shows that informational contacts do not matter much (the coefficient is insignificant), but influential contacts do matter, as the coefficient is positive and statistically significant, and job matching is also positive and significant. As compared to those whose qualifications are not matched to job requirements, workers who are matched to jobs have an 8.2 percent higher wage. Combining the results, one can conclude that in China, network information has an indirect impact on wage income through job matching, but network favoritism has both direct and indirect effects (through job matching) on wage income.

Model 4 includes the variables of hierarchical bridging and market connectedness as additional predictors. This model shows that positions of higher hierarchical bridging and positions of higher market connectedness both increase wage income significantly. More specifically, one's wage income is increased by 1.1 percent for a point increase in hierarchical bridging (an 18-point scale), and by 1.9 percent for a point increase in market connectedness (a nine-point scale). The independent effects of network favoritism and job matching on wage income remain statistically significant in this model.

SUMMARY

The data from the large-scale surveys presented in this chapter helps with resolving a number of longstanding controversies about the role of *guanxi* in job acquisition, job quality, and wage income during China's post-1978 market reforms. First, China's labor markets are full of *guanxi* influence. From 1978 to 2014, users of *guanxi* ties for job acquisition increased substantially rather than decreased. When *guanxi* ties are broken into informational ties and influential ties, both kinds grew proportionally and with a similar tendency over the thrity-seven years. This is a clear set of evidence in support of Mayfair Yang's *guanxi* as cultural repertoire view and rejecting Doug Guthrie's declining significance of *guanxi* thesis.

Second, *guanxi* influence on job acquisition is conditional upon the marketization and institutionalization of labor markets. On the aggregate level, rules of meritocracy, a measure of institutionalization, gradually increased from 1978 to 2014, though at much slower rates than the growth of non-state jobs, a measure of marketization and competition. When non-state jobs increase in numbers, so does the increase of *guanxi* usage to facilitate the acquisition of jobs; but at the same time, when merit-based screening becomes stronger, *guanxi* influence gets weaker. Individual-level analysis confirms this finding: *Guanxi* influence is stronger when both market competition and institutional uncertainty increase, but *guanxi* influence is indeed reduced substantially when institutional uncertainty drops to a low level as a result of the institutionalization of merit-based screening of job applicants. To be sure, no market or non-market economy is free of institutional uncertainty no matter how institutionalized the economy is. Logically, *guanxi* influence will persist.

Third, persistent *guanxi* influence on job quality indeed exists. On subjective measures, users of both informational ties and influential ties are more satisfied with job outcomes as well as work relations in the workplace than non-*guanxi* users. On objective measures, as compared to non-*guanxi* users, users of *guanxi* ties of otherwise equal credentials and qualifications are better able to obtain "good" jobs, and this is especially so for users of influential contacts. Here, the so-called "good" jobs are those whose technical requirements match workers' preparations in terms of education, skill, and experience; evidence shows that users of both informational ties and influential ties are more likely to have a higher degree of job–worker matching than non-*guanxi* users. "Good" jobs also are jobs with higher earning opportunities, either because these jobs allow workers to have good connections across hierarchical ranks at work, or because they give job holders a wide range of market connections. While users of informational ties can get market-connected jobs, users of influential ties can get both market-connected and hierarchy-bridging jobs.

Finally, a strong and conditional *guanxi* effect on wage income has been revealed. One piece of evidence is the strong *guanxi* effect on the entry-level wage. The *guanxi* effect on wage does not stop at the entry level, but instead continues into one's job career for no less than fifteen years after getting a new job. Yet evidence shows that this long-lasting benefit of *guanxi* is only for users of influential contacts, not for users of informational contacts; it is persistent in the state competitive sector and private sectors, but not in the state monopoly sector, where institutionalization of meritocracy rules is stronger; and it is significant across all types of jobs, but a much stronger *guanxi* effect on wage is revealed among non-skilled job holders. Once again, unlike professionals, managers, and skilled workers, non-skilled workers usually lack quantifiable measures to check on their merits, opening greater room for *guanxi* connections to influence.

4 | *Guanxi* and Business Founding

This chapter is devoted to a discussion about the roles *guanxi* plays in founding a private business. I will begin with an overview of China's business world, its history, and its current economic structure. This is the larger context within which China's private economy has emerged and grown since the late 1970s. I then shift my attention to *guanxi* as mechanisms of operating a self-employment or household business, as mechanisms of starting up a small private firm, and as mechanisms of founding a sizable business organization, and to how entrepreneurial networks affect the later success of their business ventures.

CHINA'S BUSINESS WORLD: AN OVERVIEW

As of 2017, China's GDP (gross domestic products) has increased to 80 trillion *yuan* (*RMB*), or US$12.3 trillion, making China's economy the world's second largest economy, only to the United States (Xi Jinping 2018: 3). China's GDP per capita, while still ranked seventieth among 200 economies in the world, increased from 385 *yuan* in 1978 to an estimated 58,000 *yuan* in 2017 (www.stats.gov.cn). Clearly, China is a much larger and richer economy after four decades of continuous growth. This remarkable achievement was triggered by a series of post-1978 market-oriented economic reforms to a state redistributive system inherited from the Maoist era.

Maoist Era: The Dominance of State Ownership

Public ownership was the predominant form of business organization in Maoist China. At the death of Mao in 1976 and shortly thereafter, nearly all urban labor forces were hired in the state (about 91 percent) and collective (close to 9 percent) sectors, leaving only a negligible number of "individual laborers" (个体劳动者 *geti laodong zhe*) to work in the private sector. The "reform and opening up" policy was initiated during and announced publicly at the end of 1978. Shortly thereafter, the newly implemented "rural household responsibility system" gradually dismantled collective farming under the name of People's Communes; consequently, rural households regained rights, power, and incentives as the basic units of production, distribution, and consumption (Nee 1989; Zhang 1999: 19–22). As rural products began to be sold on "free markets" in towns and cities, and under the pressure of millions of "educated sent-down youths" (*xiaxiang zhishi qingnian*) of the Cultural Revolution returning from villages back to home cities for employment, individual laborers and household businesses emerged in urban China. The rebirth of a private economy, in the forms of individual laborers and household businesses, was a great institutional breakthrough (Shi 1993), even if it was then allowed only to the extent that it "supplemented" public ownership operations in commercial and service industries in the cities (Gold 1990).

Early Reforms: Emerging Forms of Private Ownership

In orthodox Marxism, private ownership is considered the "arch-enemy" of Communist ideology. Therefore, the emergence of private ownership became a hot topic in political discourses. Are household businesses socialist or capitalist? Can a socialist China allow for class exploitation? While these issues were debated theoretically, reformers strategically shifted attention to a technical focus on what should count as class exploitation. Karl Marx's *Das Kapital* is the source of a hard-to-be-disputed proposition: in Marx's original formulation, when a business owner hires fewer than eight workers, the surplus values exploited will not make up the owner's main source of income, but his or her labor contributions will instead be the main economic support for the family. This specific formulation of Karl Marx's was used as successful rhetoric for allowing individual laborers and household businesses to operate and grow in what was still an anti-privatization political culture in the early 1980s (Wu 2003: 169).

The officially recognized Chinese domestic private sector is composed of individual/household businesses (个体经济 *geti jingji*) and private enterprises (私营企业 *siying qiye*) (Gregory, Tenev, and Wagle 2000). An entity is an individual/household business if it employs no more than seven laborers; one that hires eight or more workers must be registered as a private enterprise. In the early 1980s, however, in both rural and urban areas fast-growing individual/household businesses began to hire more than seven laborers, sounding a loud alarm among the authorities. A 1988 state document, "Tentative Stipulations on Private Enterprises," finally approved the rights of private enterprises to hire eight or more workers. But private businesses were still considered by the leftist-minded authorities as an anomaly, vulnerable to ideological attacks and economic constraints (Hershkovitz 1985; Wu 2003: 168–74). Consequently, private entrepreneurs did not have any sense of security. Immediately following the 1989 Tiananmen Square protest movements, the private economy was stymied (Kraus 1991: 2).

In the anti-privatization political culture, the "informal status of domestic private enterprises" (Gregory, Tenev, and Wagle 2000: 20–1) was a salient issue in the 1980s and early 1990s. One organizational form of private business is the "red hat" or "fake collective" firm: a firm that is registered as a collective but is in fact owned and operated through private investments and control (Liu 1992: 302–3). Another organizational form is known as *gua-kao* (挂靠"hanger-on" or subsidiary) in which a private business uses the name of a state-owned enterprise (SOE). A private enterprise can even be "adopted" by a government agency as its supervising body (主管单位*zhuguan danwei*) and thus obtain the status of public or collective ownership (Lin and Zhang 1999: 214). Zhang (1999: 15) estimated that in 1995 the number of "forged collective enterprises" nationwide was twice the number of firms registered as private enterprises.

The rise of privatization from within the SOEs is another important phenomenon in economic transition. In the early 1980s, leasing or contracting SOEs and urban collectives to managers was experimented with, and this experimentation often led to partial privatization from inside the state sector (Young 1995: 98–100), in which Communist cadres and managers became entrepreneurs. Township-and-village enterprises (TVEs), registered as rural collective enterprises, also saw mass privatization (Ho 1994: 174–200), especially in the Pearl River and Yangzi Deltas (Kung 1999; Wu 1998), where TVEs had been coordinated by local governments under the model of "local state corporatism" (Oi 1992, 1998, 1999). Often, these privatization efforts transformed SOEs and TVEs into shareholding companies without direct proprietorship.

Hiding private ownership in a disguised property arrangement, private entrepreneurs can gain the benefits of avoiding ideological discrimination and enjoying the favorable economic and financial privileges afforded state and collective enterprises. Local governments and officials – the most significant of the players connected one way or another with private enterprises – are inherently interested in having these businesses under their jurisdiction so that they can both reap financial benefits and avoid the political risks of private ownership (Zhang 1999: 51–3). Some private enterprises have disguised themselves as foreign-invested firms by funneling funds to Hong Kong and then back to the mainland for investment (Sabin 1994: 957).

Later Reforms: Growing Privatization after 1992

The Chinese private economy gained both legitimacy and new momentum only after Deng Xiaoping's Southern Inspection Tour in 1992, when he called for bolder reform measures to boost the growth of the private economy and the restructuring of SOEs (Gregory, Tenev, and Wagle 2000: 10). An important milestone was the 15th Congress of the CCP in 1997, which formed resolutions to further reduce legal and economic barriers to private ownership. A new directive implemented in 1998, termed "grabbing the big and releasing the small" (抓大放小, *zhuada fangxiao*), was to reorganize large SOEs into state shareholding business groups and to privatize small and medium-size SOEs. The privatization resolutions were formalized in the Third Plenary of the 16th CCP Congress, held in November 2003, and were confirmed and reinstated in each of the following CCP Congresses.

This wave of privatization did not arise suddenly but as the result of the past transformation of SOEs. In urban China, one transformation is the devolution of executive control rights to SOE managers, a process that Yimin Lin (2001) labeled "corporatization." Other authors have deemed corporatization to be "informal privatization" in which SOEs mimic the operations of private firms under hard budget constraints (Morita and Zaiki 1998: 105). As of 2002, 50 percent of China's 159,000 SOEs had been transformed into shareholding companies (*China Securities News*, November 19, 2003). In rural China, local cadres had long had "gray ownership" of TVEs under their jurisdiction, and when the political situation relaxed in the first years of the twenty-first century, they converted their de facto property rights into formally recognized legal rights, completing the privatization of the TVEs (Wu 1998: 165–8).

The Business World Today

In China today, individual/household businesses are predominantly run by either single persons or family units, but those that are recognized as private enterprises vary tremendously in size and capital investment. As of 2015, China had 72.64 million registered business entities, of which 51.65 million (71.1 percent) were individual/family businesses and 16.84 million (23.2 percent) private enterprises. A total of 260 million workers, or roughly 80 percent of the urban labor force, were hired in the private sectors. In the meantime, the restructured state sector was composed of giant industrial enterprises of strategic importance, leading banking organizations, and a large government sector of central and local agencies as well as nonprofit organizations at all levels, which accounted for 5.7 percent of business entities in the country, 20 percent of the urban labor force, 35 percent of the country's GDP, and 45 percent of China's business taxes (Zhang et al. 2015).

China's economic transition is still ongoing, and the country has hybrid forms of economic organization. It is in this dynamic context that we discuss the roles of *guanxi* networks in China's business world. Our attention in this chapter is given to *guanxi* as mechanisms of self-employment and business founding. In the next chapter, we will shift our attention to the role of *guanxi* in organizational governance and development.

GUANXI AS MECHANISMS OF SELF-EMPLOYMENT

Self-employment was the very first form of private ownership to emerge in China's early reforms, and it has been the cradle of the Chinese market economy and capitalism. Our analysis therefore will begin with self-employment, asking how *guanxi* ties and *guanxi* networks serve as mechanisms of self-employment. This analysis is based on two sources of data from Bian and Wang (2016). The first is in-depth interviews they conducted with self-employed persons in various locations in China. These informants are not from a representative sample, but their stories offer substantive and theoretical insights into the ways in which *guanxi* ties matter for the emergence of self-employment in China. The second source of data is the JSNET 2009 survey. In addition to data about *guanxi* and job acquisition presented in chapter 3, this survey also includes a probability sample of 584 randomly selected self-employed people (an additional data table is available from this book's webpage online*).

Compared to employees, the self-employed group tended to consist of more males than females, were younger, were less educated, and included significantly fewer CCP members. Second, the self-employed tended to have a much higher personal income, with a great variation within the group. Third, the two groups did not significantly differ in measures of tie strength (percentage of strong ties to New Year visitors) and sector-crossing ties (contacts from two sectors rather than one), but the self-employed engaged in significantly more social eating activities than employees. Let us explore how each of the three *guanxi* measures matters for self-employment in greater detail.

Weak Ties and Strong Ties

Ms. Wu was laid off a few years ago. She planned to start a self-employed business to sustain her livelihood, but she had no opportunity to do so. In her many visits to the District Government to seek help, she became acquainted with a staff member who worked in the front office receiving visitors. This staff member relayed to her the information that a printing and copying shop would be needed to offer service to many visitors to the government office. Highly motivated, Ms. Wu borrowed money from her parents and opened the shop subsequently. It has operated very well thus far.

---

* www.politybooks.com/guanxi

This story uncovers two different kinds of social ties that play different roles in starting a self-employment arrangement. The first was a weak tie to an acquaintance who worked in a government office and had access to valuable information about opening a printing and copying service shop. However, this information would not have been valuable if Ms. Wu had not had loving parents who lent her money as start-up capital. While the weak tie to a governmental staff offered informational resources, the strong tie to her parents gave her the money that enabled her to capitalize on the information. In the case of self-employment opportunities, strong ties and weak ties play different roles, supporting the hypothesis about the strength of weak ties of low intimacy and infrequent interaction for information flow (Granovetter 1973), and the hypothesis about the role of strong ties of trust and obligation for obtaining substantial assistance in the absence of market institutions (Bian 1997). The 2009 Chinese survey provides evidence of these roles.

As can be seen in table 4.1, capital investment for opening a self-employed business came mostly from the self or family. However, the larger the capital investment, the greater the probability that the capital investment had to be generated through social connections, with a roughly balanced dependence on strong ties and weak ties. In our analysis, strong ties include relatives and close friends, and weak ties include less close friends and acquaintances. As for the sources of business information and contracts, one-fourth came from within the family, more than half from mixed ties, less than 7 percent from other strong ties, and nearly 16 percent from weak ties. Strong ties seem to play a greater role in financial and contract relations.

Guanxi *Ties between Sectors*

The strength of social networks lies in the ties that bridge across structural boundaries for non-redundant information and opportunity of

Table 4.1: Start-up Capital, Business Contracts, and *Guanxi* Ties (N = 584)

	Total	Level of start-up (RMB *yuan*)		
		<10,000	10,000–100,000	>100,000
Source of start-up capital:				
Self or family	61.9%	72.7%	58.2%	47.8%
Strong ties to lender	19.4%	15.3%	19.9%	26.6%
Weak ties to lender	18.7%	12.0%	21.9%	25.6%
Number of cases	584	234	237	113
Source of first business contract:				
Self or family	25.7%	37.6%	19.4%	14.2%
Mixed ties to providers	51.7%	41.0%	55.7%	65.5%
Strong tie to providers	6.7%	8.1%	6.3%	4.4%
Weak tie to providers	15.9%	13.3%	18.6%	15.9%
Number of cases	584	234	237	113
Within/across-sector *guanxi* ties:				
Guanxi ties within one sector	35.0%	43.8%	34.2%	16.3%
Guanxi ties across sectors	65.0%	56.2%	65.8%	83.8%
Number of cases	452	185	187	80

access to scarce resources that are otherwise unavailable (Granovetter 1973; Lin 1982; Burt 1992). In transitional China, the most important structural boundary is that between the state and non-state sectors: The state sector is in control of governmental grants and projects, and the non-state sector is a source of market-related resources and opportunities. Thus, sector-crossing *guanxi* ties are resourceful for self-employment, as shown in the following two stories.

Mr. Meng is the head of a state-owned enterprise. Although his enterprise had a stable revenue, he was under strong pressure to generate extra-budgetary earnings to increase income for his employees. Through his close connection to the executive vice president of a publicly listed company, Mr. Meng developed a series of personnel training projects in collaboration with the listed company. His enterprise supplied instructors for these projects, and the publicly listed company operated them by using financially flexible arrangements. These collaborating projects became an impressive source of extra-budgetary income for Mr. Meng's enterprise and its employees.

Ms. Zeng is self-employed, and operates an interior design and decoration company. Her long-term contract is with a large state-owned construction firm, where one of the executives is her close relative. She frequently obtains reliable internal information from this relative, which helps her win the competition for the profitable interior design and decoration projects of this firm.

The special importance of sector-crossing ties is evidenced among the self-employed respondents of the 2009 JSNET survey. Of the 452 self-employed respondents, as shown in table 4.1, 35 percent had close *guanxi* ties working within one sector, state or non-state. For these self-employed people, 43.8 percent had a start-up capital of less than 10,000 *yuan*, 34.2 percent had a start-up capital of between 10,000 and 100,000 yuan, and 16.3 percent had a start-up capital of more than 100,000 *yuan*. This is a descending trend: Relatively more people had a lower level of start-up capital and significantly fewer people had a higher level of start-up capital. In sharp contrast, 65 percent of the total sample for self-employment had *guanxi* ties coming from both the state and non-state sectors. For them, an ascending trend is observed: 56.2 percent had a start-up capital of less than 10,000 yuan, 65.8 percent had a start-up capital of 10,000–100,000 yuan, and 83.8 percent had a start-up capital of more than 100,000 yuan. A simple conclusion here is that cross-sector *guanxi* ties are more helpful in mobilizing financial resources for starting self-employment than *guanxi* ties that are embedded in one sector.

Social Eating Networks

Extensive *guanxi* contacts are potentially helpful to the business success of the self-employed, but these contacts are not always available or equally willing to help. In the Chinese context, as described in chapter 2, frequent interactions through social eating, drinking, and entertainment are important opportunities for maintaining, enhancing, elevating, and deepening the relational bonding, interpersonal trustworthiness, and mutual obligations among those who are connected to each other. The more social eating activities in which one participates, the more capacity one has for mobilizing resources from social contacts, as the following case study demonstrates.

Mr. Zhang was a college teacher who became acquainted with a manager in charge of the logistics of the college. Over the years Mr. Zhang frequently invited him to dinners, where Zhang's generosity, friendliness, and interpersonal strategies helped him to develop new friends, mostly introduced to him by the manager. Through social drinking and eating, these people became Zhang's friends. When they heard of his idea of opening a Korean restaurant near the college, they all offered to help. One helped secure a good location at a low rent, another helped find food supplies of high quality but at reasonable prices, and still others helped introduce chefs and skilled workers. The issues of official inspection and business emergencies also arose, but Zhang never needed to worry because his drinking and eating friends "voluntarily" offered help to solve these problems. By the time of the 2009 survey, Zhang's restaurant had been open for several years, and both his business and his social drinking and eating networks were increasing.

Mr. Zhang's story demonstrates that social capital tends to be mobilized through social activities. In the case of self-employed people, the capacity to mobilize resources through social activities is important for their business development. On the other hand, to maintain and develop business the self-employed are much more willing to engage in such social interactions as social eating, drinking, or entertaining. The 2009 survey compares the features of the social networks of the self-employed and those of employees, as shown in table 4.2.

The first two variables in table 4.2 about resource mobilizing capacities were developed through involvement in social eating. The indicators contributing to these two composite scores (the first is the factor

Table 4.2: Features of Social Networks for Self-Employed and Employees

Variables	a. Self-employed		b. Employee		c. T-test for a − b
	Mean	SD	Mean	SD	
Resource mobilizing capacity via social eating (factor score)	0.27	1.05	−0.02	0.93	p. < .001
Resource mobilizing capacity via social eating (Likert scale)	14.05	5.32	12.54	4.74	p. <.001
Number of New Year visitors	31.72	38.85	26.79	34.84	p. <.001
Number of occupations in which New Year visitors work	5.69	4.29	5.25	3.95	p. <.01
Highest prestige of New Year visitors	−0.11	0.83	0.01	0.74	p. <.001

score from a factor analysis and the second a Likert scale summing up the values of the contributing indicators) include frequency of social eating involvement, frequency of being a social eating host, frequency of being a social eating invitee, and frequency of developing new friends through social eating. In these two variables the higher the values, the greater the capacity one has to mobilize resources through social eating networks. As can be seen, the self-employed are significantly higher in both variables than employees. The factor score is a standard score with the mean of zero and a standard deviation of one. The self-employed have a mean factor score of resource mobilizing capacity of 0.27, which is much higher than the −0.02 obtained by employees. Similarly, the Likert-scale measure shows a mean of 14.05 for the self-employed, which is significantly higher than the mean of 12.54 for employees.

Other measures in table 4.2 concern features of social networks based on New Year visitations. As can be seen, the self-employed are significantly higher in the magnitudes of all three measures than employees. Specifically, the self-employed had more visitors during the week-long celebration of the previous Chinese New Year. Not only do the self-employed have larger social networks than employees, but their social networks are also occupationally more diverse. Finally, the highest occupational prestige of visitors for the self-employed group is significantly lower than for employees. This indicates that the self-employed are connected to more and diverse people, yet these people are somewhat lower in the occupational hierarchy than employees' visitors. Note that the employees comprise an occupationally diverse group of managers, professionals, and skilled and unskilled laborers.

Summary

These case studies of a few self-employed informants and the 2009 survey show that social networks and social capital, tie strength, boundary crossing, and resource mobilizing capacity are important factors for the Chinese in starting and succeeding in self-employment. For differ-ent purposes, a self-employed individual may mobilize strong ties or weak ties, preferably from different economic sectors in order to gain access to different kinds of resources to be mobilized through these ties. But ultimately, in the Chinese context the resource mobilizing capacities are enhanced and strengthened by social activities involving social drinking and eating.

GUANXI AS MECHANISMS OF BUSINESS FOUNDING

A new business establishment emerges in response to a market demand for a specific product or service that is yet to be provided. According to this market image, equilibrium arises when the match between supply and demand in the market is perfect. Disequilibrium occurs when there are unsatisfied demands that call for the expansion of the economy, creating room for new establishments to supply the demanded products or services (McKenzie and Tullock 1989). A new establish-ment may be short-lived if that demand proves to be instantaneous or weak; but it will survive and grow if demand for the product or service is strong and continuous (provided of course that quality and price both satisfy market demand).

A network image, in contrast, is about *how* a new business can emerge out of the structural constraints it faces (Granovetter 1985). In the Chinese context, three such structural constraints are critical. The first is obtaining, intentionally or unintentionally, valuable infor-mation regarding the availability of business opportunities and the possibility of establishing an entity to exploit such opportunities. The second is obtaining start-up capital when no private entrepreneur could take loans from state or local banks during the early reform period. And the third is securing a business order when most private entrepreneurs do not have any business experience. Numerous stories indicate that a private entrepreneur's ability and success in founding a business establishment are heavily embedded in the *guanxi* networks that dominate Chinese society (Bian 2006).

Market and Network Images about Business Founding

Table 4.3 presents a typology in which a new business is considered to emerge in the interaction of network and market images. Network image depicts an economy to be relationally rooted and allows variation between network embeddedness (for past and current information and opportunities) and network cultivation (for future information and opportunities). Market image, on the other hand, depicts an economy from a supply-and-demand point of view and allows variation between continuous (strong) and instant (weak) demands. Thus, the cross-classification of these two dichotomies creates four types of start-up business.

The type I business is born out of networks in which market demands for a specific product or service are strong and continuous, and the start-up investment capital and business orders are obtained through network ties that will continue to play a long-term role in the growth of the businesses. The type II business is also born out of networks, but it differs from the former type in that there is only an instantaneous and discontinuous market demand for that specific product or service. Therefore, the maintenance of such networks will

Table 4.3: Network and Market Images of Business Founding: A Typology

Network image	Market image	
	Continuous demands	Instant demands
Network embeddedness	I	II
Network cultivation	III	IV

be crucial and the latter will continue to play an important role in the transformation and hence survival of the business.

The type III business emerges in response to strong and continuous market demand. But during the start-up phase, these businesses do not necessarily rely on network-facilitated information or opportunity, since they are readily available in the marketplace anyway. However, increased competition may force these businesses to rely on the cultivation of network ties and resources to survive and grow. Finally, the type IV business responds to an instant but discontinuous market demand for a specific product or service. As a result, these businesses may be short-lived or quickly change the products or services they provide. Although their investment capital and business orders are not necessarily obtained through network ties during the start-up, the need to cultivate network ties and resources successfully will play an important role in the transformation and eventual survival of these businesses.

What follows shortly will be the presentation of data collected from a 2003 survey of 830 firms in the Pearl River Delta region of Guangdong, where China's market reforms started early and ahead of all other regions of the country (Vogel 1990). Therefore, some of the firms surveyed were quite mature and others still in the early stages of development, giving a good range of firms to study the role *guanxi* plays at different periods from the founding of a business.

Guanxi *Networks and the Start-Up Investment Capital*

On average, the firms surveyed had a start-up investment capital of slightly more than 6 million *yuan*. This is a substantial investment for any family business, partnership, or private enterprise in the period from 1978 to 2003, and efforts to mobilize financial resources to come up with this amount should be substantial. In table 4.4, panel A indicates that 97.1 percent of the firms surveyed mobilized start-up capital from *guanxi* networks, whether the money was borrowed from non-kin

Table 4.4: Investment Capital and First Business Contract (N = 830)

Panel A Sources and channels of investment capital

Average	Source of capital	Channel of mobilization		
		Ties	No ties	Total
6,092,000 *yuan*	Non-kin ties	61.8%	0.0%	61.8%
	Kin ties	28.1%	0.8%	28.9%
	Organization	7.2%	2.1%	9.3%
	Total	97.1%	2.9%	100.0%

Panel B Forms and sustainability of first business contracts

Founder's prior tie to client	Form of contract		Business sustainability	
	Written	Oral	Continued	Discontinued
Yes (73.5%)	32.5	38.6	53.9	17.8
No (26.5%)	16.2	12.7	19.2	9.1
Total	48.7	51.3	73.1	26.9

Fuller statistical tables are available from this book's webpage online.

networks (61.8 percent), kin networks (28.9 percent), or a formal organization (9.3 percent). These figures indicate that financially *guanxi* networks are indispensable for the emergence of the Chinese private economy.

A regression analysis (not shown but available online) helps us understand what factors are more likely to be associated with specific sources of investment. First, when a firm began as a family business, a partnership, or a private company, it is more than likely to rely on kin and non-kin networks from which to mobilize start-up capital. Second, when a start-up business needs a large investment (more than a million *yuan*), it is extremely difficult to raise the money from kin or non-kin networks. Third, despite the development of market reforms from 1978 to 2003, kin and non-kin networks were not in decline as a capital mobilizing channel. Quite to the contrary: The more recent new establishments are more likely to rely on kin and non-kin networks for securing investment capital. This finding should not, however, be interpreted as evidence regarding the declining influence of formal organizations as a major source of investment capital. This perhaps instead signals that many entrepreneurs in the Pearl River Delta today might have already accumulated significant financial resources and are therefore increasingly more able to invest their own capital in new business ventures.

Guanxi Networks and the First Business Contract

The first business contract arguably constitutes the lifeblood of any new business. The key question here is where it usually comes from. As shown in panel B of table 4.4, the existence of prior ties is critical; nearly three-fourths (73.5 percent) of the firms surveyed had prior ties with their first business clients. The presence of a prior tie increases trust between the new establishments and their business clients, reducing the work of drafting a written contract to less than half. Indeed, more than a simple majority (51.3 percent) of the new establishments obtained oral contracts. Nearly three-fourths (73.1 percent) of the first business contracts were continued and renewed, and those contracts that were secured through prior ties had a close to 3:1 (53.9/19.2) advantage in continuing and renewing the contracts. The significance and the powerfulness of prior *guanxi* connections in securing and sustaining the first business contracts are clearly demonstrated.

A multivariate analysis (not shown but available online) to confirm these findings allows us to assess the "net" effect of *guanxi* networks on how a first business contract can be secured and how likely it is that it can be continued beyond the first contract term. An impressive set of positive findings has been obtained from this multivariate analysis.

First, prior *guanxi* ties offer trust that is fundamentally important for new business. When business founders had prior ties with first clients, they were 33 percent less likely to use written contracts but 43 percent more likely to have the oral contracts renewed, regardless of the types of business, the size of contract, or the period in which the business was established. This is a clear indication of the importance of the trust maintained by strong *guanxi* ties between the founders and their first business clients.

Second, the type of a new establishment matters. When a new establishment began as a family business or a partnership/private company, oral contracts are favored over written contracts. The exponential coefficients show that compared to shareholding companies, a family business was only 20 percent as likely and a partnership/private company 45 percent as likely to use a written contract. For family businesses, their first contracts are sustainable as they are more than likely to continue beyond the initial contract term. In-depth interviews show that the family businesses among the firms surveyed continued to maintain and rely on prior *guanxi* ties to operate within the established small communities.

Finally, the size and timing of a contract also matter. Firms with an initial investment of over 1 million *yuan* are significantly more likely to use written contracts than firms with lower capitalization, and these firms are less likely to continue their first contracts. Firms established more recently, in 2002 and 2003, are more likely to continue their businesses with the first business client, indicating that network embeddedness and network cultivation are still strong and important in the contemporary setting.

Summary

The data from a survey of Pearl River Delta firms indicates that Chinese private businesses were born out of the *guanxi* networks of their founders. For anyone interested in starting up a business venture, information regarding business opportunities, start-up capital, and the first business contract are all critical. These three processes are highly embedded and intertwined within the entrepreneurs' *guanxi* networks. The in-depth personal interviews reveal that many entrepreneurs learn about valuable money-making opportunities via their social contacts, either intentionally or unintentionally, which are subsequently carried through by strategic persons in the business community. Pre-existing social ties to these informants/partners prove to be indispensable. An investigation of 830 firms further demonstrates that financial investment at the start-up point is indeed highly embedded in the social networks of the entrepreneurs, not only because these investments mostly originate from family and social ties as a source of capital, but, perhaps more importantly, because the mobilization of these investments is largely operated through social ties. It is only on some rare occasions (about 3 percent) that a new firm does not have to rely on the founder's social ties to mobilize financial resources. Finally, the survey also illustrates the importance of prior ties in the first business order, and shows that these ties entail trust that helps to avoid the unnecessary complexity and hidden cost of drawing up written contracts, and that these prior ties increase the likelihood of the continuation of the business partnership rather than its discontinuation after the first order has been completed.

ENTREPRENEUR NETWORKS IN BUSINESS FOUNDING AND LATER SUCCESS

So far, we have learned that *guanxi* networks are extremely important for founding Chinese private businesses. Important *guanxi* ties offer valuable information about a business opportunity, they help "empty-pocketed" entrepreneurs to mobilize financial resources and come up with sufficient start-up capital, and they also help inexperienced business newbies to secure a first contract that sets the course for the new business to move forward. But to what extent do these *guanxi* contacts at business founding continue to be important in the later success of Chinese businesses? Ronald Burt and his associates have examined this question with the assistance of a stratified probability sample survey of 700 entrepreneurs randomly selected in the Yangtze River Delta region, including Shanghai, Jiangsu, and Zhejiang. The survey was conducted in 2012, using a "network name generator" module to collect information about business events and contacts valuable to the entrepreneurs on the events. Burt and Burzynska (2017: 249–57) provide a detailed description of this "Chinese entrepreneurial network survey" (CENS). Other publications based on the CENS dataset are available elsewhere (Burt and Opper 2017; Burt, Bian, and Opper 2018).

Business Founding as a Guanxi *Event*

Business operation is a series of network events. This is the point of departure for the CENS study. The CENS respondents are founders or non-founding owners of the businesses surveyed, and they were asked to name one contact that was "most valuable" to the founding of their business. Each of these respondents named one contact without any difficulty, resulting in 700 founding contacts. In addition, the respondents were also asked to name contacts who were "most valuable" in five other business events since founding (2,701 contacts named), and to name current contacts who were "most valuable" to their business activities in the year of the survey (2,357 contacts named). Table 4.5 shows a profile of the generated three categories of contacts, namely "founding contacts," "other event contacts," and "non-event contacts" (or general contacts not connected to any business event of the focal entrepreneurs).

As can be seen in table 4.5, founding contacts are systematically different from other event contacts and non-event contacts. Compared

Table 4.5: Founding Contacts, Other Event Contacts, and Non-Event Contacts

Variables	Founding contacts (N = 700)	Other event contacts (N = 2,701)	Non-event contacts (N = 2,357)
Trust (1–5)	4.80	4.25	3.07
Days between contacts	5.65	11.76	19.21
Years known	20.27	10.99	5.51
Percent family	31.43	6.08	1.09
Third parties (0–6)	3.10	3.26	2.73

"Founding contacts" are contacts cited as most valued for the business founding. "Other event contacts" are contacts cited as most valued for any events other than the business founding. "Non-event contacts" are current contacts who are not cited as valuable for any specific event included in the survey.
Source: Adapted from Burt and Burzynska (2017: table 7)

to the latter two categories of contacts, founding contacts are more highly trusted by the respondents (4.8 on a 5-point scale), meet with the respondents more frequently (every week), have known each other for a much longer time (more than twenty years), and are more likely to be a family member (31.43 percent). Given all these merits, the most valued founding contact is a strong tie, or simply a *guanxi* tie. Other event contacts and non-event contacts are relatively less strong ties to the respondents, with lower trust, less frequent interaction, shorter duration of the relationship, and a lower percentage of family members.

Event Contacts as Guanxi *Ties*

Table 4.5 shows one thing that does not distinguish founding contacts from the other two categories of contacts. This is the number of third parties (i.e., common friends). In network theory the significance of third parties is twofold (Burt 1992). The first element is network closure: More third parties reinforce trust between actors within the network. The second is network constraint: More third parties prevent a focal actor from obtaining the information and control benefits that would be generated by otherwise disconnected others. Burt and Opper (2017) report that founding contacts are highly trusted by Chinese entrepreneurs but relatively independent of third parties.

As shown in figure 4.1, the 700 founding contacts vary significantly in the number of third parties (top curve), from no third party at all to more than six. But this variation in the number of third parties does not matter for the high level of trust the founding contacts received from the entrepreneurs. The top curve shows that regardless of third

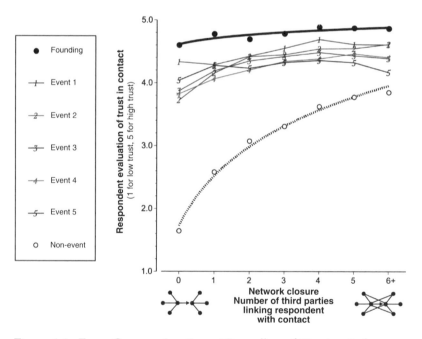

Figure 4.1: Event Contacts Are *Guanxi* Regardless of Citation Order
Source: Burt and Opper (2017: figure 7)

parties, the high trust that Chinese entrepreneurs have in their founding contacts is consistently at a level of 4.8–4.9 on a 5-point scale. In contrast, the bottom curve shows a completely different story for non-event contacts: The level of trust is now positively associated with and highly dependent upon the number of third parties there are between entrepreneurs and their non-event contacts. These findings have allowed Burt and his associates to redefine Chinese *guanxi*: "A relationship is a *guanxi* tie to the extent that trust is high and relatively independent of structural embedding" (Burt and Burzynska 2017: 240).

Further analysis of the data provides a statistical demonstration for this new definition of *guanxi* (additional data table available online). Among all different kinds of contacts, founding contacts interact more frequently with entrepreneurs, have known entrepreneurs for many more years, and are significantly less likely to be structurally embedded.

Guanxi *Contacts in Later Business Success*

Figure 4.1 visually reviews several findings for us. First, founding contacts are *guanxi* contacts who receive from entrepreneurs the highest level of trust that is relatively independent of third parties. Second, other event contacts are also *guanxi* contacts because their trust level with entrepreneurs is relatively independent of structural embedding. Third, non-event contacts are not *guanxi* contacts, as their trust level with entrepreneurs is highly dependent upon the reinforcement of third parties. When two persons are linked by a *guanxi* tie, you trust each other no matter who are the common friends in between.

These three kinds of contacts together play an important role in the later success of Chinese businesses. Burt and Opper's (2017) analyses show that business success (defined in terms of growing employment, sales, and patents) decreases with the extent to which an entrepreneur is embedded in a small, closed network; entrepreneurs are more successful when they are in large, open networks. However, this strong association between network structure and business success is seen to disappear when contacts associated with the business founding are ignored, leaving just an entrepreneur's current contacts. The comparison between these two analyses of the data indicates the importance of event contacts, which are *guanxi* ties, to the success of entrepreneurs.

Further analysis by Burt and Opper makes it more explicit that *guanxi* contacts at founding and new *guanxi* contacts at subsequent events are important to the later success of Chinese businesses. The authors show that entrepreneurs increase their business success with multiple event contacts. That is, entrepreneurs do not just rely on *guanxi* ties in a founding event, but in every other event they also mobilize and cultivate new *guanxi* ties to provide valuable support to them. Where a group of entrepreneurs began their "event sequence" with a particularly positive first move, they are even more successful, as they not only have the right kind of *guanxi* tie at founding, but also benefit from that positive move in the next business event by mobilizing new *guanxi* contacts who are either a family member or someone close to the founding contact. While new event contacts diversify entrepreneurial networks, decreasing network constraint, close *guanxi* ties matter for business success – the entrepreneurs who made a positive move in the next business event immediately after founding did not increase their network diversity as rapidly as businesses on average.

Summary

The founding and later success of a Chinese business are by and large a *guanxi* phenomenon. The 700 entrepreneurs from the Yangtze River Delta named a total of 4,464 contacts, of which more than two-thirds are *guanxi* contacts. They are *guanxi* contacts because their trust level with entrepreneurs is high and relatively independent of third parties. Entrepreneurs have a high level of trust in founding contacts, have known them for many years prior to business founding, and engage in frequent interaction with them while operating their business. The most successful entrepreneur has the right *guanxi* contact at founding, whose help wins immediate success for the new establishment, but in the next business event this entrepreneur must mobilize new *guanxi* contacts who are either from the family or are someone close to the founding contacts. This positive move can enlarge and diversify the entrepreneur network, but at the same time also maintains closeness and high trust among event contacts within the network. The later success of a Chinese business is a result of low network constraint and high trust among *guanxi* ties significant in business events.

5 | *Guanxi* and Organizational Development ————————

This chapter enlarges on the previous chapter by paying attention to the roles *guanxi* plays in the growth of businesses and the development of organizations. It begins with a review of theoretical perspectives on *guanxi*–organization relations, and then presents empirical research materials focused on three topics: *guanxi* as mechanisms of organizational governance, *guanxi* as mechanisms of organizational performance, and foreign firms' responses to *guanxi* norms.

THEORETICAL PERSPECTIVES ON *GUANXI*–ORGANIZATION RELATIONS

What Does Economic Sociology Suggest?

Our theoretical and empirical inquiry into the roles *guanxi* plays in China's organizational development during market reforms is guided by contemporary economic sociology. The premise of economic sociology's relational approach is that economic organizations and their agents are "embedded in concrete, ongoing systems of social relations" (Granovetter 1985: 487). Therefore, economic organizations are not considered as choosing between market exchanges and vertical arrangements in order to best minimize transaction costs (Williamson 1981), but instead take on various network forms of governance structure as survival and developmental strategies (Powell 1990). In such a way, the relational approach redefines the social nature of business entities.

The relational approach can also help to rewrite standard organizational theories. A few examples suffice here. Contingency theory, for example, treats organizations as open systems and emphasizes that rational decision-making must be informed about environmental circumstances (Burns and Stalker 1961). The relational approach refines this by making it explicit that important information is to be learned from network channels of interorganizational relationships (Donaldson 2001). Again, resource dependency theory emphasizes the relative power of corporate actors to extract resources from business environments (Pfeffer 1997; Pfeffer and Salancik 2003). The relational approach redefines corporate power in terms of corporate actors' centrality in interorganizational networks (Mizruchi and Galaskiewicz 1993). Taking another example, the relational approach contributes to transaction cost theory (Williamson 1981) by specifying that interorganizational networks are an essential part of government structure through which to control moral risks and establish long-term relational contracts in order to lower transaction costs (Ring and Van de Ven 1992). Finally, DiMaggio and Powell's (1983) notion of isomorphism (the similarity between various business entities in their structure or processes) integrates social and interorganizational networks into institutional theory (Scott 2005).

Relational approaches to organizational research suggest three most important mechanisms whereby social and interorganizational networks matter for organizational structure, process, and performance. The first is network ties. Network ties connect organizations and organizational actors (owners, managers, and professionals of strategic importance to organizations); they serve as channels of information, knowledge transfer, and skill learning across them (Podolny and Page 1998) and are conduits for the transfer of physical resources and moral codes of organizational behavior (Adler and Kwon 2002). The second is network structure. Organizational actors in connection with other organizational actors that are otherwise disconnected from each other enjoy information and control benefits and perform better (Burt 1992). For example, while network closure integrates new companies into scientific communities from which to obtain state-of-the-art skill knowledge, network range provides well-developed companies with evolving, non-redundant information about business opportunities (Maurer and Ebers 2006). The third is network resources. The social capital values of network ties and network structures are ultimately measured by the resources that are mobilized from the networks of interpersonal and interorganizational relationships (Lin 2001b); not just tangible resources that contacts hold in forms of technology, personnel, and money (Batjargal 2003), but also intangible resources such as information (Granovetter 1973), influence of power (Bian 1997), and social status of contacts as market signals of who should be hired, what priorities are, and how things can be handled (Podolny 2005).

Inspired by the relational approach and informed about the changing roles *guanxi* plays in Chinese business organizations during a complex, ongoing process of transition toward a market economy, sociologists and management scholars have offered diverse theoretical perspectives on the fate of *guanxi* in China's transition economy. I review a few major perspectives.

The Declining Significance of Guanxi Perspective

A detailed account of this perspective has been provided in chapter 3. Here, a brief review of its core argument with reference to Chinese business organizations is necessary. Guthrie (1998, 1999, 2002) argues that *guanxi* favoritism was essentially important in Maoist China under two structural conditions. One was the rigid bureaucratic control of resources in a shortage economy, which called for state enterprise managers to develop *guanxi* ties to state planners and redistributors from whom to obtain needed resources and approvals as personal favors in support of their production projects. The other was the mechanism of soft-budget constraints (Kornai 1986), which created a "budgetary bargaining regime" in which state enterprise managers could use *guanxi* ties to persuade higher-level authorities to adjust their budgets, provide subsidies to make up "policy-generated" losses, and get rid of deficits in accounting books at the end of the year. Are these conditions continuing into the emerging market economy?

Learning from Shanghai business managers and entrepreneurs, Guthrie concluded that these two economic conditions were giving way to market rationality: Market allocation of resources is now more and more oriented toward economic efficiency, and economic decision-making under hard budget constraints leaves less and less room for budgetary bargaining. Consequently, private property rights and hard budget constraints cause the rise of rational decision-making in the economic sphere, which in turn diminishes and eventually will eliminate irrational, *guanxi*-facilitated favor exchanges in a rationalized and globalized Chinese economy (Guthrie 1998). This is the so-called declining significance of *guanxi* hypothesis.

The Entrepreneur–Bureaucrat Connection Perspective

The entrepreneur–bureaucrat connection perspective denies any claim that the emergence and growth of the Chinese market economy is coupled with the decline of the political control and influence of a durable Communist party-state. Quite the contrary: Based on his Chengdu study, Bruun (1993) argues that China's political elites have not retreated from economic life as markets have spread. Instead, they have survived in political positions in the party-state apparatus and, more impressively, have also taken active roles in the emerging market economy that grew in the shadow of the robust, self-adjusting, and influential state and local bureaucratic systems. The cultivation and maintenance of *guanxi* connections to state and local officials have therefore been crucial for the development of private business.

Bruun (1995) identified multiple types of entrepreneur–bureaucrat connections. The first was that private entrepreneurs build favor-exchange *guanxi* with SOE managers and state bureaucrats for obtaining business opportunities and projects as well as political protection and official recognition from the latter. The second was that household businesses had one spouse registered as the owner while the other maintained employment in a local government office through which to win favors from local state authority. And the third was that local officials were de facto partners with private entrepreneurs, from whom they regularly collected profit shares in the form of kickbacks for any business contracts they helped secure for the entrepreneurs. These various connections were the backbone of emerging private businesses and illustrate the "dependent development" nature of the private economy at local levels, suggesting that China may have returned to its pre-1949 pattern of "petty capitalism," a mode of industrial production and commercialization that is subordinate to and subsumed within the state-dominant economic system.

The Official–Entrepreneur Symbiotic Relations Perspective

While Bruun sees the growth of China's entrepreneurship as being dependent upon and in thrall to a strong officialdom, Wank (1995, 1996, 1999) offers a different vision of interdependence between local state officials and private entrepreneurs. Based on his research in the increasingly marketized coastal city of Xiamen, Wank argues that the connections between entrepreneurs and bureaucrats are "symbiotic" patron–client ties. While these ties characterized pre-reform SOEs, in which party secretaries exercised authority over political activists in a culture of "party clientelism" (Walder 1986), in reform-era Xiamen Wank found similar clientelist ties now connecting local bureaucratic patrons and private business clients in the emerging market economy. "They are patron–client relations between actors who control asymmetrical resources and forge alliances for mutual benefit. The alliances ... are embedded in personal ties between entrepreneurs and officials who know and trust each other" (Wank 1995: 69–70). "The intertwining of Communist legacies and new market activities created a distinct configuration of state power in China's emerging market economy that constrains commercial trade networks" (Wank 1999: 33).

For Wank, entrepreneurs and officials survive and grow with interdependence, working together to capitalize on the business opportunities increasingly generated in the marketplace. These two players are pursuing not only "utility-maximizing interest calculations but also the rationality of social trust" (Wank 1995: 31). Thus, clientelist capitalism implies neither the forcefulness of "hard budget constraint" and economic rationalization (as for Guthrie) nor the subjection of private entrepreneurs to government officials (as for Bruun); rather, it points to the relational and symbiotic nature of the emerging socioeconomic order.

The symbiotic perspective is consistent with the "local corporatism model" (Oi 1992, 1999; Walder 1995). In this model, local governments act as business corporations, exercising control rights over the enterprises under their jurisdictions to achieve economic and political benefits both for themselves and for the localities they lead. Walder (1995) found that, compared to those in higher jurisdictions, governments in lower jurisdictions far from the central government are more capable of monitoring enterprises and of achieving good economic performance. Indeed, mutually beneficial exchanges between private entrepreneurs and local officials result in clientelist ties that facilitate contract enforcement, market competition, and local growth (Wank 1999). These are the economic contexts of a transition economy in which entrepreneurs and officials value the *guanxi* connections between them.

The Institutional Substitute Perspective

Xin and Pearce (1996) provide a plausible explanation of why China's private entrepreneurs value *guanxi* connections more than state and collective managers. These authors point to the weak and largely uncertain institutional protection that the state institution provides to the emerging private economy. In-depth interviews with private-company executives offer several insights. First is an underdeveloped legal framework that makes private-company executives more dependent on *guanxi* than executives in state-owned or collective-hybrid companies. In a fully developed market economy, a private company can formally obtain company registration, secure bank loans, and collect profits from business operations, but in an anti-privatization political culture in the 1980s and early 1990s, access to these "market" rights and resources was not readily available to Chinese private entrepreneurs. "A weak rule of law is problematic for all who do business in China, but such unreliability would prove particularly burdensome for newer, smaller private companies" (Xin and Pearce 1996: 1642). In a sample of 258 company executives, private-company executives (N = 72) perceived *guanxi* connections to be much more "important" than state (N = 120) and collective (N = 66) executives.

Another important insight is about the protective role *guanxi* ties to government officials play in helping private entrepreneurs to face fundamental threats, such as expropriation and extortion (Redding 1990). These threats are an everyday phenomenon of the Chinese private economy even today: Small commodity retailers, grocery sellers, and other mobile traders run around the city streets to get away from the harsh "market managers" sent by the city government; small and medium shops, stores, and factories must deal with local police, public health officials, and tax officers who can stop or even terminate any business for real or fictional reasons any time; and large and even giant companies have to be mindful of the predatory behaviors of powerful officials and especially their ruthless and money-thirsty children. No wonder private-company executives in Xin and Pearce's sample feel more strongly than state- and collective-company executives that "connection defends against threats" and that they "trust in connection" more than formal institutional arrangements (Xin and Pearce 1996: table 2).

The Institutional Hole Perspective

While the institutional substitute perspective focuses on the weak legal institutions facing the Chinese private economy, the institutional hole perspective more broadly looks at market functions that *guanxi* networks provide in the absence or ineffectiveness of formal institutions (Bian 2002). These are the information-flow, trust-building, and obligation-binding functions. In the case of private entrepreneurs, they must have the necessary information about suppliers, customers, and competitors before they can approach each other; must achieve a minimal level of trust in each other's accountability before they cut a deal and sign the contract; and must apply obligation-binding measures to ensure that the contractual terms be fulfilled. In the fast removal of hierarchical institutions and the slow growth of market institutions, the Chinese market economy is full of "institutional holes," causing formal channels to be ineffective for transmitting information, building trust, and binding obligations among economic entities, especially private entrepreneurs. *Guanxi* networks of interpersonal relationships are the informal mechanisms to fill in these holes.

Information asymmetry is a problem facing both planned and market economies, but in different ways. The problem of information asymmetry in the planned economy is the control and distortion of information by government agencies oriented to attaining political goals and completing ideal-typical plans. In China's emerging markets, the problem concerning information diffusion is that formal channels are either restricted or ineffective. The information restriction scenario applies to private entrepreneurs and international joint ventures, to which the government has no obligation to provide timely or truthful information about factor resources and future assessment. The information ineffectiveness scenario applies more broadly. In the labor markets, for example, all businesses outside the state confine lack formal means of diffusing employment information, as "only bad, undesirable jobs" that "nobody wants" would be advertised through such formal channels as newspapers and employment services (Bian 2002: 129).

A minimum level of trust is necessary for entrepreneurs to do business with each other. The greater the mutual trust between economic actors, the greater the confidence they have in their future commitment to each other, and the more likely it is to prevent opportunism. But the Chinese transitional economy is full of opportunistic behaviors, as widely evidenced by faulty contracts, delayed payments, false accounts, counterfeit articles, pirated software, shoddy constructions, harmful powdered milk, fake and inferior drinks and foods, manipulated statistics, and official corruption – to name just a few. All these problems would be under control given high standards of business ethics and/or effective formal institutionalization, especially the legal system. The economic realities are that none of these moral and institutional measures are effective, creating room for *guanxi* networks to help build trust and enforce relational control over economic opportunism.

The Network Capitalism Perspective

Despite their differences in perspectives about *guanxi*–business connections in China's market transition, the views described so far share an implicit assumption that a Weberian legal-rational institutional order, which values and protects private property rights above anything else and which is relatively free of *guanxi* prevalence, is the high end to achieve in developing a "modernized" market economy for China. Questioning this assumption, Boisot and Child (1996) take a "causal empiricism" approach to examining the working logic of China's economic takeoff. Their conclusion is that China is by no means taking the Western path to modernization. Quite the contrary: The Chinese market economy is distinctive and can be labeled "network capitalism."

These authors' institutional analysis can be summarized with reference to two dimensions. One dimension is the degree of codification of information about knowledge, technology, and any other forms of productive asset. Codified information takes on a level of abstraction by sacrificing contextual specificities, and in so doing can be diffused more easily and more widely than uncodified information. The other dimension is the variation in the diffusion of information, codified or uncodified. All human societies are assumed to start "low" in both dimensions, in "fiefs" that retain among themselves tacit knowledge that never spreads further. Consequently, economic growth is limited. Europe is believed to have taken a path from fiefs to bureaucracies, which increase the level of information codification but, due to centralization, make no real progress in information diffusion, and finally to markets, a "modernized" system in which codified information is diffused widely and openly. Growth and development characterize advanced market economies because of the diffusion of codified information.

China has taken a completely different path to modernization. The imperial system is considered to operate under the "iron law of fiefs" (Boisot and Child 1988), but industrial China in the late Qing period and thereafter never really moved to bureaucracies that would have codified the domestic industrial system to a higher level of abstraction. Instead, industrial firms in late imperial times usually depended on the patronage of senior government officials (Faure 1994). In reform-era China today, similar institutional arrangements are observed: SOEs in practice negotiate with government authorities for how to exercise public property rights (Child and Lu 1996), urban collectives are subject to local government jurisdictions for supervising their operation (Nee 1992), and private entrepreneurs value customary uncodified norms and conduct business through their *guanxi* ties to local officials (Wank 1995). Each of the three types of property rights – state, collective, and private ownerships – is not defined as in the West, but these different forms of economic organization all develop patronage ties to central, provincial, and local governments, as well as strategic alliances with other firms, banks, and foreign capitalists. These various ties are cultivated and maintained within the reach of economic actors, around whom is built a "clan-like" business network through which to define and redefine property rights, to manage economic dynamics, and, more generally, to diffuse uncodified information (though to a less widespread degree than Western market capitalism). This clan-based socioeconomic order is termed "network capitalism" (Boisot and Child 1996), a theoretical framework of fairly low codification and medium diffusion that has inspired fruitful theoretical rethinking (Wang and Rowley 2016) as well as empirical analysis of China's economic transition (Snell and Tseng 2002; Haveman et al. 2017).

The Centrally Managed Capitalism Perspective

There appears to be an internal contradiction in the network capitalism perspective. The perspective acknowledges the role of government, especially local governments, in clan-like patronage ties with economic actors, but at the same time it regards China as lacking "bureaucracies," which seemingly ignores a well-codified, quite elaborated, and self-adjusting state-party hierarchy. Recognizing China's strong party-state is the point of departure for Lin's (2011) "centrally managed capitalism" perspective.

For Lin, there is no doubt that China has developed capitalistic capacities (private property rights, international joint ventures, banking system, labor markets, etc.). Along with market growth, however, the party-state has, he argues, increasingly tightened control of the economy and synchronized political and economic stratification. Two elements are key to this centrally managed capitalism (CMC) perspective. First, the party-state itself acts as a capitalist. The party-state "commands the economy by controlling personnel, organizations, and capital in both political and economic arenas. At the same time, it delegates fiscal and administrative authorities to multiple and diversely formed corporations to compete in the marketplace" (Lin 2011: 63). Second, economic activities are heavily embedded in *guanxi* networks. Ties to government officials at all levels, for example, are the key channels through which to acquire economic resources (Li et al. 2011), operate business groups (Keister 2000), and govern relational contracts (Zhou et al. 2003). "The combination of state guidance with informal *guanxi* enables Chinese businesses to connect with each other and with officialdom at various levels and build trust and harmony for long-term mutual benefit and stability in both business and social aspects" (Wang and Rowley 2016: 110).

The Social Roots Perspective

Any view on the importance of *guanxi* networks in China's business world will come down to the social roots of *guanxi*–business connections. Analytic attention is focused on the family and kinship networks. Despite the three decades of state socialism that dismissed and denounced the productive function of the family and the social-political functions of kinship in village society under Mao, the family and kinship immediately resumed these functions and the family became the major form of private business during early reforms (Gold 1990). Later, in a more organized production system at village and higher levels, kinship networks are found at the core of the governance structure in township and village enterprises (Lin 1995) and function well in the absence of property rights laws (Peng 2004). By 2012, among entrepreneurs in Yangtze River Delta the family had continuously accounted for one-third of the "most valuable" contacts at business founding and had been the one stable source for the supply of helpful contacts at critical events in the history of business development (Burt and Burzynska 2017; Burt and Opper 2017). Even in some of China's giant corporations, conglomerates, and business groups, family, kinship, and pseudo-kin networks make a great deal of contribution one way or another (Keister 2000).

In theory, the Chinese family contains a mixture of positive and negative elements with reference to business development (Whyte 1995, 1996). Family solidarity and loyalty are certainly positive elements at business founding (Shi 1993), but reliance on the family without developing large, open networks beyond the immediate family is detrimental to business growth (Guo and Miller 2010; Burt and Opper 2017). Mao's era had weakened the senior generation's power within the extended family while to a large extent family solidarity and loyalty survived (Whyte 1995), giving the more energetic, prosperity-seeking younger generations both the personal freedom and the family support to work away from home and become the real drivers of a family-based economy (Peng 2004). The social roots perspective rests on the assumption that people do not merely pursue personal interests; instead, they conform to the ethics and norms of family, kinship, and larger social networks. The social extension of familiar sentiments and obligations to interfirm networks and entrepreneur–bureaucrat patronage networks is, by and large, consistent with the perspectives of network capitalism (Boisot and Child 1996) and centrally managed capitalism (Lin 2011).

Summary

Among these diverse perspectives on the role of *guanxi* networks in China's business world reviewed here, one scholar assumes that *guanxi* favoritism will be on the decline with the rise of the rationalized market economy, but all other scholars argue the opposite while focusing their analysis on different working logics of the Chinese market economy. While scholars will continue to debate about the roles of *guanxi* networks in China's business world, one consensus emerging from this literature review is that *guanxi* networks have been nearly indispensable mechanisms to explain the emergence, development, and governance structure of Chinese businesses during market reforms. We now turn to the empirical analysis of *guanxi* mechanisms in China's organizational governance and organizational development.

GUANXI AS MECHANISMS OF ORGANIZATIONAL GOVERNANCE

Kinship Networks as Governance Structure

Township and village enterprises (TVEs) are a significant part of China's emerging market economy. TVEs experienced tremendous development during the early reforms in the 1980s, growing from 1.5 million in 1978 to 12 million in 1985. Their economic outputs increased from 37 percent of agricultural GDP in 1978 to 104 percent in 1987. As of 2007, TVEs hired 29 percent of the rural labor force, made 69 percent of rural economic value, and accounted for 29 percent of China's total GDP (Naughton 2007; Huang 2008). Studies show that kinship networks function as the governance structure of TVEs.

One of the most successful TVEs is the corporation of Daqiuzhuang village (大邱庄), located in north China 80 kilometers south of Tianjin. Lin (1995) conducted an-depth study of the village corporation. The village head and Party secretary Yu Zuomin had been the chairman of the corporation, with one of his sons serving as the CEO and president. Other members of the Board of Trustees were vice presidents of the corporation and CEOs of the five component companies of the corporation, all of them being Yu's other sons, sons-in-law, cousins, grandsons, or close confidants. Clearly kinship networks function as the governance structure of Daqiuzhuang corporation; the village economy exemplified Boisot and Child's (1996) clan model of network capitalism.

Peng (2004) provided a plausible explanation of why kinship networks are the key governance mechanism of TVEs. In the absence of property rights laws, TVEs rely on kinship networks in producing and enforcing informal norms and asset protection. In villages where rural industrialization take place, kin solidarity and kin trust played an important role in protecting the property rights of private entrepreneurs and reducing transaction costs during the early stages of market reform, when formal property rights laws were ineffective and market institutions underdeveloped. An analysis of 366 villages throughout China shows two pieces of supportive evidence. First, in villages where a large lineage becomes dominant, private enterprises are likely to emerge and survive. Second, in these villages, private enterprises are highly likely to grow in size and maintain a stable market position. These effects are insignificant for collective enterprises.

Guanxi *Circles as Organizational Governance*

Influenced by Fei Xiaotong's (1947/1992) concept of "the mode of differential associations" (*chaxu geju*), several scholars have used the image of *"guanxi* circles" to study business networks of private firms in transitional China (Guo and Miller 2010; Luo 2011). Fei's concept can be understood as egocentric networks in social network analysis today: An ego develops multiple layers of alters extending from the core to the periphery of his or her egocentric network. In Fei's original metaphor, this network is like circles of water ripples (layers of alters) being made after a rock (ego) is thrown into water, and the circles of water ripples extending from the center (ego) change in magnitude from thick (stronger ties) to thin (weaker ties) ripples. For Chinese culture and society, Fei firmly believes that the family is at the core of everyone's egocentric network, and that the overlapping of egocentric networks is the basic social structure through which Chinese individuals socialize with others, norms of morality are learned and reinforced, social resources are mobilized, and, more generally, the social order is maintained.

Adopting Fei's imagery, Luo (2011; Luo, Cheng, and Zhang 2016) argues that a private Chinese firm is made of "*guanxi* circles." Any focal player of the organization can establish his or her *guanxi* circle through which to exercise power and govern organizational processes. At the center of Luo's *guanxi* circle is an inner ring of real and pseudo-family members, and this ring of *guanxi* applies "need rules" in which within-ring members satisfy each other's needs without asking for return. The next is a middle ring composed of good friends who follow the "*renqing* rule" of long-term favor exchanges for expressive support and instrumental resources under the principles of reciprocity. Beyond the middle ring are acquaintances on the periphery, where instant return and bargaining in favor exchanges are expected by the "equity rule" in which trust comes from fair exchange. Beyond the periphery boundary there are no rules.

The *guanxi* circle image puts organizational members into four categories. The first is the core members, who are inside the inner ring of the *guanxi* circle of one or more powerful persons of the organization. The second is the periphery members, who have familiar ties with one or more core members of the identified *guanxi* circle. The third is the bridges, who are the periphery members of several *guanxi* circles. Finally, the fourth is the outsiders, who are not insiders of the *guanxi* circle of any powerful person within the organization. In a large Taiwanese company operating in mainland China, Luo and Cheng (2015) find that employees' trust in organizational governance is a function of their roles in reference to *guanxi* circles within the organization. Among equally qualified employees with the same level of organizational commitment, organizational trust is the highest for core members of the top supervisor's *guanxi* circle, but lower for bridges connecting between *guanxi* circles of several supervisors, and lowest for outsiders who belong to none of the *guanxi* circles of supervisors.

Guanxi *Circles and Network Dynamics in Organizational Growth*

While Luo's *guanxi* circles seem static, Guo and Miller (2010), drawing on a study of six ventures, discuss how *guanxi* circles evolve in the process of organizational growth. Each venture goes through three critical stages of development, and the network structures, rules of social exchange, and contents of *guanxi* circles evolve accordingly. The first stage is the creation of a firm. A small core circle is made of family members, relatives, and close friends, who supply start-up capital, advice, and critical feedback for creating the firm. Network closure is the immediate result of affection-based strong ties, which keep within the core circle all the members who interact according to the *"ganqing* rule" of contributing to each other without being overly burdened by payback obligations.

The second stage begins with the early growth of the firm. At this point, a medium-sized intermediary circle is added around the core circle. The intermediary circle has a sparse network structure, and the added new members are government officials, bank investors, key clients, and business associates who bring to the firm additional resources for firm growth. These new members have strong ties to each another, but they interact according to the *"renqing* rule" by which to fulfill social obligations of gift-favor-banquet exchanges, while making contributions to the firm with valuable information, needed knowledge transfer, and resource mobilization.

The third and final stage is the later growth of the firm. During this stage, the firm is sizable, so is in need of a large, open, and indefinitely expanding periphery circle. The network structure of the periphery circle is sparse, and new members of the circle are random, previously unknown individuals from diverse backgrounds. Weak ties connect these people, who are there to offer diverse information and resources for instrumental exchanges and therefore are opportunistic. There is no affection and no long-term commitment, but these people are surely using the "*jiaoqing* rule" to build acquaintance for future business cooperation.

Guo and Miller (2010: 284) conclude that "the *guanxi* ties in the core circle remain highly stable over the venturing process, and it is the periphery circle that experiences constant change and continuous expansion." Ties included in the periphery circle as described by the authors are exceptional *guanxi* ties. Commonly known *guanxi* ties are the strong ties linking people who are familiar with each other, are intimate with each other, and have high trust in each other. Exceptional *guanxi* ties are obligatory or contractual ties, which are likely to link, though not confined to, opportunistic people for rent seeking, power–money exchange, and illicit transactions.

The Internal Dynamics of Guanxi *as Governance Mechanisms*

Implicit in the study of *guanxi* circles is the proposition that *guanxi* mechanisms decline as an organization has fully developed. Fu, Tsui, and Dess (2006) question this proposition in a study of knowledge management in Chinese high-tech firms. A high-tech firm is missioned to "create high-capacity information links between organizations and engender a motivation for information sharing, thus mitigating uncertainty and allowing the focal organization to vicariously benefit from the insights and experiences of its peers" (Kraatz 1998: 638). Thus, a high-tech firm is centrally concerned with two organizational goals of knowledge management: (1) the management of knowledge protection and control and (2) the management of knowledge generation and application. While the first goal requires close-knit *guanxi* networks of intimate and high-trust ties to implement protection and control, the second goal relies on sparse networks of acquaintances and strangers for information diversity and greater knowledge generation and application. As a high-tech firm is constantly in this dual-goal attainment process, it is inherently involved in the internal dynamics of *guanxi* as governance mechanisms.

Fu, Tsui, and Dess (2006) identify three types of social relations facing any high-tech firm. The first is *qinren*-based social relations, or kin and pseudo-kin ties of intimacy and high trust. The second is *shuren*-based social relations, or non-kin ties of high acquaintance and familiarity, which are by definition also of high trust. The third is *shengren*-based social relations, which refer to the activation of new social relations without prior ties of any nature. For a high-tech firm, these are managers, professionals, technicians, and other employees who are neither relatives nor acquaintances of the focal players of the firm. A series of propositions were developed about the internal dynamics of *guanxi*. For knowledge protection and control, young and small Chinese high-tech firms primarily rely on intimate *guanxi*, especially in the technical core or the upper echelon of the firm. But excessive reliance on intimate *guanxi* will eventually slow down knowledge exploration and increase the need for information diversity and new knowledge generation, which increase the reliance on non-*guanxi* relationships inside the firm and decrease the reliance on intimate *guanxi*. In the next process of the internal dynamic, excessive reliance on non-*guanxi* relationships will lead to a decrease in attaining shared goals and an increase in the need for cooperation in knowledge application, which will lead to more intimate *guanxi* than non-*guanxi* relationships inside the firm. When the firm grows large and becomes structurally complex, it does not decouple from this internal dynamic of *guanxi*: The need for greater decentralization of decision-making will lead to greater involvement of individuals with non-*guanxi* relationships in the firm's decision-making processes, but excessive reliance on non-*guanxi* relationships in decision-making processes will result in weakened top management control and a rising need for tighter control, which will lead to increased reliance on intimate *guanxi*.

Success for Chinese high-tech firms is, therefore, finding an equilibrium in which dense and sparse networks are utilized to meet different organizational goals throughout the development and growth of organizations. The

> growth and development of entrepreneurial firms may fall victim to the dynamics of *guanxi* as they attempt to manage knowledge acquisition and application and the decision-making processes. ... If the firm is able to move beyond the continuing need to control and protect its special knowledge, and able to move forward to including more *shengren*-based relations (more professional managers), then the growth trajectory will be good. Otherwise, the firm falls into the vicious cycle by revolving back to *qinren* and this would restrict the growth or even survival of the firm. (Fu, Tsui, and Dess 2006: 296–7)

In practice, successful Chinese entrepreneurs are expected to have the ability to know what type of *guanxi* to recruit, use, cultivate, and dismiss as their organizations develop to scale and maturity.

Supervisor–Subordinate Guanxi *in Organizations*

Supervisor–subordinate relations are an important component of organizational governance. In the Western workplace context, what is commonly referred to as leader–member exchange (LMX) is found to be positively associated with employment outcomes such as job satisfaction, turnover, and organizational commitment, while commitment to supervisor (CTS) is positively associated with job performance

(Scandura and Graen 1984). While both of these Western concepts – LMX and CTS – are confined to work relations, the Chinese concept of supervisor–subordinate *guanxi* involves both work-related and non-work aspects of the supervisor–subordinate relationship and significantly affects employment outcomes (Law et al. 2000).

In a study of 189 supervisor–subordinate dyads randomly selected from two companies in Hangzhou, China, Law et al. (2000) used a six-item battery to measure supervisor–subordinate *guanxi*, including:

1 frequent social contact during non-working time;
2 social eating together;
3 gift exchange at events of personal significance;
4 frequent personal conversations;
5 care about the supervisor's family;
6 standing on the supervisor's side when opinions conflict.

Each item was a 0/1 dichotomy. The 189 supervisor–subordinate dyads generated a mean of 3.86 and a standard deviation of 1.53. These figures indicate a high average degree of *guanxi* closeness and a significant inter-dyad variation.

The measure of personal *guanxi* closeness is highly correlated with but not identical to measures of LMX (a correlation coefficient of .54) and CTS (.58). This means that those supervisors and subordinates whose work relations are positive are also highly positive to each other in terms of personal *guanxi* relationships. A covariance structure analysis shows three sets of interesting results. First, LMX, but not personal *guanxi* closeness, has direct and positive impacts on performance ratings and job assignment. Second, personal *guanxi* closeness significantly increased a subordinate's probability of getting bonus allocation and chances of promotion. Third, it is the employees whose performances are rated high who are more likely than others to get promotion and high job assignment. Together, these results indicate that supervisor–subordinate *guanxi* elevates leader–member exchanges at work through which to increase subordinate performance ratings, chances of promotion, and job assignments.

Similar results are obtained from a study of a large insurance company in Taiwan (Farh et al. 1998). Of the 560 supervisor–subordinate dyads, measures of prior *guanxi* relations significantly increase a subordinate's trust in his or her immediate supervisor. At the same time, a stronger effect of prior *guanxi* relations on the trust between managers was revealed. These effects held true even when similarities and differences in personal attributes such as gender, age, and education were statistically controlled for. These study results confirm that in Chinese culture *guanxi* plays a significant part in maintaining vertical dyads between supervisors and subordinates and horizontal dyads between managers of equal rank.

Guanxi *Culture and Career Performance in Organizations*

Collective harmony is a social norm in *guanxi* culture (Bian and Ikeda 2014/2016). Under this norm, emotional support, resource sharing, and relational reciprocity are strongly expected by people who are connected to each other by *guanxi* ties (Yan 1996; Lin 2001b). On the individual level, however, building a strategic network to reap benefits from otherwise disconnected others (known as "structural holes"; Burt 1992) is a basic strategy used to achieve career success in Western organizations (Podolny and Baron 1997). To what extent does *guanxi* collectivism affect career network and career performance in Chinese organizations?

Xiao and Tsui (2007) examined this question by conducting a survey in four high-tech companies in China. Two of these companies maintained an organizational culture of "high commitment," which required and rewarded employees' devotion to the company as well as support to each other, punishing selfish or opportunistic behaviors. The other two companies were "low commitment" companies that encouraged competition under weak collective norms. On career network, the authors followed a standard name generator approach developed in the West to measure an employee's egocentric network, which contains superiors and other colleagues perceived to be important alters to the employee (ego). Within the company, these alters are a source of mentorship, task advice, strategic information, political aid, and social support. When some of these alters are disconnected with each other, the employee is believed to have a good number of "structural holes"; the employee has fewer or no "structural holes" when his or her alters are closely connected among themselves (an additional data table is available from this book's webpage online*).

Salary and bonus are used to measure employee career performance in organizations. In general, the more structural holes an employee has in his or her career network, the lower salary and bonus the employee earns. But this effect is stronger and more significant in high commitment companies, and it is insignificant in low commitment companies. The quantitative differences that structural holes make in salary and bonus between high and low commitment companies are impressive. Working in a high commitment company, as compared to someone whose career network lacks structural holes, otherwise equally qualified employees whose career network retains structural holes will face a 47 percent salary reduction and 49 percent bonus reduction from the company average. These huge punishments in salary and bonus make it explicit that *guanxi* collectivism matters tremendously in Chinese organizations, especially when the organizations are under strong collective norms.

The Negative Effect of Guanxi in Organizations

While *guanxi* is a mechanism of organizational governance, its practice is against procedural justice. If, for example, job assignment, reward allocation, promotion, and performance appraisal are based

---

* www.politybooks.com/guanxi

on *guanxi* with managers rather than merit and work outcomes, these kinds of *guanxi*-altered human resource management (HRM) practices will reduce employees' trust in management. Chen, Chen, and Xin (2004) examined this issue in a study of 140 Chinese executive MBA students.

The MBA executives were asked to evaluate their companies in terms of, among other items, *guanxi*-altered HRM practices, the prevalence of informal *guanxi* relations, and employees' trust in management. When companies have concentrations of informal *guanxi* relations at work, their *guanxi*-HRM practices are dense, and their employees' trust in management is low. When companies are strong in procedural justice in HRM practices, the negative effects of *guanxi* prevalence and *guanxi*-altered HRM practices are reduced to insignificance. The more the managers' HRM decisions favor someone with particular ties (such as relatives and hometown fellows), the lower the employees' trust in management; conversely, the greater the relational neutrality of HRM decisions, the higher the employees' trust in management.

Interfirm Relations and Chinese Business Groups

The formation of business groups is one of the most important reform measures in China's transition toward a market economy. Under the policy of "grabbing the big, releasing the small," China's largest SOEs were transformed into business groups around the late 1990s. Keister (1998, 2000) examined the first wave of Chinese business groups, and her empirical analysis of forty separate business groups and more than 500 component firms provides a clear set of findings about the importance of two kinds of interfirm relations in the formation of business groups in China.

The first is interfirm relations outside a business group. These include direct and indirect ties between managers of different firms across business groups. The more direct and indirect ties a firm's managers have with managers of other firms outside the business group, the more likely it is for the firm to exchange labor, product, and financial resources with these other firms. This impact is stronger when labor, product, and financial markets are less developed in the region in which the firm operates its business, but the impact is decreasing along with the growth and enhancement of the markets.

The second is interfirm relations inside a business group. These refer to direct and indirect ties between managers of different firms within the business group. As with interfirm relations across business groups, the more direct and indirect ties a firm's managers have with managers of other firms within the business group, the more likely it is for the firm to exchange labor, product, and financial resources with these other firms. The longer the duration of these direct and indirect ties, the stronger the impact of the ties on market exchanges between the firms; the higher the centrality of a firm's position within the business group, the greater the probability for the firm to keep trading and lending relations with these other firms. But unlike interfirm relations across business groups, the impact of direct and indirect ties within business groups is not decreasing but increasing with time, as these ties are the internal structures through which to operate market exchanges within business groups. These findings hold true when transaction costs are controlled for. Thus, Keister's analysis reveals that "firms select exchange partners of known reputation and solicit relations that reduce uncertainty, even when there is a cost involved" (Keister 2000: 336).

Interfirm Contractual Relationships under Guanxi Norms

Interfirm contracts specify terms of responsibility of economic actors involved in an anticipated business transaction between and among them. While interfirm contracts in Western countries are observed to be carried out through informal social relations (Macaulay 1963), Zhou et al. (2003) examine how social relations facilitate interfirm contracts under economic transition in Beijing and Guangzhou. Three findings are summarized here.

First, interfirm contracts are based heavily on prior relations of business and social acquaintance. Of the 622 firms studied, 877 interfirm contracts were identified, and 61 percent of these contracts were with partners of prior acquaintance from recurrent social or business relations. Second, networks of ongoing social relations are one of the most frequently used and most effective channels through which to search for contractual partners. This is especially true for new firms with private or hybrid forms of ownership. Third, business contracts are carried out through the assistance of social interactions in such forms as personal contact, gift exchange, and social banqueting. This is especially so when contracts are of larger value, for longer duration, or involving fewer partners.

Summary

Guanxi is a core component of governance structure in Chinese organizations. The focal player of a Chinese organization, whether it is the founder or general manager, establishes a *guanxi* circle of kin and pseudo-kin ties of high trust through which to manage the organization. But the focal player's *guanxi* circle will diversify to include acquaintances and strangers of managerial and professional competence when an organization grows in size and becomes complex in organizational structure. High-tech organizations involve the internal dynamic of *guanxi*, in which close-knit networks of intimate and high-trust ties are required to manage knowledge protection and control, whereas sparse networks of low intimacy and low acquaintance are needed to manage knowledge generation and application. Successful Chinese organizations must develop a capacity of knowing when to do what or otherwise fall into a "vicious cycle" (Fu, Tsui, and Dess 2006) through excessive reliance on kin and pseudo-kin relations, which restricts the growth or even survival of the organization. Nevertheless, maintaining a certain degree of personalized *guanxi* is an important part of good supervisor–subordinate relations as well as good manager–manager relations, and the *guanxi* culture for social harmony is against an individual's taking advantage of his or her social contacts. But overt *guanxi* practices in favoring particular ties in human resources management are against procedural justice, thus decreasing employees' trust in management.

GUANXI AS MECHANISMS OF ORGANIZATIONAL PERFORMANCE

Guanxi *and Economic Performance of Guangzhou Firms*

A probability sample survey was conducted in Guangzhou in 1998 (Bian and Qiu 2000; Bian 2006). Of a total of 2,000 member firms registered with the city's Labor Management Association, 188 were selected, with 119 state-owned, 30 collectives, and 39 private. The great majority of these firms were under the jurisdiction of the municipal government (166), and only a small number (22) were under the lower level of district government within the city.

Given the hierarchical structure of economic organization in Guangzhou, the study measured three *guanxi* ties of each firm: (1) vertical ties with the government, measured by whether or not the firm CEO previously held a government position (11 percent had); (2) horizontal ties with other firms across the industry, measured by whether or not the firm CEO had previously held a managerial position in other firms (35 percent had); and (3) broad social ties, measured by a five-point self-evaluated scale of the extent to which the firm CEO had a broad range of *guanxi* connections (14 percent "very extensive," 59 percent "quite extensive," 28 percent "so-so"). Since these measures are highly correlated with one another, a composite measure of "network social capital" was obtained through a factor analysis, resulting in a mean of 2.19 and a range from 1 to 4.704 standard-deviation points (SDs). The variation is huge. Did network social capital increase a firm's economic performance?

The results from a regression analysis of the survey data (not presented here but available online) are impressive in two ways. First, a firm's network social capital increases by 12.2 percent for private firms (compared to state and collective firms), by 11.4 percent for new firms in tertiary industry (compared to other industries), by 5.7 percent for each level of increase in the CEO's education, and by 7.9 percent for each rank increase in the CEO's administrative rank in the hierarchy of organizational management in the city. Second, the effect of network social capital on a firm's economic performance is considerably large and significant: One SD point in network social capital produces a 43.3 percent increase in the firm's per capita output value. This increase margin tells us how significant vertical, horizontal, and social connections were to firms in Guangzhou in the 1990s.

Guanxi *and the Conditional Effect of Political Ties*

Guanxi ties to government and government officials are political ties. What are the institutional conditions under which political ties affect organizational performance? Findings were obtained by Nee and Opper (2010) from a 2002 survey of 1,764 firms randomly selected in the Yangze River Delta region. The firms surveyed were 26 percent state-owned, 16 percent collective, 18 percent shareholding, 28 percent private, 10 percent joint venture, and 2 percent unspecified ownership. This represents the mixed ownership structure of China's transitional economy (summary results are presented in a table available online).

These firms vary in the political ties they had cultivated and maintained by the time of the survey. Less than one-third (31 percent) of the firm CEOs held a formal position in the Party apparatus, 6 percent had previously held a position in the government, and 16 percent had been appointed directly by the government. On a six-item index of perceived government support, the average was 0.64 items but the standard deviation was 1.21, indicating a large variation in perceived government support (additional data table available online).

Are firms with political ties and government support doing better than the other firms? Several results can be summarized here. First, a previous position in the government increases the firm's probability of getting a government grant and shortens the waiting period of local custom clearance of export goods, but reduces the chance of getting tax exemptions. Second, the government appointment of a firm CEO had negative results: a reduced sales margin in 2002, a longer waiting time for local custom clearance of expert goods, and a lower chance of obtaining an export license. Finally, government support is a positive political capital for the firm only in the government-sheltered areas. On the whole, political ties matter only partially: They make a significant difference in government-sheltered domains, but their influence is much weakened in economic markets from which government intervention is either constrained or taken away.

Guanxi *and the Dynamics of Political Embeddedness*

In the modern era, publicly listed companies are a window onto the dynamics of the market economy. For China, the transition of state-owned enterprises to publicly listed shareholding companies is of fundamental importance because reformers consider it as one of the key indicators of the success of economic reforms (Wu 2003). By design, publicly listed companies are driven by market signals and incentives and thus are less politically embedded (Paulson 2015). Haveman et al. (2017) demonstrate, however, that China's listed firms are increasingly embedded in political ties to the party-state, which improve, rather than worsen, their economic performance.

These authors analyzed the growth pattern of firms listed on the domestic exchanges from 1992 to 2007. During this period, the number of listed firms grew from 26 to 1,371, and politically embedded listed firms, defined by a firm's having former bureaucrats as executives and directors, increased from 27 percent in 1992 to 69 percent in 2002 and to 66 percent in 2007, the year when China finally adopted laws to fully proclaim the rights to private property in business. Therefore, the period studied had two features highly important to listed firms. First, this was a period of tremendous market development, as evidenced by the increase of listed firms. Second, it was also a period of growing uncertainty, characterized by the fast pace of change in economic transition, the ineffectiveness of legal enforcement, and the persistence of bureaucratic power to interfere frequently and abruptly. The authors' central argument is that China's listed firms maintained and cultivated political ties to reduce the uncertainties that grew as market development proceeded.

For all the firms studied (N = 1,054), political embeddedness had a statistically significant and positive impact on listed firms' economic performance measured by return on assets, and this impact was greater when the firms were operated under greater marketization, whether it was measured by proportion of non-state workers ("labor marketization") or by proportion of capital investment not through government channels ("capital marketization"). Furthermore, this impact of political embeddedness is significant in more competitive industries where uncertainty was great, and not significant in less competitive industries where uncertainty was reduced by the high concentration of giant firms; and it was significant among small firms that constantly faced uncertainty, and not significant among large firms whose higher capacities to mobilize resources, more stable market position, and greater power to negotiate with government help them reduce uncertainty.

Haveman et al. (2017) identify two causal mechanisms whereby political embeddedness affects listed firms' economic performance. The first causal mechanism is a firm's access to bank loans, a critical condition for firms' economic performance. In an underdeveloped capital market, Chinese firms face a great deal of uncertainty in loan applications, but the results show that this uncertainty can be reduced as firms with political ties are more likely to increase their borrowing ratio, especially in areas of greater labor marketization. The second causal mechanism is the constraint that the listed firm is pressured to provide loan guarantees to the controlling shareholder or other firms controlled by that shareholder. The results show that firms with political ties are better able to reduce the propensity to provide such loans, lowering their "related-party loan ratio" significantly, and more so in more marketized areas (additional data tables available online). In the more marketized areas such as Guangdong, Jiangsu, and Zhejiang, while pressure to make related-party loans increases, public-listed firms with political ties have greater capacities than those without such ties to defend themselves against such pressure. This is a monopoly effect: Public-listed firms are giant companies of strategic importance and their political ties to government officials are protective of themselves. In contrast, political ties are less effective when governmental influence is significantly reduced in competitive markets (Nee and Opper 2010).

Guanxi *and Organizational Performance*

Many organizational studies have been conducted to examine the effects of *guanxi* on organizational performance. These studies were conducted in different localities, at different time periods, and with varying sample sizes of different kinds of organizations, producing mixed and sometimes contradictory results. Is there a generalizable pattern emerging from the organizations studied for the *guanxi*–performance link? Luo, Huang, and Wang (2011) answer this question with a meta-analysis of fifty-three studies encompassing 20,212 organizations.

Two kinds of *guanxi* ties are measured. The first is business ties, including ties with suppliers, customers, competitors, and other business intermediaries. The second is government ties, including ties with central and local government, industrial bureaus, tax bureaus, state banks, and other governmental organs. Some firms may have one kind of ties over the other kind of ties, but other firms may have a combination of both ties. Another complication is that some of these ties are direct, while in other instances they are indirect. But no matter what kinds of ties organizations have mobilized, these ties are believed to affect two dimensions of an organization's performance: the economic performance that is measured in market and financial terms, and the operational performance that is measured in competitive and social/societal terms. A summary of the analytic results is presented in a table not given here but available online.

A strong positive relationship is found between business ties and organizational performance. Specifically, business ties have a greater impact on an organization's operational performance than on economic performance, the impact is greater among firms operating within China than among firms operating overseas, and this pattern holds true for both state-owned and non-state-owned firms and does not vary over time. These *guanxi*–performance associations are more significant for direct ties than for indirect ties, and more significant on subjective than objective performance measures. This means that business ties sharpen an organization's competitive edge as well as improving its social and societal orientation, and their impact on organizational performance is robust across institutional contexts and across reform periods.

A significant positive association is also found between governmental ties and organizational performance. But in contrast to business ties, governmental ties are found to have greater impact on economic performance than on operational performance. Such impact is much stronger among state-owned firms than among non-state-owned firms, is much stronger among firms operating within China than operating overseas, and decreases in magnitude over time. These findings are clearer when the studies applied direct measures of *guanxi* than indirect ties, but the results are equally strong whether the studies use subjective or objective measures of performance. The decrease over time in the impact of governmental ties on organizational performance is similar to the finding from another study by Nee and Opper (2010), indicating the declining significance of political ties in economic domains where state intervention and political influence are gradually going away.

Guanxi *Ties and Their Causal Effects*

Is *guanxi* effect causal? Because well-positioned organizations are better able than poorly positioned organizations to use *guanxi* and use it more successfully, the causality of the *guanxi* effect is questionable (Mouw 2003). Statistically, a more convincing analysis should be conducted under an experimental condition: Equally competent organizations are randomly assigned to experimental and control groups, but only the organizations in the experimental group use *guanxi* for boosting organizational performance. If measured organizational performance is significantly higher for organizations in the experimental group than in the control group, then one can confidently say that the *guanxi* effect is causal. While organizational studies usually do not establish this experimental condition, Zhang (2016) does a propensity-score analysis (Rosenbaum and Rubin 1983) that matches firms in treatment (high *guanxi*) and control (low *guanxi*) conditions under which to assess the causal effect of *guanxi* on organizational performance, with a Pearl River Delta sample of firms in 2003.

The firms surveyed were labor-intensive, concentrated in textile (24.8 percent), metal processing (21.4 percent), garment (16.2 percent), ceramics (14.2 percent), furniture (12.5 percent), and construction materials (10.9 percent). Most firms were family-owned (83.1 percent), with relatively small sizes in terms of employment (mean = 63), fixed asset (1.2 million RMB), and value-added tax (VAT, 2.631 points after natural logarithm conversion). These firms were established during the reform period, with 22.6 percent in the early reforms before 1991, 52.2 percent between 1992 and 1999, and 25.3 percent after 2000 when the World Trade Organization regulations began to apply to the area.

Three sets of model estimates were generated. First, in terms of particularism (whether a company had "many" particular ties from the business ties to the three top partners), the high *guanxi* level companies have a much higher performance index than the low *guanxi* level companies. Second, in terms of multiplexity (whether "many" business ties to the top three partners are multiplex ties), the high-level companies also have a much higher performance index. Finally, in terms of reciprocity (partners perceived to be free of opportunism), high-level companies do much better on the performance index than low-level companies (additional data table available online). These are consistent results demonstrating the causal effect of *guanxi* on a company's economic performance.

FOREIGN ORGANIZATIONS IN *GUANXI* CULTURE

China is increasingly globalized. How do foreign firms perceive *guanxi* practices in China within which they conduct business? Do they reject or are they adapting to certain *guanxi* norms? Let me begin with my personal observation before a presentation of research results.

I gave a lecture on China's social environment to a delegation of forty or so bankers from Denmark, Finland, Norway, and Sweden in Xi'an in May 2016. The delegates paid the visit on behalf of their Northern European banks intending to open operations in China. To satisfy their interest in "the social and cultural elements important to the

Chinese economy," I chose to talk about market reforms and the evolvement of *hukou*, *danwei*, and *guanxi*, the three unique characteristics of Chinese society. Respectively, these are the household registration institution, the work-unit system, and networks of favor exchange ties. During the Q&A period, the delegates raised a good number of questions, paying much more attention to *guanxi* than anything else. Later that day, the delegation head, a 40-plus gentleman, sent me a short thank-you message: "Dear Professor Bian, thank you very much for your lecture. On the return trip back to the hotel, my colleagues were talking about your lecture with great appreciation. We concluded that we have a lot of *guanxi* in our countries!"

Western Bankers' Response to Guanxi *Practices*

As of 2007, sixty-nine Western banks operated in China, with fifty-three from Europe, thirteen from North America, and three from Australia. Nolan (2011) interviewed twenty-six foreign bankers covering all three regions. The interviewees were all male, aged 37–63; twenty-three were Caucasian and three second-generation Chinese-American. Two findings are highly interesting.

First, Western bankers make a fine distinction between good *guanxi* and bad *guanxi*. Good *guanxi* refers to social networks functioning for *voluntary* information exchange. Although this is considered to occur everywhere around the world, China's *guanxi* networks are thought to flow a lot more business information than, for example, American social networks, because in China "we don't have the *Wall Street Journal* or the *Dow Jones* to tell us what's going on" (Nolan 2011: 3364). Bad *guanxi*, in contrast, is about the *intentional* use of social networks to generate illicit and illegal personal favors in the forms of bribery and official corruption: "corrupt *guanxi* because you have to pay them" (p. 3365), and "in some way it hurts their national image" (p. 3363). These quotes from the foreign bankers interviewed by Nolan are self-explanatory about what bad *guanxi* is and how bad it can be.

Second, there is a process of "bricolage" where Western bankers reinterpret the norms of *guanxi* practices to justify their actions. There is the ongoing discourse in which Western bankers talk about *guanxi*, not just what it is, but how to adapt to it in order to win in business competition under the weak rule of law in China. They understand and are willing to accept that *guanxi* means network building for long-term commitment and mutual trust between business partners. To some but not all Western bankers, it is also acceptable to hire people recommended by Chinese officials or "people of influence" as long as the candidates go through a formal process of screening to examine their merits. A small minority of Western bankers conduct direct favor exchanges with Chinese officials. In this case, the Western bankers offer the requested financial advice and loan support to the Chinese officials, who, in turn, provide assistance with licensing issues, which are difficult to deal with and which would otherwise take a long time to resolve. Therefore, as one Western banker admitted, "you have to do what you have to do" (Nolan 2011: 3367).

Guanxi *as a Core HRM Concept in International Joint Ventures*

More recent studies in human resource management (HRM) have paid great attention to the culturally specific nature of *guanxi* (Warner 2014). For example, Wong, Wong, and Wong's (2010) study of 292 employees in joint ventures in Southern China showed that the culture of *guanxi* influences the nature of Chinese employees' trust in both their supervisors and their organizations. These authors argue that good subordinate–supervisor *guanxi* is a core HRM concept in China because it can increase employees' perceptions of procedural justice and job security and, consequently, reduce their turnover intentions.

Western-based HRM concepts and practices are widely taught through management programs in Chinese universities and business schools, but they are also developing clearly identifiable national guises and incarnations (Zhu, Warner, and Rowley 2007). From the phasing out of the "iron rice bowl" (*tie fan wan*) in the 1980s to the development of contemporary HRM practices used in large organizations in the 2000s, Warner (2014) identifies the emergence of "Confucian HRM," which takes harmony as its template for interpersonal relationships.

In the case of *guanxi*, HRM correlates can be both positive and negative in terms of their outcomes. On the one hand, *guanxi* may lead to "benign horizontal communication or a less benign form of corruption" (Warner 2010: 2059). Warner notes, however, that the identification of Confucian principles in HRM practices in China cannot be explained simply through the "cultural differences" argument. The terms must also be contextualized against the backdrop of the current popular discourse on Confucianism in China, which coexists with Sino-Marxism and the CCP's adoption of the concept of the "harmonious society" to legitimate its current political agenda. Thus, Warner also foregrounds the importance of institutional influences adapting seemingly stable "traditional" elements of Chinese thought to modern HRM practices.

Guanxi *and Sino-Israeli Business Relationships*

Barnes, Yen, and Zhou (2011) and Yen, Barnes, and Wang (2011) created a *guanxi* measurement scale, labeled the "GRX scale" (*ganqing, renqing, xinren*), from the angle of Taiwanese firms doing business with Western companies. This scale shows that these three constructs of *guanxi* make a significant contribution to Taiwanese–Western business relations. Berger et al. (2015) reevaluated this scale from the angle of Western firms doing business with mainland

Chinese companies. In a study of 329 Israeli high-tech export-ers and importers that trade with China, these authors find that a great majority of these Israeli firms have adopted *guanxi* norms in their business relations with Chinese counterparts. Two findings are summarized here.

First, Israeli managers recognized the importance of *guanxi* norms in their Sino-Israeli business relations. On *ganqing* or affective attach-ment, an Israeli manager tends to "talk openly as friends" with his or her Chinese contact person and "have a brotherly feeling toward the contact person," and "would try my best to help out my contact person when he/she is in need." On *renqing* or favor exchange, they admit that the practice of "give and take" of favors "is a key part of the relationship between this contact person and myself," stating "I would feel embar-rassed if I was unable to provide a requested favor for this person" and "I know that it is bad business not to return favors for this contact person." On *xinren* or trust, they admit that "the contact person I do business with has been frank in dealing with us" and "the contact person I do business with does not make false claims."

Second, the three *renqing* items were found to be the most impor-tant practices of *guanxi*. To many Israeli businesspeople, the exchange of gifts and favors is considered as bribery. In the Chinese context, however, they understand the importance of giving a gift as a ritual of empathy or fellow feeling. Therefore, how to give a gift is more impor-tant than what the actual gift is. "It is important to grant favors in a humble manner so as to save face for the other party," and this *renqing* aspect of business conduct is "fundamental for building good long-term relationships" (Berger et al. 2015: 172).

Cultivating Guanxi *as a Foreign Investor Strategy*

Based on the success of three Sino-American joint ventures and the experiences of their Chinese partner companies, Pearce and Robinson

(2000) argue that cultivating *guanxi* is *the* top foreign investor strategy. The point of departure is that business success requires an adequate understanding of cultural preferences of the people in context. In China, "people do business only with those they know and trust. ... People who share a *guanxi* network are committed to one another by an unwritten code. ... Thus, developing and expanding *guanxi* is a form of social investment that enriches the executive's current resources and future potential" (Pearce and Robinson 2000: 31). In business communication, for example, Westerners are used to exchanging facts and information relevant to closing a business deal, while Chinese are accustomed to exchanging affection, gifts, and favors through which to establish a sense of trust and security for a long-term relationship. To Westerners, this is clearly an inefficient way of generating business opportunities, because time and energies are spent to cultivate *guanxi* with potential business partners, but *guanxi* cultivation is nevertheless believed to be the effective way to conduct business in China because, once established, well-maintained *guanxi* networks of long-term relationships can keep business going.

The *guanxi* cultivation strategy applies to many areas of business development. It starts with *guanxi* marketing, in which consultants are hired through *guanxi* contacts to marketize the products and services concerned. It is extended to *guanxi* lending, with which to negotiate favorable loan terms and flexible payment schedules through the assistance of *guanxi* contacts from Chinese partner companies. It is also recommended to be used to deal with employee relations, where manager–staff-member friendships are maintained to facilitate and promote good collegial relations. Finally, the *guanxi* cultivation strategy is used to deal with business disputes in the legal system, in which law enforcement by courts is relied on less than by appointed individuals who are in positions to make decisions.

Corruption is likely to arise when a foreign investor ought to cultivate *guanxi* with government officials at various levels of the party-state.

And *guanxi* can also be "a source of frustration for expatriates who are not accustomed to developing close personal relationships with their customers and clients before conducting business. It also takes a great deal of time and energy for Western managers to maneuver among the complicated *guanxi* webs. Nevertheless, the energies put into developing *guanxi* are well invested" (Pearce and Robinson 2000: 37–8).

6

Guanxi and Politics ⎯⎯⎯⎯⎯⎯⎯⎯⎯

The main question to be answered in this chapter is what role *guanxi* plays in China's political sphere. Politics is broadly defined as the process of making decisions that apply to members of a group, and it more narrowly refers to the decision-making process when applied to positions of governance in a community and especially the state polity (Hague and Harrop 2013). China is a Communist party-state, and its central feature is political control of citizenship (Yang 2004). Therefore, politics is relevant to all forms of group life in China past and present. In this chapter, I use empirical findings from various studies to examine the forms of *guanxi* influence on local politics in a county government, on politics of career promotion and elite selection at local and national levels, and on the politicized legal system.

NEPOTISM AND *GUANXI* NETWORKS IN A LOCAL GOVERNMENT

Feng (2010) conducted a two-year participant observation study of a local government in Central County, a large county with a population of 800,000 in Henan Province. In the first year, he was a deputy head of a township government in the county. In the second year, he became an assistant county magistrate. Taking advantage of these leadership roles, he completed 161 in-depth interviews with county- and township-level officials, both incumbents and retirees. He also read a large number of personnel documents and personal dossiers. From this data, he drew a detailed picture of the *guanxi* networks of government officials in Central County.

The Hierarchy and Selection of Government Officials

China has a five-level hierarchy of government administration: central, provincial, prefecture-level municipal, county/city district, and township/city subdistrict. Confined to the mainland, as of 2017 China had 31 provincial-level governments, 333 prefecture-level municipal governments, 2,862 county-level governments, and 41,636 township-level governments (http://www.gov.cn). Roughly, these five levels of governments hire 12 million staff members formally called 公务员 (civil servants), from whom government officials are screened and selected through a political-appointee system.

This political-appointee system is characterized by the Party leadership. That is, it is the Communist Party apparatus at each level of the government hierarchy that nominates, examines, screens, and selects candidates for vacant official positions. Age, education, work seniority, current and prior work experiences, and political and work performances on the current job are the main aspects of candidacy evaluations. While equal-level colleagues and higher-level superiors are invited to evaluate candidates nominated by the Party organization department, the immediately higher level of the Party standing committee and its secretary have the authority to make the final selection.

Despite the elaborate process designed to screen candidates, merit evaluations and performance appraisals can hardly be "scientific" and are therefore open to human influence. One popular jingle vividly describes the key features of this political-appointee system: youth is an asset, diploma a must, competence only a point of reference, and *guanxi* the most important

(年龄是个宝， 文凭不可少， 能力作参考， 关系最重要， *nian-ling shige bao, wenpin buke shao, nengli zuo cankao, guanxi zui zhongyao*). What does the last verse "*guanxi* the most important" refer to? It refers to a candidate's *guanxi* ties to the decision-makers, most importantly the Party secretary. The importance of political *guanxi* is evidenced in the following patterns of official selection.

Political Families of Elitism

A political family is defined as a family in which the majority of its members hold official positions in the government system. As of 2010, Central County's government system had four main levels of official positions (the full-*chu* level, the half-*chu* level, the full-*ke* level and the half-*ke* level), each split into further positions, adding up to 1,000 positions. In a county of 200,000 families, on average every 200 families would have one member appointed a government official. Thus, when a family of three has two members who are government officials, argues Feng (2010: 151), it beats the odds and is becoming a political family. If an extended family of ten has five or more members holding official positions, then the family is surely a "big" political family.

Thanks are due to Feng for his diligent fieldwork on political families of a local elite. As of 2010, Central County had 21 "big" political families, each having five or more members who were government officials. In addition, there were 15 families with four officials, 35 families with three officials, and 90 families with two officials. Altogether, these 161 political families occupied 500 official positions, or 50 percent of the total official positions in the county.

Let us take the biggest political family as an illustration. The extended Zhang family (containing three nuclear families) had a total of eighteen adult members in official positions. These positions include the standing members of the county Party committee, the chairman of the county Political Consultative Conference, the deputy county magistrates, the heads of the county Party organization depart-ment at different time periods, several township Party secretaries, several township heads, and several chiefs of many resource bureaus of the county. These positions were occupied by the father Zhang, Zhang's eight children, Zhang's younger sister and her husband, their three children, and Zhang's younger brother and his wife and their two children.

Guanxi *Networks of Political Ties*

Immediate family ties and lineage ties are of most importance to *guanxi* networks of government officials. This importance is exemplified by the notion of political families and is well illustrated by the extended Zhang family. Since 50 percent of official positions in Central County are occupied by political families, and we assume that Central County is China in microcosm, nepotism is widespread in official society at local levels.

Marriage ties to positions of political influence are next in order of importance. Marriage ties are formed through two routes. One is the "self-selection" route: An ambitious and competent college graduate (E) dates and marries the daughter (A1) of a close confidant (A2) of the county Party secretary (A3), who then paves the way for E's promo-tion to an official position. Another route is the "arranged marriage" in which E, now in an influential position, hires the daughter (A4) of the county executive deputy magistrate (A5) to work in an office under his jurisdiction. He then persuades his nephew (A6), a staff member in the county government, to date and marry A4. Through this "arranged marriage" E's nephew, A6, becomes a son-in-law of A5, the country executive deputy magistrate, who then promotes A6 to official posi-tions. Because of the political influence of A3 and A5, the county Party secretary and the county executive deputy magistrate respectively, E is quickly appointed as a township's Party secretary.

When someone is not in a kinship or marriage tie to elites of political influence, developing a ritualized kin tie (干亲*ganqin*) is of instrumental importance to one's political career. In this case, an ambitious young staff member recognizes a politically influential superior and his wife as ritualized parents (干爹干娘*gandie ganniang*). There has been a tradition of forming ritualized kin ties in village societies in Henan Province, and thus doing it does not surprise official society at township and county levels. Feng does not provide an estimate of the quantity of ritualized kin ties among government officials, but he gathers a number of stories showing the effectiveness of these ties in handling work tasks of operational difficulty and their impact on promotion to official positions.

What can you do when you don't have any kin, ritualized kin, or marriage ties to political elites? You find common relational bases with people in official positions and transform them into pseudo-family ties. In Central County, the most important common relational bases include native place, birthplace, classmates, and army comrades. These relational bases provide opportunities for personalized communication and social exchanges, through which to strengthen emotional attachment to each other, exchange favors of substantive and instrumental value with each other, and formulate network cliques and long-term strategic alliances. But these opportunities would be wasted if one did not do the "right things" at the "right times." What are the right things and when are the right times to do them?

Guanxi *Cultivation in Everyday Activities*

Alcohol drinking (喝酒) is on top of a list of the "right things" to do in *guanxi* cultivation and network building in everyday life. "Drinking is the stimulus of official society, and it is the most frequent mode of social exchange among officials. During drinking, strangers become acquaintances, and mutual emotional attachments are strengthened; it is an occasion to not only establish *guanxi*, but also flow information and pave the way to get things done" (Feng 2010: 164). Since drinking makes people relax and share secrets with each other, it is friends who are invited to drinking parties. Therefore, turning down a drinking invitation is a signal of not being willing to become someone's friend. In his first month of stay in a township where he was a new deputy township head, Feng, a Peking University doctoral student and a totally inexperienced drinker, got drunk and spilled the wine all the time on drinking occasions. But he was considered to be a friend (够朋友) because he attended and did the "right things" at these drinking parties. Subsequently, Feng gained trust and received cooperation from his colleagues with whom he conducted his interviews. His interviewees told him a lot.

Card-playing and mahjong-playing are next on the list of the "right things" to do. These are the popular leisure activities favored by Central County officials. Playing cards is a game during drinking, and it is used as a mechanism to encourage drinking more; the rule is that with each game played, winners skip drinking but losers must drink to the bottom. When you reach your upper limit of drinking, you become a "free soul" – free to tell the truth (Foucault 1983). Unlike card-playing, mahjong-playing takes place before and after drinking. Feng was told to "better schedule" all his interviews in the mornings because at about 11:00 am all the officials would leave the office for lunch meetings, there to drink with old and new friends; they spent the afternoons playing mahjong or taking a nap, thus preparing for dinner gatherings and nighttime leisure activities. Wow, what a life! If you do not drink and play cards or mahjong with officials, how could you survive in a local government?

But still, do not forget about gift giving, one of the most important items on the list of the "right things" to do. Gift giving is in a one-way direction: juniors to seniors, subordinates to superiors, officials of lower rank to those of higher rank, and favor requestors to potential favor granters. Gift giving must be done at the "right times." These include public holidays such as the Spring Festival and the Mid-Autumn Festival. During these holidays, Central County officials are absent from their offices because "they are on the roads to the municipal government in Beishan City, to provincial government in Zhengzhou, and to central government in Beijing, there to meet and give gifts to *guanxi* contacts of political influence" (Feng 2010: 165). Other "right times" for gift giving are when someone is promoted, especially when someone moves to a higher position outside the county. The financial values of gifts are well understood among insiders within a given *guanxi* network and in a given context, and cash in a red envelope (红包*hongbao*) is also a popular form of gift giving. The most critical time to give gifts is when there is an event (有事*youshi*) to celebrate. Events of personal importance include one's birthday, a family member's wedding, and children going to key schools. But the most critical time for gift giving is at someone's career promotion. As career promotion is highly competitive, the *guanxi* network of a candidate's close ties becomes the canvassing net created to try to win the competition.

The Canvassing Net in Electoral Politics

In 2002, the Party central committee published the "Regulations on the Selection and Appointment of Party and Administrative Officials." In its 2014 revised version of the Regulations, Article 14 specifies the following: "The selection and appointment of party and government leading cadres must be recommended through a democratic process. Democratic recommendations include the recommendations made at meetings and those by individuals in private consultations; these recommendations serve as an important reference for the selection and appointment [of leading official positions] and are valid for one year" (CCPCC 2014).

By design, this "democratic recommendation" regulation is aimed at minimizing the problem of promotion decisions being monopolized by a small minority of authorities. It is intended to give some weight to a wide range of equal- and higher-level officials invited to recommend the most qualified candidates for vacant positions. This regulation, however, has been interpreted by local officials as the "voting system" (票决制 *piao jue zhi*), in which those who win most "votes" become candidates for career promotion. Subsequently, canvassing nets are created by potential candidates to mobilize support and generate votes. Person-to-person contact, banqueting in a small group, and cash in red envelopes are some of the popular methods used to initiate and secure recommendations.

Feng (2010) observed that in Central County the canvassing nets are most frequently used by township Party secretaries, whose next promotion to a deputy county leadership position is of fundamental importance for their political career. To make this critical promotion successful, the people targeted from whom to pull votes are some 260 half-*chu* and full-*ke* officials; these people are consulted to make recommendations. One opening position for promotion to a deputy county leadership position would involve three to five potential candidates, each of whom has a canvassing net ready to work for the goal of trying to pull votes.

The core of a canvassing net consists of the potential candidate's deputies at work, his relatives and close confidants, and his close superiors as consultants. All voters are targeted to be contacted, except for those who are in the core networks of other potential candidates. "Pulling votes has become a norm in Central County now. You try to pull every possible vote, even openly; if you do not pull votes, you give up promotion. Vote pulling does not guarantee your success [of becoming a candidate], but not making efforts to pull votes means a failure for sure, a hundred percent" (quote from a township Party secretary interviewed by Feng 2010: 169). Feng's interviews make it explicit that pulling a vote actually involves giving a red envelope of cash to a poten- tial voter. In 2008–9 when Feng was in Central County, the cash amount for this "vote to be appreciated" gift was 1,000 *yuan* for a full-*ke* level voter and 2,000 *yuan* for a half-*chu* level voter. The average monthly salary for a full *ke*-level official in the county then was about 1,000 *yuan*. To pay 230 full-*ke* voters and 30 or so half-*chu* voters, a candidate had to prepare and spend 300,000 *yuan*, or twenty to twenty- five years' salaries for a full-*ke* official. No wonder so many government officials become corrupt! To generate this money, they must and have to be corrupt. *Guanxi* networks of close ties that connect people of shared interests are themselves not corrupt, but the internal logic of *guanxi* as an informal mechanism of ingroup favoritism has both the structural tendency and cultural values to permit official corruption to emerge and operate under the weak rule of law. I will revisit this point in the next, concluding chapter.

GUANXI FAVORITISM AND THE POLITICS OF PROMOTION

The politics of promotion is not confined to local governments. It is everywhere. It is in the civilian workplace. It is in the military system. It is in the selection of national elites in science and engineering. And it is in the selection of political elites at regional and national levels. When the process of elite selection becomes political, *guanxi* favoritism is invited to influence it. *Guanxi* favoritism is a form of ingroup bias and ingroup favoritism, which are widely observed around the world (Hewstone, Rubin, and Willis 2002). While general ingroup favorit- ism draws on the dichotomy of ingroup and outgroup members, such as whites and blacks in the United States (LeVine and Campbell 1972; DiTomaso 2013), *guanxi* favoritism emphasizes particular sentiments, reciprocal obligations, and interpersonal trust that are built up between individuals connected by *guanxi* ties (DiTomaso and Bian 2018). In the Chinese context, the effect of *guanxi* favoritism on career promotion is possible because career promotion is highly political (Pye 1992, 1995). Although meritocracy is a chief criterion in all career promotion decisions, candidates' qualifications, credentials, and especially performances are evaluated by human actors, thus opening up the space for *guanxi* favoritism to emerge and operate.

Guanxi *Favoritism and Job–Worker Matching*

Chapter 3 presented a series of empirical findings about job-search processes and outcomes obtained from the JSNET project. Here, we use this project data again for one analysis: the effect of *guanxi* favoritism on job–worker matching. There is a large research literature on job–worker matching in market economies. In addition to the human capital mechanism that matches qualified workers to the required credentials of a job position (Jovanovic 1979; Kalleberg 2007), personal networks also are considered as a matching mechanism because they offer information (Granovetter 1981) and influence (Rees 1966; Prendergast and Topel 1996) to increase or decrease, respectively, job–worker matching. For China, our question is the extent to which *guanxi* favoritism *distorts* job–worker matching. For example, *guanxi* influence from a powerful government official can press a state or non-state employer to hire someone with low education, simple skills, or thin work experience in a job position that requires candidates with high education, complex skills, and rich work experience. The JSNET datasets show evidence that there is indeed a distorting effect of *guanxi* influence on job–worker matching, but this effect occurs only under a high degree of competition over jobs.

Figure 6.1 shows job–worker education matching during China's reform era since 1978. Education matching at job entry (the "Matched" curve) was as low as 10 percent of all new jobs in 1978, but it increased steadily across subsequent years, reached a high point of 60.8 percent

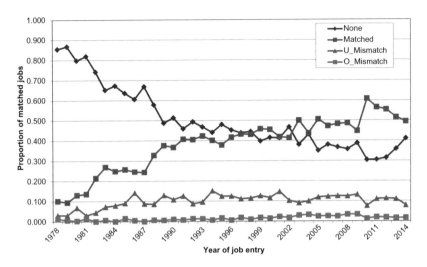

Figure 6.1: Education Matching by Year of Job Entry

in 2010, and then experienced a gradual decline to 50 percent in 2014. Meanwhile, jobs for which no credentials were specified by employers (the "None" curve) decreased from 85.4 percent in 1978 to 41 percent in 2014. The contrasts between these two tendencies indicate the improvement of China's labor markets during the reform era. During this era, higher-credential mismatches ("O_Mismatch") have been extremely low, in the range of 1–2 percent across the years, but lower-credential mismatches ("U_Mismatch") increased from 1 percent in 1978 to 18 percent in 2006 and decreased and stabilized at about 10 percent during 2007–14. Skill matching and work-experience matching produce highly similar tendencies (figures not shown).

We focus our attention on the lower-credential mismatches. This is where *guanxi* favoritism generates a distorting effect. In table 6.1, panel A shows OLS (ordinary least squares) regression results: When job competition is low to none, *guanxi* information or *guanxi* influence makes no difference between job–worker matches (reference category)

Table 6.1: *Guanxi* Effects on Job–Worker Matching (Coefficients Converted to %)

	No–low competition			High–higher competition		
	Higher credential	Lower credential	None specified	Higher credential	Lower credential	None specified
Panel A: OLS regression						
Guanxi information	0.0%	0.0%	0.0%	0.0%	0.0%	72.0%
Guanxi influence/favoritism	0.0%	0.0%	0.0%	77.0%	180.0%	72.0%
Guanxi resource unspecified	0.0%	0.0%	0.0%	0.0%	131.0%	80.0%
Panel B: Propensity score matching regression						
Guanxi information	0.0%	0.0%	0.0%	0.0%	0.0%	0.0%
Guanxi influence/favoritism	0.0%	0.0%	0.0%	0.0%	230.0%	0.0%
Guanxi resource unspecified	0.0%	0.0%	0.0%	0.0%	0.0%	0.0%

Percentage-point differences are calculated from the logistic coefficients by taking the anti-logit of each coefficient, but statistically insignificant coefficients are converted to 0.0 percent. A further statistical table is available from this book's webpage online*.
Source: Hao (2016: tables 3.8, 3.12, 3.18, 3.22)

*www.politybooks.com/guanxi

or mismatches. But under a high degree of job competition, while *guanxi* information reduces one's probability of getting a job for which no credential is specified by an employer, *guanxi* influence significantly increases one's probability of getting a lower-credential mismatched job by a large margin of 180 percent. In fact, *guanxi* influence also prevents a job seeker both from getting a higher-credential mismatched job in which one is overqualified for the job, and from getting a no-credential-specified job in which one's credential might be wasted.

Panel B presents propensity score matching regressions. This model equates *guanxi* users with non-*guanxi* users by matching individuals of the two groups in terms of personal, family, and work-related characteristics. While the matching procedure reduces the sample size, it gives us greater confidence in whether or not *guanxi* favoritism really has a causal effect on job outcomes. Panel B confirms a key finding in panel A: *Guanxi* influence boosts one's likelihood of getting a lower-credential mismatched job by a huge margin of 230 percent. This finding means that *guanxi* favoritism indeed distorts China's labor markets by matching lower-credential job seekers to positions of higher education, skill, and work-experience requirements. Since lower-credential mismatches have increased from 1978 to 2014, as shown by figure 6.1, this distorting effect has been increasing in its scope of influence as well.

Guanxi *Favoritism and Promotion in the Civilian Workplace*

Career promotion is competitive in the civilian workplace. In Mao's era (1949–76), although the Cultural Revolution decade (1966–76) saw the rise of egalitarian ideology throughout China (Parish 1984), the first seventeen-year period from 1949 to 1966 observed the rise of credentialism and meritocracy in career promotion, salary increases, and performance appraisals. In the meantime, however, Mao's workplace was a politicized arena in which party clientelism or "principled particularism" ruled the worker's life (Walder 1986). Under this model, political activists, the clients, developed "instrumental particular ties" to the Party secretaries as their patrons, from whom to win personal favors for political promotion as well as material rewards. This resulted in a pattern of sponsored mobility in which Party-favored youths moved quickly up the ladder of a political or administrative career (Li and Walder 2001). This sponsored mobility has continued into the reform era, in which one's personal *guanxi* ties to his or her immediate leaders affect one's job assignments, performance appraisals, and promotion opportunities. Lei (2018) analyzes the JSNET 2014 data and provides empirical evidence.

In the pre-reform state sector, of the 1,022 respondents to the 2014 JSNET survey, 30 percent had "so-so" *guanxi* with immediate leaders, 40 percent "good" *guanxi*, and 30 percent "very good" *guanxi* (additional data table available online). On average, about three in ten employees would be promoted. But compared to those employees with "so-so" *guanxi* to their immediate leaders, employees with "good" and "very good" *guanxi*, respectively, enjoyed a much greater probability of getting promoted. Assume that "so-so" *guanxi* give someone a 10 percent chance of getting promoted. The propensity score matching model indicates that "good" and "very good" *guanxi* give equally qualified and equally performing employees 50 percent and 146 percent, respectively, more promotion opportunities.

As for the state sector of the reform era, the pattern we have just analyzed under Mao continued into the post-Mao period. While the distributions of employees by their *guanxi* to immediate leaders are about the same as in Mao's period, the effects of *guanxi* to leadership on one's promotion opportunities are much stronger than in Mao's period. Interestingly, similar results were found for the reform-era non-state sector, in which the magnitudes of *guanxi* effects on promotion opportunities are about the same as those for the reform-era state sector. These findings lead to the conclusion that *guanxi* favoritism in promotion in the civilian workplace during the reform era is widespread in both the state and non-state sectors.

Guanxi *Favoritism, Bribery, and Promotion in the Military*

The People's Liberation Army (PLA) under Mao was known for its political purity as well as disciplined organization (Nie 2007). Even during the chaotic decade of the Cultural Revolution and shortly thereafter, the PLA was able to maintain its revolutionary tradition and resist the decay of morality that was spreading in larger society (Geng 2009). During the reenergized reform period since 1992, however, a large number of the highest-ranking PLA officers have been convicted of corruption (Mulvenon 2006), including two vice chairmen of the Central Military Commission (CMC), Xu Caihou and Guo Boxiong. The amount of bribes each accepted was an astronomical figure, and much of the bribery money was from the selling of military positions behind the scenes (Mulvenon 2015). Wang (2016), a sociologist based in Hong Kong, conducted interviews with twenty retired and near-retiring officers and one military researcher, from whom to collect hard-to-come-by data about the role *guanxi* played in the buying of promotions and the selling of positions within the PLA. Before and after retirement, his interviewees were relatively free of organizational constraints and had little risk to career advancement for their participation in interviews.

Wang's impressive research findings begin with an observation on a gap between rules on paper and operational practices. The rules on paper are clearly specified to select and appoint military officers on the grounds of political integrity, formal schooling, professional competence, and measurable performance. Under the principle of "democratic centralism" the decision-making process on promotions must consist of consultation before formal meetings, decisions through formal meetings, and all major issues being decided upon by Party committees after deliberation. Since no formal procedures of the PLA are subject to any external monitoring by the media or civic groups, practically the evaluation of candidates for promotion is concentrated in two key decision-makers at each level of the military hierarchy: the political commissar (i.e., the Party secretary) and the military commander. Consequently, good *guanxi* ties to them, as well as to other relevant officers participating in the decision-making process, are informally developed and maintained by lower-level officers. It is these *guanxi* ties that are decisive in promotion nominations.

For a lower-level officer to be promoted, cultivating good *guanxi* ties to his senior officers is of fundamental importance. But some *guanxi* ties are certainly better and more useful than others for obtaining promotion opportunities. The most privileged are "three types of princes" (三爷 *san ye*): a senior officer's son (少爷 *shao ye*), son-in-law (姑爷 *gu ye*), or personal secretary (师爷 *shi ye*). These princes do not necessarily work or get promoted under the command of the focal senior officer, but all "senior officers have an immense incentive to employ all their [*guanxi*] resources to assist in the promotion of their relatives [and personal secretaries]" (Wang 2016: 978). Hometown ties are next in order of importance, since they contain no communication barriers and are the available bridges through which to build sentimental, obligational, and high-trust ties with senior officers. But ties of these characterizations cannot be built if *guanxi* cultivators do not do "dirty/bad things" with their senior officers. These include "selling scarce resources monopolized by the military on the open market, embezzling military assets (money or property), creating false accounts, and aiding promotion by violating regulations" (Wang 2016: 980). The earnings and benefits of these dirty things certainly go into the pockets of the focal senior officers. Consequently, the lower-level officers who have repeatedly done the dirty things quickly become key members of their senior officers' *guanxi* networks.

Being a member of their senior officers' *guanxi* networks does not cut the deal for promotion. Since corruption had been widespread and systematic in the PLA for years, bribing decision-makers becomes necessary to pave the way of getting promoted. While each level of promotion has a general price known to the briber and the bribed, to win the competition, the greater the amount of money paid and accepted, the greater the probability of getting promoted. But no bribe can be given without a channel of *guanxi* networks. The importance of *guanxi* networks in military promotions is multidimensional: in identifying buyers and sellers, in getting reliable information about each other, and in assessing the credibility and trustworthiness of buyers and sellers. Bribery is illegal, operates in private, and has no guarantee of return. Therefore, *guanxi* networks are the channels through which to give or accept a bribe while reducing the risks to the minimum. Do highly competent candidates still need to bribe senior officers in order to get promoted? Wang was told by his interviewees that "a bribe payment is an indispensable, although not sufficient, element to gaining career advancement, even for competent officers" and that "PLA officers are less likely to get promoted without payment [no matter who you are]" (Wang 2016: 983).

Guanxi *Favoritism in the Selection of National Scientific Elites*

The Chinese Academy of Sciences (CAS) and the Chinese Academy of Engineering (CAE) are China's most prestigious societies and their memberships are recognized as the highest honor for elite scientists in the country. Cao (2004) studied elite Chinese scientists and found that mentoring relationships, among other factors, significantly increased one's probability of becoming a member of the CAS. Shi and Rao (2010), both having returned to China after successful careers in top universities in the United States, were surprised by a significant proportion of Chinese scientists who spent "too much" time on building *guanxi* connections through which to win competition for government funding, regional and national prizes, and election into the CAS and CAE. Fisman et al. (2018) conducted a statistical analysis of favoritism effects on the selection of CAS and CAE members. Their summary results are presented in table 6.2.

A profile was compiled for 4,921 nominees for CAS/CAE member elections from 2001 to 2013. Of these nominees, 14.3 percent were elected to the CAS/CAE (column A in panel A). The nominees were divided into two groups. One group consisted of 10 percent of the nominees having hometown ties (同乡 *tong xiang*) to the CAS/CAE standing members who evaluated them, and their rate of success for membership election was 19.6 percent (column B). The other group consisted of 90 percent of the nominees who had no hometown ties

Table 6.2: Favoritism Effects on the Selection of Chinese Academicians

Panel A Average election rates (%)	(A) Total sample	(B) Hometown ties (10%)	(C) No hometown ties (90%)	(D) Comparison (B/C)
Elected	14.3%	19.6%	13.7%	+43.1%***
First stage passed	40.4%	38.8%	40.6%	−4.4%
Elected/First stage	33.8%	49.4%	32.2%	+53.4%***
Panel B Tie effects on election	First-stage election		Final-stage election	
Committee tie = 1	0.0%		17.4%	
Log (1 + H-index)	7.7%		0.0%	
Has homerun	14.0%		5.0%	

Percentage-point differences are calculated from the reported logistic regression coefficients by taking the anti-logits of the coefficients. When a coefficient is statistically insignificant, it is converted to 0.0 percent. A further statistical table is available from this book's webpage online.

Source: Fisman et al. (2018: tables 1, 3, 4)

to the CAS/CAE standing members, and their rate of success was only 13.7 percent (column C). The comparison of the two groups shows that a hometown tie increases one's probability of becoming a CAS/CAE fellow by 43 percent (column D).

A multivariate analysis was conducted to assess the "net" effect of hometown ties on election along with two criteria of merit evaluation, namely research productivity and influence. Panel B shows that the favoritism effect did not occur at the first stage of evaluation as a committee tie made no difference at all. At this stage, evaluations were done by mail by a broader set of CAS/CAE members within each subject department, and variables of a nominee's merit rather than anything else mattered for taking one's candidacy into the next and final stage: Candidates with higher research productivity (measured by H-index) were 7.7 percent more likely to move to the final stage than the less productive candidates, and those with a measured research influence ("Homerun") were 14 percent more likely than other candidates lacking this influence to move to the final stage.

At the final stage, however, in-person meetings created opportunities for personal lobbying (Shi and Rao 2010). The results show that the effect of research productivity (H-index) became insignificant, that of research influence ("Homerun") substantially reduced, and the most significant determinant was membership ties. Quantitatively, while candidates with a "homerun" impact on research were 5 percent more likely to be elected than candidates lacking such impact, those candidates with a tie to committee members were 17.4 percent more likely to be elected than their counterparts without such ties. The influence of a committee tie was more than three times stronger than a significant, "homerun" contribution to society's knowledge system.

This interpretation must be understood within the context of Chinese academia election. Candidates having passed the first stage of evaluation were equally productive and equally influential whether or not they had committee ties. At the end of the final stage, however, the newly elected members with committee ties were significantly less productive and less influential in research than those other newly elected members without committee ties. Clearly, favoritism through hometown ties to the CAS/CAE standing members has distorted the selection of Chinese academicians.

Guanxi *Networks in the Selection of National Political Elites*

Communist Party membership and educational credentials have been found to be the two most important personal attributes affecting individuals' mobility into political elites (Bian, Shu, and Logan 2001; Li and Walder 2001). China's political elites of national recognition include four main levels of cadre rank in the Party personnel management system, from higher to lower: the full-*guojia* leadership level, the half-*guojia* leadership level, the full-*bu* level, and the half-*bu* level. Zang (2001) compiled a profile of 1,664 top Chinese leaders (ranked at half-*bu* level and upward) and confirmed this finding. That is, political virtue and loyalty, measured by Communist Party membership and its seniority, and competence, measured by a degree of higher education, explain a great deal of variation in career mobility into national elite positions. Zang's findings are important because he analyzed the highest ranked Party and government officials, whose data is very hard to come by. But one thing that is missing in all these scholarly works is how *guanxi* connections matter for promotion into national elite positions. In the geographically confined Central County, we have learned that nepotism and *guanxi* favoritism matter for promotions to elite positions at local levels. Here, we ask what kinds of *guanxi* ties matter for mobility into national political elites.

The selection of national political elites is operated by the central Party. The Organization Department of the central Party is missioned to examine candidates at the half-*bu* level and upward; once promoted to this level, the cadres are deployed by the central Party to vacant positions in the central Party's organs and the State Council and its ministries and bureaus in Beijing, as well as provincial-level Party and administrative positions around the country. The selection of these "centrally administered" cadres still follows the "Regulations on the Selection and Appointment of Party and Administrative Officials" reviewed in the section of this chapter on "The Canvassing Net in Electoral Politics." In practice, in a ministry or provincial government, all cadres at the half-*bu* level and upward are consulted to nominate candidates for promotion to a half-*bu* or higher rank. But most importantly, the nominations by the central Party and state leaders as well as by the Organization Department of the Party central are given the greatest weight. So *guanxi* connections to central and provincial leaders are the channels of influence.

Li (1994) delivered an analysis of the impact of prestigious university connections on the selection of national political elites. Special attention was paid to Tsinghua University, where a score of China's leaders earned their Bachelor's or higher degrees and held political positions during years of study or post-graduation. These include the Party politburo's standing committee members, such as Xi Jinping (China's current paramount leader), Hu Jintao (China's top leader preceding Xi), Zhu Rongji (past premier), Wu Bangguo (past CPCSC chair), Yao Yilin (past vice premier), Song Ping, Hu Qili, Huang Ju, Wu Guanzheng, and politburo members such as Chen Xi (current head of the Organization Department of the central Party), Huang Kunming (current head of the Propaganda Department of the central Party), Liu Yandong (current vice premier), Kang Shi'en (past vice premier), Zeng Peiyan (past vice premier), and Hu Qiaomu (past ideology leader). A large number of Tsinghua alumni have been ministers, provincial governors, and presidents of the CAS and CAE. In its post-1949 history, Tsinghua has established a strong tradition of training "red experts" or "red engineers." This was facilitated by the establishment of political counselors in the 1950s, who were taught according to the motto "听话出活" (*tinghua chuhuo*, be obedient and productive). From a total of 682 political counselors on campus between 1953 and 1966, two-thirds were later transferred out of Tsinghua, and a considerable number rose to positions as governors, ministers, general managers of large industrial enterprises, or presidents of other universities. This trend has continued into the reform era; from 1978 to 1984 Tsinghua transferred 1,757 of its officials, faculty, and staff members to other educational institutions. Of the top fourteen universities, from which had seventy-two alumni served on the fourteenth central Party committee, Tsinghua took the lead with twenty-nine alumni. All other universities on the list had from one to six.

Tsinghua's impact on the selection of China's top leaders is well understood within *guanxi* logics. One of these logics is that close ties are developed from relational bonds, such as schools and workplaces, where there are plenty of opportunities to develop and maintain durable and intimate relationships. Another important relational bond is colleague relations, where people work together for a long period of time. Guo (2001) studied the first generation of Chinese Communist revolutionaries and found that top military and administrative leaders were significantly more likely to come from Mao Zedong's First Front Army than from any other fraction of the Party or the military. Guo's analysis indicates that similar revolutionary career tracks and direct working relations as superiors and subordinates are the two mechanisms of forming *guanxi* networks of top Chinese leaders, and these *guanxi* networks have four theoretical dimensions that make them work in practice. The first is the emotional dimension. This connects revolutionaries of equal rank through *ganqing* (mutual affection) and those of unequal rank through *enqing* (owing a great favor to a superior who paves the way for subordinates to move up). The second is the moral dimension, which connects military generals and civilian officials through the values of *zhong* (personal loyalty) and *yi* (brotherly obligation). The third is the etiquette dimension, which connects colleagues through the notions of *renqing* (human feeling) and *li* (politeness and respect). And the fourth is the instrumental dimension, which connects people with reciprocal obligations to each other at work. Guo (2001) used numerous examples to illustrate how these dimensions of *guanxi* networks worked for leaders like Mao Zedong, Zhou Enlai, Zhang Guotao, He Long, Lin Biao, Kang Sheng, and Jiang Qing, to name just a few. Mao and Zhou were considered the masters of mixing these different dimensions while working with revolutionary colleagues with different personalities and different cultural and family backgrounds. Researchers into Chinese politics have agreed that *guanxi* is "the central term in our conceptualization of informal politics" (Dittmer 1995).

Summary

Career promotion is an arena of politics because candidacy evaluations cannot be totally quantifiable and are subject to the influence of *guanxi* favoritism. In the civilian workplace, *guanxi* favoritism mismatches lower-credential job seekers to positions of higher requirements, and stronger ties with immediate supervisors increase an employee's probability of getting promoted. In the military system, the effect of *guanxi* favoritism becomes uglier as potential candidates must give bribes in the widespread corruption throughout the PLA hierarchy. *Guanxi* favoritism also has invaded the field of science, in which membership selections to the most prestigious CAS and CAE are heavily influenced by candidates' hometown ties to evaluators. In the selection of national political elites, while political virtue and educational credential increase one's chances of promotion, these formal criteria along with performance appraisals are conditional upon candidates' *guanxi* ties to decision-makers in the process of promotion nominations, evaluations, and decisions. While school connections and subordinate–supervisor relations are the two most important network bridges to mobilize support and transmit influence, mixing the emotional, moral, etiquette, and instrumental rules of *guanxi* is a skill set that must be used to cultivate elite *guanxi* networks in the first place. Such a skill set is a cultural toolkit for career advancement, not just for elite politicians and scientists but also for all levels of strategic players in Chinese society today.

GUANXI FAVORITISM IN THE POLITICIZED LEGAL SYSTEM

Numerous scholars have studied *guanxi* favoritism in China's legal system. This is a politicized system in which the party-state exercises total control over the legal branches of the government as well as legal practitioners, such as judges, lawyers, and lay assessors. *Guanxi* favoritism is widespread and deep in this politicized legal system, as evidenced by empirical findings, now to be examined, on a rural dispute pagoda under the influence of political *guanxi*, the survival of lawyers through political *guanxi* in the cities, *guanxi* influence of political and social ties in the court, and *guanxi* tactics in bribery to judges.

Lack of Guanxi *and the Dispute Pagoda in Rural China*

To what extent do rural villagers appeal to the official justice system for resolving a dispute with a village head? A winner of the 1992 Golden Lion Award in Italy, the Chinese film *Qiuju Fights a Lawsuit* (秋菊打官司) is an interesting fiction on this point. Qiuju was the young, illiterate, pregnant wife of an ordinary villager who had a land dispute with, and was kicked and severely injured by, his bully of a village head. Qiuju's husband did not want to do anything about it but instead submitted to humiliation. But Qiuju, firmly believing in social and legal justice, demanded a public apology from the village head in order to save her husband's face – the humanistic respect from villagers that would allow him to live a dignified life within the village. In a politicized local culture, this move by an ordinary villager would have challenged the authority of a village head, and the bully refused to compromise. Qiuju therefore took action to file a lawsuit against him in the township and eventually the county and municipal courts. What she was not prepared for, however, was a series of harsh struggles she had to fight against the *guanxi* networks of the village head in and beyond the village and the favor-exchange norms spreading throughout the bureaucratic, corrupted legal system. A 2016 popular Chinese film *I'm Not Madame Bovary* (我不是潘金莲, *wo bushi pan jinlian*) has a similar storyline, signifying the pervasiveness of political *guanxi* and legal injustice at local levels in China today.

Michelson (2007a) provided a systematic analysis of the social barriers that constrain rural villagers from appealing to the official justice system. Besides financial capacity, lack of *guanxi* to stakeholders in the legal system is the most important barrier that prevents villagers from filing a lawsuit. Consequently, most disputes are dealt with locally within the village, and only a small number of cases go to court at the county or higher levels. Michelson finds a dispute pagoda as shown on the left-hand side of figure 6.2. Among 4,757 disputes gathered from

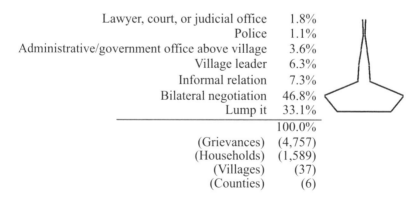

Lawyer, court, or judicial office	1.8%
Police	1.1%
Administrative/government office above village	3.6%
Village leader	6.3%
Informal relation	7.3%
Bilateral negotiation	46.8%
Lump it	33.1%
	100.0%
(Grievances)	(4,757)
(Households)	(1,589)
(Villages)	(37)
(Counties)	(6)

Figure 6.2: Dispute Pagoda by Political Connections, Rural China, 2002
Source: Michelson (2007a: figure 1)

a survey of 37 villages and 1,589 families, the overwhelming majority (93.5 percent) were solved within the village and did not go to court. These included 33.1 percent where complainants had to "lump it," 46.8 percent settled through "bilateral negotiation," 7.3 percent through "informal relation," and 6.3 percent through the involvement of the "village leader." Above these local resolutions are three higher levels of the dispute pagoda: 3.6 percent through the government, 1.1 percent through the police, and only 1.8 percent through the use of a lawyer, the court, or a judicial office.

Who is likely to go a higher level of the pagoda to resolve a dispute? It is those who have political connections to that level of the pagoda. Michelson shows that among those villagers without any political connections, only 1.6 percent used the highest level of legal means to try to solve a dispute. The fictional figure Qiuju does indeed exist in the countryside. Among those who have political connections to the village head, there is a much higher probability than average of using the village head, above village government and the highest-level legal channels, to solve disputes. Finally, among those who have political connections to both village heads and higher-level cadres, the probabilities of using above-village government (19.1 percent) and the highest-level legal channels (19.1 percent) are much higher than among those villagers in the other two groups. While lack of political *guanxi* prevents a villager from using the official justice channels, having political *guanxi* increases a villager's likelihood of going all the way to reach the highest level of the dispute pagoda.

Political Guanxi as a Survival Strategy of Chinese Lawyers

China's state legal system consists of three branches, namely the police, the procuracy, and the court. Michelson (2007b) studied Chinese lawyers, who are emerging players in China's legal system during the reform era. He paid special attention to how lawyers' political *guanxi* ties to the branches of the state legal system help them survive in their jobs. His point of departure is the critique of the "naive legal formalism" in which law is assumed to operate as a transparently and predictably enforceable set of rules (Suchman and Edelman 1996). Instead, studying legal realities in transition China, Michelson (2007b: 355) argues that "the law on the books tells us little about the law in action." A 2000 survey of 980 lawyers from Beijing and twenty-four smaller cities shows empirical evidence on the importance of *guanxi* for Chinese lawyers in the 1990s. Summary results are presented in figure 6.3.

First, Chinese lawyers are not given professional autonomy but instead depend totally on access to information and documents controlled by the courts, the police, and the procuracy of the government. In general, officials from these governmental organs do not always work cooperatively with lawyers; the reverse is actually the case. In criminal cases, for example, a great majority of lawyers agree that "public security organs always find ways to obstruct lawyers' investigation work" and that "the prosecution has an advantage over the defense." At the same time, a great majority of lawyers disagree that "the laws are sufficient to guarantee that lawyers' functions are brought into full play," "lawyers get the full cooperation of related government offices," and "lawyers get the full cooperation of related individuals and civil organizations." "If lawyers have trouble getting in through the front door, they try the back door" (Michelson 2007b: 358). Therefore, a great majority of lawyers "spend a lot of time fostering personal *guanxi* with judges" and they do not believe that "personal *guanxi* between a lawyer and a judge will not influence how a court case is tried."

Second, lawyers' evaluations of their institutional environment are associated with their structural positions in the hierarchy of the legal system as well as their personal relations with relevant government officials. As compared to lawyers from partnerships, lawyers from state-owned firms express greater positive response (18 percent more positive) and significantly less negative response (13 percent less

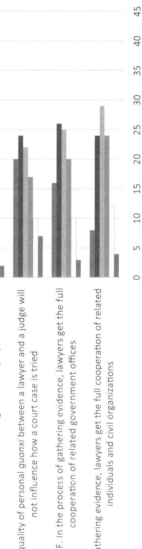

Figure 6.3: Lawyers' Evaluations of Their Institutional Environment
Items D–G are rearranged from the author's original order to honor the frequencies of "0" responses.
Source: Data from Michelson (2007b: table 4)

negative) to the support received from government officials (additional data table available online). When working on a case or with a client assigned by the court, perceived support from government officials is much more positive than negative (27 percent positive vs. 13 percent negative), and prior work in court significantly boosts a lawyer's perceived support from the government (20 percent more likely). As compared to full-time lawyers who are professional practitioners of law and less likely to have political *guanxi* ties, part-timers and specially appointed lawyers are clearly advantaged in greater access to support from the government (about 30 percent more positive). Since full-time lawyers take a 72 percent share of the profession, China's professional lawyers by and large work in an unpleasant and difficult legal environment.

Guanxi *Influence of Political and Social Ties in the Court*

"Everywhere we are embedded in *guanxi*. Indeed, *guanxi* has become part of our lives. We make use of *guanxi*; as a chain of the network, we are also being used by others in *guanxi*." This quote is from a trial judge interviewed by He and Ng (2018: 841). While studying Chinese courts, He and Ng gained a high level of trust from a wide range of judges in coastal and inland regions, rural and urban. The authors interviewed forty of them, from whom they gathered a great number of stories, experiences, and insights about *guanxi* influence on the trial processes and judicial decision-making behind the scenes. The central lesson learned is already expressed in the trail judge's quote: *Guanxi* is an indispensable part of Chinese courts and judicial decision-making.

Two kinds of *guanxi* ties have been found effective in and out of court. The first is a superior–subordinate mentorship tie within the court. Both past and current mentoring relations are counted in, and these include junior–senior judge dyads, senior judge–division chief dyads, division chief–court leadership dyads, court leadership–high court judge dyads, and court leadership–government official dyads. Strong mentoring relations are maintained effectively as patron–client relations, in which a superior's care, opinion, and advice on a particular case serve as the guideline for a junior, frontline, and caseworker judge to handle and decide on the case. The second is social relations trial judges maintain out of court. These are ties to kin, friends, neighbors, former classmates, army comrades, and former colleagues, direct and indirect. When these people have strong ties to the judges and especially their superiors, the trial processes and case decisions are considerably altered; when these ties are less strong but the relative parties do the "right things" in the "right ways" at the "right times," immediate favor exchanges come into play and affect the trial processes.

To what extent does *guanxi* influence matter? A survey shows that 52 percent of the judges admitted that they were frequently approached by *guanxi* contacts when handling cases, and "in the scope of discretion" 61 percent of them would favor the plaintiffs or the defendants who are connected to them directly or indirectly (Wang 2016). Surveys, unlike personal interviews, tend to be able to estimate the effect of *guanxi* when it is considered immoral, illicit, or unlawful. Of interest here is the notion of "the scope of discretion," a gray area in which a case can be evaluated one way or the other because any judgment made would not be against the law. To take examples from only a few of the many cases He and Ng described and analyzed: The formal procedure requires that a case be examined a week after submission of the full materials, but it can be taken care of on the first day when the caseworker judge is advised by her division chief to do so. A case that should be closed within three months is still unfinished after five years of a trial process simply because the defendant, a well-known entrepreneur in town, is a close friend of the city mayor as well as the court president. A jaywalker-injury case is judged to favor the jaywalker and punish the truck driver because the jaywalker's daughter is a former classmate of the judge responsible. These cases show that key to *guanxi* influence in the court is a large gray area in which judges have consider-able scope of discretion to handle and make decisions on legal cases. The limit of *guanxi* influence, He and Ng argue, is that judges do not make unlawful decisions one way or the other, and this is especially true in developed coastal regions.

Guanxi *Tactics in Bribery Performance*

Judges interviewed by He and Ng dealt with cases of low financial value, in the range from 1,000 *yuan* to 30,000 *yuan*. Li (2011) studied lawyer–judge *guanxi* in bribery involving cases of much greater finan-cial value. Most of these cases started with no prior relations, direct or indirect, from a lawyer to a caseworker judge. Thus, Li's research atten-tion was paid to how a bribing lawyer developed a favor-exchange relation of high trust "from scratch" with the judge, potentially the bribed. Li discussed two scenarios of how bribery was performed, and the results are completely different.

In the first scenario, a new lawyer Zhai in Beijing in 2003 sent a letter to five judges from three different courts. In the letter, he asked each of the judges to do him a favor by introducing him to potentially winning litigants when the claim of the dispute was more than 300,000 *rmb*. He promised "I will let you share 40% of the retainer as your commission fee" (Li 2011: 2). This is an open act of bribing the judges. One of the judges "found it funny at first but then felt it was over the top" (p. 2) and decided to forward the letter to the Beijing Bureau of Justice (BBJ). Zhai was summoned by the BBJ, which subsequently issued an administrative decision to disbar him on the grounds of violation of the Chinese Lawyers' Law.

The second scenario is more common and discloses the hidden code of conduct in the performance of bribery through "adequate" *guanxi* cultivation and "acceptable" *guanxi* practices. Zhang, a central figure from a quasi-autobiography *Celadon* (Fushi 2006), ran an auction house in a provincial capital city. His business primarily came from court commissions. A stranger in the city, Zhang knew no court judge on a personal level. But he took initiatives to develop *guanxi* with a judge handling an auction commission in which he was interested. First, Zhang learned about the drinking habits of the judge, delivering him a full case of new "health preserving liquor" not yet on sale and asking him to evaluate the product for its marketability. Second, Zhang showed his "sincere" care about the interest of the judge's son in Chinese calligraphy, paying a professional calligrapher to coach him, arranging a friend to bid for his calligraphy during an "open" auction, and sending the "earned" money to the judge. After half a year's *guanxi* cultivation, Zhang became a friend of both the judge and his wife, gaining the personal power of paying visits to their home without an appointment.

The ultimate result of the second scenario is obvious. Zhang obtained valuable information from the judge about court commissions, competitors, and decision-making processes on the selection of auctioneers. Subsequently Zhang become a successful auctioneer. To Li (2011), Zhai and Zhang were doing the same thing in trying to bribe court judges who had power, but the reasons for the completely different result lay in the internal logic of *guanxi* cultivation and *guanxi* practice: A "good" gift of a particular type is chosen to draw the bribed into a personal relationship; the exchange value of the gift is not so great that the briber risks economic loss in case there is no future return from the bribed, but it is not so low as to invite rejection either; and more personal favors are voluntarily offered to the bribed to satisfy the latter's needs. All of these *guanxi* practices build up mutual sentiments and reciprocal obligations between the briber and the bribed, resulting in bribery performed through gift giving "with a human face."

This illicit feature of gift giving and bribery can be traced back to imperial times, when "humanistic bribery" became a widespread informal norm in official society (Wu 2009). In reform-era China, however, bribery holds risks of both external (detection and punishment) and internal (opportunism of briber or bribed) safety. To reduce these potential risks to the minimum, *guanxi* cultivation and *guanxi* practices are in fact a trust-building process, in which sensitive terms about bribery are completely avoided. What arise are euphemisms used to legitimize and facilitate briber–bribed interactions, such as "Money for cigarettes and liquor" (烟酒钱 *Yanjiuqian*), "Benefit-earning" (好处费 *Haochu fei*), and "Earning for the effort" (辛苦费 *Xinku fei*). The normalization process is made possible through *guanxi* actions phrased in euphemisms such as "Handle *guanxi* contacts" (打点关系 *Dadian guanxi*) and "Go to find *guanxi*" (托关系 *Tuo guanxi*), in which Mayfair Yang's (1994) art of *guanxixue* was utilized to target, mobilize, and secure "right" *guanxi* contacts for illicit assistance from favor granters of power through gift/cash giving. From this perspective, lawyer Zhai was seen as being "funny" by a judge because he violated all the internal logics of *guanxi* cultivation and *guanxi* practices, and auctioneer Zhang became a "good friend" of another judge because he followed the internal logics of *guanxi*.

Summary

Guanxi influence is widespread and deep in China's legal system. At local levels, lack of political *guanxi* prevents a villager from going out of the village to resolve a dispute through an official legal means, such as the court and hiring a lawyer. In the politicized legal system, however, even lawyers are constrained by lack of political *guanxi* in practicing law. Those lawyers who are well connected to the legal branches of the government perceive stronger support from the government than their poorly connected counterparts. Court judges, on the other hand, are also influenced by their political as well as social *guanxi*: While subordinate–superior relationships within the politicized legal system influence a frontline judge's decisions on cases, social connections outside the court alter these decisions to favor the strongly connected. Bribery that does not follow the *guanxi* logic of building sentiments, obligations, and trust with the potentially bribed is publicly denounced, but bribery behind the scenes survives under *guanxi* logic. *Guanxi* logic in itself is not corrupt, but official corruption in the legal system indeed cannot be decoupled from *guanxi* networks of political and legal players of strategic importance.

To reduce corruption and develop public confidence in the legal system, since the Fourth Plenary of the CCP in 2014 China has strengthened its lay assessor institution (人民陪审制度 *renmin peishen zhidu*), expanding the participation of the citizenry in judicial processes. In formal terms, lay assessors and their involvements in tribunals have increased dramatically. In reality, however, He (2016) found that lay participation under China's authoritarian regime has failed to meet its intended goals. On the one hand, the authoritarian regime exercises total control over professional judges, even if the judges may use their expert knowledge to challenge the authority of the state. On the other, judges exercise firm control over lay assessors, whose role in the judicial processes is consequently next to nonexistent. Legal reforms have a long way to go.

7

Guanxi and Social Structure

In this last and concluding chapter of the book, I discuss the central roles *guanxi* plays in social structure in China. Social structure is a broad sociological concept. It generally refers to the patterned social arrangements that constrain the actions of social actors, whether they are individuals, groups, or organizations (Parsons and Shils 1951). Since Parsons, contemporary sociology has offered two different approaches to defining social structure. The positional approach defines social structure as the patterned arrangements of positions of social distinction, such as class, power, and status (Sorensen 2001). The relational approach, in contrast, defines social structure as the enduring networks of ongoing social relationships among actors (Wellman 1988). Both approaches are relevant to Chinese social structure (Bian 2002). In this chapter, I follow the positional approach by discussing the relationship between *guanxi* networks *and* social structure, and in addition I follow the relational approach by discussing *guanxi* networks *as* social structure. To contextualize these discussions, I will first sum up the materials of the previous chapters by focusing on the internal and external logics of *guanxi* favoritism. In closing the book, I will suggest a research agenda meant to further advance *guanxi* scholarship in the social sciences.

THE INTERNAL AND EXTERNAL LOGICS OF *GUANXI*

Guanxi in its most basic form is a dyadic tie linking two individuals (chapter 1). In this sense, *guanxi* and network building (chapter 2) are an interpersonal phenomenon in the private sphere, within which we can examine the internal logics of *guanxi*. However, the internal logics of *guanxi* are not confined to the private sphere. As individuals socialize with one another in broader social structures beyond personal worlds, their *guanxi* ties and *guanxi* networks go across the private–public boundary to affect social actions and interactions in economic, political, and legal spheres (chapters 3–6). What are the internal and external logics of *guanxi* that the previous chapters have implied?

The Internal Logics of Guanxi

I use the term "internal logic" to mean the inherent and inseparable components of a *guanxi* tie that necessarily affect actors connected by the tie. To be sure, there is no single internal logic of *guanxi*. What have emerged from the previous chapters are multiple logics all internal to the formation and operation of *guanxi*. I discuss four.

The first internal logic of *guanxi* is the formation-necessity logic. This refers to a shared community that serves as the structure from which two actors develop a *guanxi* tie that connects them. The most traditional forms of community are the family and kinship. For an average Chinese individual today, family and kinship ties still make up one-third of daily contacts, one-fifth of social eating contacts, two-thirds of holiday contacts, and more than two-thirds of business founding contacts (chapters 2 and 4). Native place, birthplace, workplace, neighborhood, school, and the military are the most frequently cited examples of non-kin communities from which emerge *guanxi* ties (chapters 2 and 6). In the internet age, the extent to which "concrete" communities may give way to interest-based, "virtual" communities as the structures for forming *guanxi* ties is an empirical question for future research (Wellman 2001).

The second internal logic of *guanxi* is the formation-sufficiency logic. A shared community of any type provides only the structural *potential* to develop a *guanxi* tie between focal actors, but no *guanxi* tie whatsoever can be formed without meeting a sufficient condition: Sentiments or affections flow mutually between focal actors. I consider "sentiment" and "affection" as equivalent terms; I enlist both above because different *guanxi* researchers prefer one term over the other. I myself do not have a preference. To me, sentiment (情感) and affection (感情) are the same thing, and their manifestations include sympathy, care, and love, all of which translate into frequent interaction, emotional attachment, familiarity/intimacy, mutual trust, and altruistic actions taken by one party to benefit the other party of a *guanxi* relationship.

The third internal logic of *guanxi* is the indebtedness-reciprocity logic. For any dyads, *guanxi* ties exist and sustain to the extent that focal actors satisfy each other's emotional and instrumental needs or, worded differently, material and spiritual interests. The mutuality of need satisfaction between focal actors in a *guanxi* relationship is mediated by the exchange of favors. Small favors are handy or inexpensive and therefore are granted to each other as an expression of mutual affections, but substantial favors are granted to satisfy someone's special needs in events of personal significance, and they generate costs to favor granters, to whom social debts are accumulated and obligations to pay back are built up for favor receivers. One gains moral and social respect from granting favors, to which an immediate return is against the affection logic. Favors are returned when favor receivers have the opportunity to do so, thus gaining moral and social respect later on. This time-lagged, indebtedness-reciprocity logic does not operate alone, the reason for which becomes clearer in the next logic of *guanxi*.

The fourth internal logic of *guanxi* is the status-inconsistency logic. That is, *guanxi* ties and *guanxi* networks tend to connect actors of unequal status, power, or resources (chapter 2). According to Yan (2006), an established social anthropologist on *guanxi* scholarship, the unequal nature of *guanxi* ties and *guanxi* networks is to a large degree inherited from the Confucian ethics of five cardinal relations (chapter

1), in which each dyad matches the general characterization of superior–subordinate relations. In cases of career advancement (chapter 6), for example, superiors are of higher status, more powerful, or more resourceful, and they grant favors to their trusted subordinates; in return, career-oriented subordinates pay personal loyalty and provide services of a secret nature to their superiors, from whom they obtain special treatment. The superior–subordinate relations are patron–client relations; they are durable, institutionally contextualized, instrumentally oriented, and maintained within *guanxi* networks of particular ties and trust-loyalty bonds.

The External Logics of Guanxi

I use the term "external logic" to mean the external conditions that create the propensities for persistent *guanxi* influence in the public sphere. Four such conditions are identified here and each is about a long-lasting and underlying property of Chinese social structure: (1) the cultural repertoire of relational beliefs and values, (2) the disjunction between formal norms and actual behavior, (3) the discretional power of strategic players, and (4) the institutional space created and recreated for informal norms to rule.

China has a long history of imperial rule. The imperial court organized society through the principles of nepotism, lineage virtue, and *guanxi* favoritism (Yang 1959), and these principles were legitimized by the Confucian ethics of particularism (King 1991). China's postimperial paths to modernization after 1911 significantly deviated from those of Western countries (Boisot and Child 1996), and the country has been able to reserve a cultural repertoire of relational beliefs and values (Yang 2002). With these beliefs and values, going through *guanxi* ties to do things of importance becomes a mindset for Chinese people across all levels of the socioeconomic and political hierarchies, not just for ordinary job seekers (chapter 3) but also for petty entrepreneurs (chapter 4), corporate managers (chapter 5), and other strategic players in the scientific, military, political, and legal systems (chapter 6).

Cultural beliefs and values cannot work alone. The beliefs and values in *guanxi* favoritism are effective in a social structure that is characterized by the disjunction between formal norms and actual behavior. Chinese social structure has always been like that. Under imperial rule, formal norms projected court officials as ideal-typical gentlemen following the Confucian codes of behavior; in the Communist party-state, both officials and ordinary citizens are taught to follow Communist role models and become altruistic and devoted Communists, and this ideological idealism did not just exist under Mao but still does today. Ideological idealism, past and present, disregards private rights and private interests, thus causing informal norms to emerge in unofficial societies. *Guanxi* logics of sharing, affection, favor exchange, and trust-loyalty bonds are the informal norms that recognize private rights and satisfy the interests and needs of individuals, who then treat formal norms only as political slogans and ideological propagandas and behave differently. Kipnis (1997) observed a pattern of insincere presentation and social behavior: Chinese people say things one way and behave the other way. This is a pattern of self-protection under coercive regimes of ideological idealism where formal norms are unrealistic.

The disjunction between formal norms and actual behavior makes significant room for strategic players to exercise their discretional powers. Since the Qin dynasty (221–207 BC), Chinese empires had been large in geography, diverse in ethnic people and cultures, and complex in government hierarchy. Therefore, the laws and rules of the imperial court could not be specific, but instead local officials were given significant discretional powers to rule in provincial and county governments. The same problems face China's central government today (Xueguang Zhou 2017); Deng Xiaoping's piecemeal reforms and trial-and-error tactics rely on reform-minded local officials to break away from Mao's redistributive rules (Shirk 1993), thus increasing the discretional powers of Communist cadres in strategic positions. Their discretional powers, however, do not just serve the interest of the central government; the Communist cadres also use these discretional powers to serve the interests of their functional constituents, their *guanxi* networks, and, after all, themselves. While official power corrupts to the extent that public office is used to serve the private interests of the incumbents and their *guanxi* networks, the *guanxi* logics of sharing, affections, favor exchanges, and trust-loyalty bonds create informal structures through which to nurture and permit official corruption (Granovetter 2007; Luo 2008). The materials in chapters 3–6 in this book indicate the following tendency: The greater the discretional powers of cadres and other strategic players, the greater the influence of *guanxi* favoritism.

The final discussion about the external logics of *guanxi* comes down to the issue of institutionalization. The greater the institutional uncertainties there are in the domains of the public sphere, the greater the space that will be created and recreated for informal norms to rule in those domains, and the greater the discretional powers that will be granted to or retained by cadres and other strategic players, resulting in the greater influence of *guanxi* favoritism. Chapter 3 in this book provides one case scenario about institutional uncertainty and *guanxi* favoritism in China's labor markets during the reforms: When institutional rules are unspecific or mixed about screening job candidates, *guanxi* favoritism plays a great role in job allocation; conversely, when job candidates are screened by strict meritocracy rules, the influence of *guanxi* favoritism decreases significantly.

GUANXI NETWORKS AND SOCIAL STRUCTURE

Social structure is defined here as the patterned arrangements of positions of social distinction. In this section, I sum up the materials from the previous chapters by paying special attention to *guanxi* influence on four positions of social distinction: positions of economic power, positions of scientific power, positions of political power, and positions of legal power.

Guanxi *Influence on Positions of Economic Power*

Chapter 3 presented a series of pieces of evidence about persistent *guanxi* influence on job positions of high quality. On subjective measures, users of *guanxi* contacts for job searches are more satisfied with job outcomes as well as work relations in the workplace than non-*guanxi* users. On objective measures, users of *guanxi* ties of otherwise equal credentials and qualifications are better able to obtain jobs that match candidates' human capital and jobs that offer great earning opportunities. Indeed, a strong *guanxi* effect on wage income was revealed: As compared to non-*guanxi* users for job searches, users of *guanxi* contacts enjoyed a higher entry-level wage, higher success rates of mobility into better-paid jobs, and a higher overall wage in the first fifteen years of their job career. These effects were stronger and more significant among jobs of lower technical specificity and in smaller rather than larger work organizations, state and non-state.

Guanxi influence on entrepreneurs is evident in several ways (chapters 4 and 5). Petty entrepreneurs, or those who are self-employed and household business owners, rely on their *guanxi* contacts for access to resources instrumental to starting their small businesses from scratch. Private companies, on the other hand, are born out of the *guanxi* networks of their founders; most business founders obtain from their *guanxi* networks start-up capital and first business contracts. A company's focal player, whether it is the founder or general manager, establishes a *guanxi* circle of kin and pseudo-kin ties of high trust through which to manage the organization from within. When the business develops and secures a stable market position, the focal player's *guanxi* circle will diversify to include acquaintances and strangers of professional competence to manage organizational complexities and advanced innovations. Outside the organization, however, owners and managers continue to rely on their *guanxi* ties to government bureaucracies and officials, local and central, for information, opportunities, and resources in China's political economy. These conclusions are true for state as well as non-state entities, and political embedded ties are effective for local firms as well as publicly listed firms. Political embedded ties are more effective in economic sectors in which government intervention is observable and strong.

The wide spread of *guanxi* business culture has affected foreign companies from advanced capitalism (chapter 5). While they draw a moral distinction between the "good *guanxi*" of information exchange and the "bad *guanxi*" of power-for-money exchanges, foreign companies develop different strategies to adapt to, rather than resist, *guanxi* norms in order to maintain a competitive edge in China's markets. In international joint ventures, for example, foreign investors and managers are quite willing to include *guanxi* as a core concept in their human resources management. Foreign companies also have modified their Western business values by recognizing the *guanxi* norm of establishing a long-term commitment to and high level of trust with Chinese partner companies. Consequently, Western scholars of business administration have developed a completely new scheme to advise foreign companies to more consciously use *guanxi* cultivation as a business strategy when operating in China.

Guanxi *Influence on Positions of Scientific Power*

Scientists gain positions of prominence not merely depending on their research creativity and achievements. Scientists live and work in social-political environments and are exposed to human influence. In a top national university in China, for example, a great research project of international significance must get approval from three stakeholders before it can be submitted for major government grants: (1) the university lead scientist in the area, who has the professional authority as well as within- and between-university networks to ascertain the scientific value of the project; (2) the director of the functional office having operational authority to select one project over other projects; and (3) the Party secretary or the president, who has final decision-making power over the allocation of internal resources. Beyond the university boundary, *guanxi* ties to key government officials are decisive because these officials wield the authority to approve projects.

The selection of members of the prestigious CAS/CAE is influenced by *guanxi* favoritism. Mentoring relationships, among other factors, significantly increase one's probability of becoming a member of the CAS. Lobbying CAS/CAE members for nominations and votes is also widespread. During the thirteen-year period from 2001 to 2013, China had 4,921 nominees for CAS/CAE member elections and 14.3 percent were elected. Fisman et al. (2018) show that hometown ties to the CAS/CAE standing members significantly boosted a nominee's probability of getting elected, with more than a 40 percent advantage over other nominees lacking hometown ties to the voting members. While nominees were equally impressive in track record, research productivity, and scholarly influence, the well-connected winners of CAS/CAE elections were lower achievers than their poorly connected counterparts. Clearly, *guanxi* favoritism through hometown ties to the CAS/CAE standing members has distorted the selection of Chinese academicians.

Guanxi *Influence on Positions of Political Power*

Chapter 6 presents evidence on the wide spread of nepotism in the selection and appointment of local government officials. While political virtue and work performance are the formal criteria announced to screen candidates, the effectiveness of the formal criteria is conditional upon candidates' *guanxi* ties to decision-makers in the process of promotion nominations, evaluations, and decisions. In practice, *guanxi* networks of political ties to decision-makers and other stakeholders in career promotion processes are mobilized to boost one's probability of success for career promotion. Under the new regulation of "democratic selection" in which cadres of equal and higher ranks are invited to participate in the selection process, canvassing nets are created to pull votes from relevant parties. Money-for-vote exchange is the mechanism to make the canvassing nets work, and this practice even openly operates in Chinese electoral politics at local levels.

The selection of national political elites is by and large a *guanxi* phenomenon. The first internal logic of *guanxi* works very well in the selection of national political elites, as they are disproportionately distributed among a few leading national universities, with Tsinghua University in the lead. The second and third internal logics of *guanxi* – the affection and favor-exchange logics – are also effective, as national political elites are nominated by top politicians who favor those who are their close confidants. The fourth internal logic of *guanxi* works most effectively in the selection of national political elites. This refers to the trust-loyalty bonds already built up in past superior–subordinate relations, and this internal logic is behind the nominations and appointments of nearly all elite politicians. On both sides of the trust-loyalty bonds, exercising different *guanxi* logics is a skill set needed in political life; this is a cultural toolkit for career advancement, not just for elite politicians but also for all levels of strategic players in Chinese society today.

Guanxi *Influence on Positions of Legal Power*

The conclusion just reached does not exclude legal professionals and officials. On the contrary, *guanxi* influence is widespread and deep in

China's legal system. At local levels, lack of political *guanxi* prevents a villager from appealing to the court or hiring a lawyer. But lawyers are also constrained by lack of political *guanxi* in practicing law. Those lawyers who are well connected to the legal branches of the government perceive stronger support from the government than their poorly connected counterparts. Court judges, on the other hand, are influenced by their political as well as social *guanxi*: while subordinate–superior relationships within the politicized legal system influence a frontline judge's decisions on cases, social connections outside the court alter these decisions to favor the strongly connected. Their decisions are not illegal but within the discretional powers of trial judges.

Bribery is a huge problem in China's legal system. Bribery is always publicly denounced, but behind the scenes it survives under the *guanxi* logic of favor exchange. This *guanxi* logic in itself is not corrupting, so far as the exchanges of favors are confined to personal worlds and do not invade the public sphere. But the hard realities are that the favor-exchange logic does indeed go beyond personal worlds and operates strongly as an informal mechanism to permit official corruption among legal players of strategic importance. To reduce corruption and restore public confidence in the legal system, China has recently strengthened its lay assessor institution, expanding the participation of the citizenry in the judicial processes. In formal terms, lay assessors and their involvements in tribunals have increased dramatically. In reality, however, lay participation under China's authoritarian regime has failed to meet its intended goals. Legal reforms have a long way to go.

GUANXI NETWORKS AS SOCIAL STRUCTURE

Here, social structure is defined as the enduring networks of ongoing social relationships. In the West, this definition is rooted in the works of Lévi-Strauss (1949/1969) and Bott (1957), who pioneered the study of family and kinship as networks of lineage and marriage ties. It was not until the 1970s that we saw this definition fully accepted in structural sociology (Blau 1975). Since then, social network analysis (SNA), a multi- and interdisciplinary field of study, has been a contemporary version of this relational approach to social structure (Wellman 1988). Independent of and long before this Western tradition, however, Confucianism was an ancient Chinese philosophy of human relations and interpersonal ethnics (chapter 1). In the modern era, the late Chinese anthropologist and sociologist Fei Xiaotong (1947/1992) was the very first to define Chinese social structure in a relational approach. In this section, I will begin with a review of Fei's theory before discussing its contemporary significance for analyzing today's Chinese social structure as *guanxi* networks of particular ties.

The Mode of Differential Associations as Chinese Social Structure

"The mode of differential associations" is my translation of Fei's original Chinese phrase "差序格局" (*cha xu ge ju*). Elsewhere, the phrase was translated as "the differential mode of association" (Hamilton and Zheng in the 1992 English translation of Fei) or "the configuration of differentiated associations" (Yan 1996). None of these translations, including my own, can be understood without elaboration because an equivalent phrase is unavailable in the English-language literature in sociology or anthropology. To me, what Fei meant by the phrase is what we describe in today's SNA terminology as a system or structure emerging from "the overlapping of egocentric networks." Working on his innovative conceptualization of Chinese social structure from a relational (rather than positional) approach in the mid-1940s, Fei then lacked a standard SNA concept to use since the field of study was nonexistent. Had he redeveloped his conceptualization before his passing in 2005, Fei would, I imagine, have used "the structure of overlapped egocentric networks" to define and characterize Chinese social structure.

Fei's original vision was brilliant and pathbreaking. A sociology major in Beijing in the first half of the 1930s, Fei was taught by, in addition to his Chinese teachers, Ernest Burgess and Robert Park, visiting American sociologists from the University of Chicago. Fei then became a doctoral advisee of British anthropologist Bronislaw Malinowski at the London School of Economics during 1936–8. From his American and British teachers, Fei learned much about a positional approach to defining social structure as groups of interest-oriented individuals, or in his words "团体格局" (*tuanti geju*, or the mode of grouped individuals). In this group-based social structure, argued Fei, individuals are recognized for their equal citizen rights as well as their private interests as the primary order of social organization, and individuals with similar interests are socially grouped together to exercise their rights and realize their interests, structurally leading to the emergence of individualism as a moral system in society at large. While this group-based social structure matched Fei's observation on Western societies such as the UK and the US, it did not at all fit his image of Chinese social structure. For him, social structure in rural China, on which he focused his analytic attention, was fundamentally different; it had never been group-based, but instead it had since before the Qin dynasty been based on the overlapping of egocentric networks of family, kinship, and extended particular ties.

Writing originally in a popular essay for a newspaper, Fei used a metaphor to describe his ideas. When a rock (the ego) is thrown into water (society), circles (networks) of water ripples (relationships with significant others) will be made and pushed by the rock from the center to the periphery, with the magnitudes of water ripples changing from thick (stronger ties closer to the ego) to thin (weaker ties distant from the ego). The circles of water ripples as a whole look like a cobweb, elaborated by Fei, and this cobweb is like the web of social relations for all villagers. In a village community, Fei argued, each individual makes his own network of stronger and weaker ties through which to learn about how to perform in social roles, to mobilize resources via favor exchanges with closer and distant others of social relevance, and thus to realize their private interests and satisfy private needs. The descriptions in parentheses above are mine to help readers understand what Fei implied in his metaphorical analysis.

Fei maintained that this egocentric network had a fundamental implication for how a village community or the entire traditional Chinese society was structured. For him, the ego and his alters are not aware of "citizen rights" but know each other very well in terms of family, kinship, and extended particular ties that connect them. Structurally, the underlying logic of a village community as a social system does not lie in the patterned arrangements of social positions occupied by villagers, but instead is in the overlapping of egocentric networks of villagers. At this point, Fei coined the phrase "the mode of differential associations" to define Chinese social structure.

Fei forcefully argued that the social structure of differential associations has no way of generating a Westernized version of "individualism" (个人主义, *geren zhuyi*). A moral system of individualism recognizes citizens' private rights and interests as the underlying logic of social structure. In sharp contrast, what emerges from the social structure of differential associations is a moral system of "egoism" (个体主义, *geti zhuyi*) in which selfishness drives the dynamics of egocentric networks of particular ties. For Fei, egoists are totally different from individualists because egoists have no "society" in mind but care only about the personally networked communities around them. These personal communities are adjustable in size and composition depending on the ego's needs to keep alters of social relevance in his on her network. In Fei's view, a universal notion of public morality never has existed in Chinese society, which has been full of relational morality of particularism.

The Contemporary Significance of Fei's Network Theory

Fei's network theory of Chinese social structure is not confined to China's village communities. It is generalizable about all communities in Chinese society, past and present. Classic sociology has made the theoretical distinction between a "community" of densely networked familiar persons and a "society" of interest-oriented, rational strangers (Tönnies (1887/1957). In contemporary sociology, this distinction is frequently operationalized as that between rural villages and urban cities. For Fei, a Chinese rural village is a densely networked community in which the underlying structure is the overlapping of family and kinship networks. Since, Fei argued, dynasties were all modeled after and mimic the Chinese family and kinship, the overlapping of family, kinship, and extended particular ties was the underlying social structure throughout imperial Chinese history. In his essay on "the mode of differential associations" Fei cited Confucian scholars, used fictional stories, and analyzed social facts to support his theoretical position. We omit the details but turn our attention to the contemporary significance of Fei's theory in Chinese society today.

To be sure, Chinese society today is full of the personally networked communities of Fei's characterization. There are many examples that can be cited here to qualify this proposition. Villages that were studied by Yang (1959), Jacobs (1979), Lin (1995), Yan (1996), Kipnis (1997), Michelson (2007a), and Chang (2010) are all a rich source of evidence on how *guanxi* networks of villager ties rule in socioeconomic exchanges, political governance, and legal processes in rural communities. Mao's factories studied by Walder (1986), on the other hand, show how Communist cadres formed patron–client networks of trust-loyalty bonds with political activists through which to allocate economic incentives and exercise political control on the shop floor. For China under reform today, the previous chapters of this book have presented evidence on how *guanxi* networks of particular ties have become the effective informal structures through which to obtain desirable jobs (chapter 3), start businesses (chapter 4), govern and develop organizations (chapter 5), and secure opportunities of career advancement in various domains of society (chapter 6).

There is a structural reason why China today, rural and urban, is still a *guanxi* society. The reason is, I argue, that any larger society of interest-oriented, rational strangers is ruled through personally networked communities of governing elites. Giddens (2001) defines governing elites as the uniform elites holding hegemonic power or the established elites holding democratic power. China's Communist cadres fit Giddens's first type of governing elites, as they are missioned to govern a village, a school, a university, a company, a corporation, or a certain level of government by following the uniform rules of the central government under the hegemonic Communist party-state. Yet governing elites in various domains of Chinese society and at different levels of the government hierarchy cannot perform their jobs without densely networked communities around them. The canvassing net described in chapter 6 is a perfect example for illustration. A local official wanting to win a promotion competition forms a canvassing net consisting of his or her deputies, superiors, relatives, close subordinates, and equal-ranking colleagues to work for him or her. This canvassing net is also the personally networked community through which any Communist cadre performs his or her governing job every day. In fact, governing a society of citizens or managing a sizable organization of employees is always done through the personally networked communities of governing elites, whether the society or organization in question is a public entity or a private venture. Consequently, Fei's image of the overlapping of egocentric networks of particular ties is of contemporary significance in every corner of Chinese society today.

Empirical and theoretical research conducted by China-based sociologists has presented a series of pieces of evidence in support of my argument. Sun (1996) observed that when resources were allocated through the bureaucratic system of work units in Mao's era, an ordinary worker could obtain these resources through two channels: the "vertical" channel of trust-loyalty relations with superiors within one's own work unit, and the "horizontal" channel of direct or indirect ties to redistributors of other work units. Sun argued that this overlapping of the vertical and horizontal channels is the basic social structure through which to obtain vertically allocated resources in all post-Mao regimes. Chen and Chen (1998) observed that in Chinese villages and townships under reform, particular ties of high intimacy were the basic social structures through which to realize the private interests of individuals, who then made efforts to construct and reconstruct their *guanxi* networks of particular ties. One explanation of why Fei's mode of differential associations still rules village communities under reform is that villages are not only interpersonally networked communities but also the power structures through which to allocate lands and other basic rural resources (He 2007). Even in a larger society of urbanites, *guanxi* networks are extended from personal worlds to invade the "small" publics within which to satisfy people's basic needs (Xiao 2014) under the ethics of affection, sharing, and reciprocity (Feizhou Zhou 2017).

A RESEARCH AGENDA

This book has confined its examination of *guanxi* favoritism and *guanxi* influence to several, not all, domains of social life in China, and the long bibliography at the end of this book provides only an incomplete list of social science publications on *guanxi* research. The discussion of the existing *guanxi* scholarship has implied several lines of theoretical and empirical analysis that will further advance our understanding of the *guanxi* phenomenon in China in the years ahead.

The Personal Worlds of Guanxi *and Cohort Variation*

There is a set of norms, values, and beliefs that characterize the cultural system of *guanxi* favoritism. Are these cultural elements of *guanxi* favoritism invariably internalized by individuals of new cohorts? The resilience of *guanxi* thesis calls for attention to not only a period analysis of changing *guanxi* practices but a cohort analysis of persistent *guanxi* favoritism as a cultural system. At what ages do children internalize the beliefs and norms of *guanxi* favoritism and in what contexts? Is the transition from school to work also the transition from the internalization of "good *guanxi*" values for information exchanges to the recognition and acceptance of "bad *guanxi*" values for money-for-power exchanges? Or are the new generations breaking away from all these *guanxi* values and becoming more rationalized and less relationally embedded? What is the relative efficacy of individualism and egoism among the new generations in an increasingly globalized China?

Guanxi *Favoritism's Crossing of the Private–Public Boundary*

Key to the prevalence of *guanxi* influence in public life is that *guanxi* ethics travel from the personal worlds into the public spheres. We understand that governing elites and other strategic players must necessarily perform their public duties through the personally networked worlds of deputies and close confidants, kin and pseudo-kin contacts included. This tendency makes *guanxi* logics of intimacy, affection, favor exchanges, and trust-loyalty bonds inevitable and inseparable from the social and political behaviors of governing elites and other strategic players. While job-search networks broadened to contain more weak ties from 1978 to 2014, ties to leaders have remained in a stable range of 50–70 percent over those thirty-six years of the reform era. This makes it explicit that trust-loyalty bonds between superiors and subordinates are the core of *guanxi* favoritism in the public spheres, and that they seem to be strengthened in the new wave of political centralization under Xi Jinping's leadership. The question for future *guanxi* researchers is: To what extent can the rule of law and other formal norms prevent the misuse of *guanxi* networks for private gains? This calls for an analysis of the interplay between the discretional powers of governing elites and the *guanxi* logics.

Different Public Domains and Different Guanxi Practices

Institutional contexts matter greatly for *guanxi* influence. Between "good *guanxi*" and "bad *guanxi*," what public domains support the former and disallow the latter, and why? This book has shown persistent and increasing *guanxi* influence in the labor markets, in the business world, in the scientific sphere, in the government system, in the military system, and in the legal system. What about other domains of social life? Is *guanxi* influence persistent and increasing in the educational sector? In the public health industry? In non-government organizations? In the area of social movements? Overall, is the rise of the market economy with Chinese characteristics creating external conditions that oppose nice *guanxi* in favor of naked favoritism? Have "bad *guanxi*" practices stayed within the confines of business and political circles? Or are they spreading to all public spheres in a fast-changing China?

Cross-Cultural and Cross-National Analysis of Guanxi Influence

The notion of "generalized particularism" (Lo and Otis 2003) calls for a cross-cultural and cross-national analysis of *guanxi* influence. A framework for a China–US comparative analysis of labor markets has been suggested in the literature (DiTomaso and Bian 2018). This framework identifies three general elements for a cross-cultural and cross-national analysis of *guanxi* influence between and among societies of cultural, economic, and political differences: the effectiveness of formal institutions that constrain social actors, the differentiation between primordial and generalized particularisms that govern social interactions, and the interplay between the formal and informal institutionalizations.

Looking Forward

Guanxi connections and *guanxi* networks are central to understanding how China works. For ordinary people, network building and rebuilding are an everyday phenomenon, and information, influence, and other forms of favoritism from *guanxi* contacts are prevalent for obtaining scarce resources, such as good jobs, wage increases, and promotion, as the economy continues to develop in its current direction. For entrepreneurs and business elites, *guanxi* networks of trust and favor exchanges are the backbone of business founding and development because they are the basic channels through which to learn confidential information, mobilize otherwise unavailable resources, and, crucially, to reduce institutional uncertainties and future risks in what is an increasingly competitive economy. This means *guanxi* will continue to play an important role in the future, even as China's businesses move further into the global economy – indeed, as we have seen, businesses outside China are also turning toward *guanxi* practices in order to facilitate global cooperation with China. For political elites at all levels, *guanxi* networks of trust and loyalty are the social mechanisms whereby appointments of strategic importance are made, opportunities for upward mobility are distributed, and cooperation, alliances, and cliques are formed and reformed. As is widely commented on, China's rise to economic and industrial prominence on the global stage has not mirrored the accepted Western path to modernization, in which growing economic prosperity accompanies growing electoral democratization. China's internal politics remain China's affair and, for the most part, untouched by global interactions, and thus the *guanxi* model persists and will continue to do so. Students of contemporary China must acquire basic knowledge about how China works through *guanxi* mechanisms; otherwise they will get lost when trying to understand Chinese social behavior and social structure. Researchers into Chinese culture, economy, politics, and society are missioned to explore the dynamics of *guanxi* in a fast-changing China while enriching the stock of *guanxi* literature of empirical and theoretical significance.

Bibliography

Adler, Paul, and Seok-Woo Kwon. 2002. "Social Capital: Prospects for a New Concept." *Academy of Management Review* 27: 17–40.

Albrow, Martin. 1996. *The Global Age*. Cambridge: Polity.

Arrow, Kenneth. 1998. "What Has Economics to Say about Racial Discrimination?" *Journal of Economic Perspectives* 12: 91–100.

Barbalet, Jack. 2018. "*Guanxi* as Social Exchange: Emotions, Power and Corruption." *Sociology*.

Barnes, Bradley, Dorothy Yen, and Lianxi Zhou. 2011. "Investigating *Guanxi* Dimensions and Relationship Outcomes: Insights from Sino-Anglo Business Relationships." *Industrial Marketing Management* 40: 510–21.

Batjargal, Bat. 2003. "Social Capital and Entrepreneurial Performance in Russia: A Longitudinal Study." *Organization Studies* 24: 535–56.

Beckman, Christine, Pamela Haunschild, and Damon Phillips. 2004. "Friends or Strangers? Firm-Specific Uncertainty, Market Uncertainty, and Network Partner Selection." *Organization Science* 15: 259–75.

Berger, Ron, Ram Herstein, Avi Silbiger, and Bradley Barnes. 2015. "Can *Guanxi* Be Created in Sino-Western Relationships? An Assessment of Western Firms Trading with China Using the GRX Scale." *Industrial Marketing Management* 47: 166–74.

Bian, Yanjie. 1994a. *Work and Inequality in Urban China*. Albany, NY: State University of New York Press.

Bian, Yanjie. 1994b. "*Guanxi* and the Allocation of Urban Jobs in China." *The China Quarterly* 140: 971–99.

Bian, Yanjie. 1997. "Bringing Strong Ties Back In: Indirect Connection, Bridges, and Job Search in China." *American Sociological Review* 62: 266–85.

Bian, Yanjie. 1999. "Getting a Job through a Web of *Guanxi* in Urban China." Pp. 255–77 in *Networks in the Global Village*, edited by Barry Wellman. Boulder, CO: Westview Press.

Bian, Yanjie. 2001. "*Guanxi* Capital and Social Eating: Theoretical Models and Empirical Analyses." Pp. 275–95 in *Social Capital: Theory and Research*, edited by Nan Lin, Karen Cook, and Ronald Burt. New York, NY: Aldine de Gruyter.

Bian, Yanjie. 2002. "Institutional Holes and Job Mobility Processes in the PRC: *Guanxi* Mechanisms in Emergent Labor Markets." Pp. 117–36 in *Social Connections in China: Institutions, Culture, and the Changing Nature of Guanxi*, edited by Thomas Gold, Doug Guthrie, and David Wank. New York, NY: Cambridge University Press.

Bian, Yanjie. 2006. "*Guanxi.*" Pp. 312–14 in *International Encyclopedia of Economic Sociology*, edited by Jens Beckert and Milan Zafirovski. London: Routledge.

Bian, Yanjie. 2008a. "Urban Occupational Mobility and Employment Institutions: Hierarchy, Market, and Networks in a Mixed System." Pp. 165–83 in *Creating Wealth and Poverty in Postsocialist China*, edited by Deborah Davis and Feng Wang. Stanford, CA: Stanford University Press.

Bian, Yanjie. 2008b. "The Formation of Social Capital among Chinese Urbanites: Theoretical Explanation and Empirical Evidence." Pp. 81–106 in *Social Capital: An International Research Program*, edited by Nan Lin and Bonnie Erickson. London: Oxford University Press.

Bian, Yanjie. 2009. "Sociology." Pp. 2031–5 in *The Berkshire Encyclopedia of China*, edited by Karen Christensen. Great Barrington, MA: Berkshire.

Bian, Yanjie. 2017. "The Comparative Significance of *Guanxi.*" *Management and Organization Review* 13: 261–7.

Bian, Yanjie. 2018. "The Prevalence and the Increasing Significance of *Guanxi.*" *The China Quarterly*.

Bian, Yanjie, and Soon Ang. 1997. "*Guanxi* Networks and Job Mobility in China and Singapore." *Social Forces* 75: 981–1005.

Bian, Yanjie, Ronald Breiger, Deborah Davis, and Joseph Galaskiewicz. 2005. "Occupation, Class, and Social Networks in Urban China." *Social Forces* 83: 1443–68.

Bian, Yanjie, Deborah Davis, and Shaoguang Wang. 2007. "Family Social Capital in Urban China: A Social Network Approach." Pp. 219–32 in *Social Change in Contemporary China*, edited by Wenfang Tang and Burkart Holzner. Pittsburgh, PA: University of Pittsburgh Press.

Bian, Yanjie, and Xianbi Huang. 2009. "Network Resources and Job Mobility in China's Transitional Economy." *Research in the Sociology of Work* 19: 255–82.

Bian, Yanjie, and Xianbi Huang. 2015a. "The *Guanxi* Influence on Occupational Attainment in Urban China." *Chinese Journal of Sociology* 1: 307–32.

Bian, Yanjie, and Xianbi Huang. 2015b. "Beyond the Strength of Social Ties: Job Search Networks and Entry-Level Wage in Urban China." *American Behavioral Scientist* 59: 961–76.

Bian, Yanjie, Xianbi Huang, and Lei Zhang. 2015. "Information and Favoritism: The Network Effect on Wage Income in China." *Social Networks* 40: 129–38.

Bian, Yanjie, and Ken'ichi Ikeda. 2014 original/2016 2nd edition. "East Asian Social Networks." Pp. 417–33 in *Encyclopedia of Social Network Analysis and Mining*, edited by Reda Alhajj, and Jon Rokne. New York, NY: Springer.

Bian, Yanjie, and John Logan. 1996. "Market Transition and the Persistence of Power: The Changing Stratification System in China." *American Sociological Review* 61: 739–58.

Bian, Yanjie, and Lulu Li. 2012. "The Chinese General Social Survey (2003–2008): Sample Designs and Data Evaluation." *Chinese Sociological Review* 45: 70–97.

Bian, Yanjie, Xiaoling Shu, and John Logan. 2001. "Communist Party Membership and Regime Dynamics in China." *Social Forces* 79: 805–41.

Bian, Yanjie, and Wenbin Wang. 2016. "The Social Capital for Self-Employment in Transitional China." Pp. 21–35 in *Rethinking Social Capital and Entrepreneurship in Greater China*, edited by Jenn-Hwan Wang and Ray-May Hsung. London and New York, NY: Routledge.

Bian, Yanjie, and Lei Zhang. 2008. "Sociology in China." *Contexts* 7: 20–5.

Bian, Yanjie, and Lei Zhang. 2014. "Corporate Social Capital in Chinese *Guanxi* Culture." *Research in the Sociology of Organizations* 40: 417–39.

Bian, Yanjie, Lei Zhang, Wenbin Wang, and Cheng Cheng. 2016. "Institution-Spanning Social Capital and its Income Returns in China." Pp. 344–57 in *Handbook of Research Methods and Applications in Social Capital*, edited by Yaojun Li. London: Routledge.

Bian, Yanjie, Lei Zhang, Yinghui Li, Yipeng Hu, and Na Li. 2018. "Income Inequality and Class Stratification." Pp. 1022–41 in *The Sage Handbook of Contemporary China*, edited by Weiping Wu and Mark Frazier. New York, NY: Sage.

Blau, Peter M. (ed.). 1975. *Approaches to the Study of Social Structure*. New York, NY: Free Press.

Blau, Peter, Danching Ruan, and Monika Ardelt. 1991. "Interpersonal Choice and Networks in China." *Social Forces* 69: 1037–62.

Boase, Jeffrey, and Ken'ichi Ikeda. 2012. "Core Discussion Networks in Japan and America." *Human Communication Research* 38: 95–119.

Boisot, Max, and John Child. 1988. "The Iron Law of Fiefs: Bureaucratic Failure and the Problem of Governance in the Chinese Economic Reforms." *Administrative Science Quarterly* 33: 507–27.

Boisot, Max, and John Child. 1996. "From Fiefs to Clans and Network Capitalism: Explaining China's Emerging Economic Order." *Administrative Science Quarterly* 41: 600–28.

Bott, Elizabeth. 1957. *Family and Social Network*. London: Tavistock.

Bourdieu, Pierre. 1986. "The Forms of Capital." Pp. 241–58 in *Handbook of Theory and Research in the Sociology of Education*, edited by John Richardson. New York, NY: Greenwald Press.

Brass, Daniel, Joseph Galaskiewicz, Henrich Greve, and Wenpin Tsai. 2004. "Taking Stock of Networks and Organizations: A Multilevel Perspective." *The Academy of Management Journal* 47: 795–817.

Bruun, Ole. 1993. *Business and Bureaucracy in a Chinese City*. Chinese Research Monograph 43, Institute of East Asian Studies, University of California at Berkeley.

Bruun, Ole. 1995. "Political Hierarchy and Private Entrepreneurship in a Chinese Neighbourhood." Pp. 184–212 in *The Waning of the Communist State: Economic Origin of Political Decline in China and Hungary*, edited by Andrew Walder. Berkeley, CA: University of California Press.

Burns, Tom, and George Stalker. 1961. *The Management of Innovation*. London: Tavistock.

Burt, Ronald. 1992. *Structural Holes: The Social Structure of Competition*. Cambridge, MA: Harvard University Press.

Burt, Ronald. 2000. "The Network Structure of Social Capital." *Research in Organizational Behavior* 22: 345–423.

Burt, Ronald, Yanjie Bian, and Sonja Opper. 2018. "More or Less *Guanxi*: Trust is 60% Network Context, 10% Individual Difference." *Social Networks* 54: 12–25.

Burt, Ronald, and Katarzyna Burzynska. 2017. "Chinese Entrepreneurs, Social Networks, and *Guanxi*." *Management and Organization Review* 13: 221–60.

Burt, Ronald, and Sonja Opper. 2017. "Early Network Events in the Later Success of Chinese Entrepreneurs." *Management and Organization Review* 13: 497–537.

Cao, Cong. 2004. *China's Scientific Elite*. London: Routledge.

Chan, Ta-Chien, Tso-Jung Yen, Yang-chih Fu, and Jing-Shiang Hwang. 2015. "ClickDiary: Online Tracking of Health Behaviors and Mood." *Journal of Medical Internet Research* 17: 147–67.

Chang, Kuang-chi. 2011. "A Path to Understanding *Guanxi* in China's Transitional Economy: Variations on Network Behavior." *Sociological Theory* 29: 315–39.

Chang, Xiangqun. 2010. *Guanxi or Lishang Wanglai? Reciprocity, Social Support Networks, & Social Creativity in a Chinese Village*. Taipei: Airiti Press.

Chen, Chao, Xiao-Ping Chen, and Shengsheng Huang. 2013. "Chinese *Guanxi*: An Integrative Review and New Directions for Future Research." *Management and Organization Review* 9: 167–207.

Chen, Chao, Ya-Ru Chen, and Katherine Xin. 2004. "*Guanxi* Practices and Trust in Management: A Procedural Justice Perspective." *Organization Science* 15: 200–9.

Chen, Wenhong, Justin Tan, and Fangjing Tu. 2015. "Minding the Gender Gap: Social Network and Internet Correlates of Business Performance among Chinese Immigrant Entrepreneurs." *American Behavioral Scientist* 59: 977–91.

Chen, Yunsong. 2011. "The Causal Effect of Social Capital in the Labor Market: Identification Challenges and Strategies." *Chinese Sociological Review* 44: 76–100.

Chen, Yunsong. 2012. "Do Networks Pay Off among Internal Migrants in China? An Instrumental Variable Analysis." *Chinese Sociological Review* 45: 28–54.

Chen, Yunsong, and Beate Volker. 2016. "Social Capital and Homophily Both Matter for Labor Market Outcomes: Evidence from Replication and Extension." *Social Networks* 45: 18–31.

Cheng, Lucie, and Arthur Rosett. 1991. "Contract with a Chinese Face: Socially Embedded Factors in the Transformation from Hierarchy to Market, 1978–1989." *Journal of Chinese Law* 5: 143–244.

Chiao, Chien. 1982. "*Guanxi*: A Preliminary Conceptualization." Pp. 345–60 in *The Sinicization of Social and Behavioral Science Research in China*, edited by Kuo-shu Yang and Wen-chong Yi. Taipei: Academia Sinica.

Child, John, and Yuan Lu. 1996. "Institutional Constraints on Economic Reform: The Case of Investment Decisions in China." *Organization Science* 7: 60–77.

Coleman, James. 1988. "Social Capital in the Creation of Human Capital." *American Journal of Sociology* 94: S95–S120.

Davis, Deborah. 1990. "Urban Job Mobility." Pp. 85–108 in *Chinese Society on the Eve of Tiananmen*, edited by Deborah Davis and Ezra F. Vogel. Cambridge, MA: Harvard University Press.

Davis, Deborah. 1992. "Job Mobility in Post-Mao Cities: Increase on the Margins." *The China Quarterly* 132: 1062–85.

Davis, Deborah, and S. Friedman (eds.). 2014. *Wives, Husbands, Lovers: Marriage and Sexuality in Hong Kong, Taiwan, and Urban China*. Stanford, CA: Stanford University Press.

DiMaggio, Paul, and Walter Powell. 1983. "The Iron Cage Revisited: Institutional Isomorphism and Collective Rationality in Organizational Fields." *American Sociological Review* 48: 147–60.

DiTomaso, Nancy. 2013. *The American Non-Dilemma: Racial Inequality without Racism*. New York, NY: Russell Sage Foundation.

DiTomaso, Nancy, and Yanjie Bian. 2018. "The Structure of Labor Markets in the U.S. and China: Social Capital and *Guanxi*." *Management and Organization Review* 14: 5–36.

Dittmer, Lowell. 1995. "Chinese Informal Politics." *The China Journal* 34: 1–34.

Donaldson, Lex. 2001. *The Contingency Theory of Organizations*. Thousand Oaks, CA: Sage.

Farh, Jiing-Lih, Anne Tsui, Katherine Xin, and Bor-Shiuan Cheng. 1998. "The Influence of Relational Demography and *Guanxi*: The Chinese Case." *Organization Science* 9: 471–88.

Faure, David. 1994. "China and Capitalism: Business Enterprise in Modern China." Occasional Paper No. 1, Division of Humanities, Hong Kong University of Science and Technology.

Fei, Xiaotong. 1947 Chinese original/1992 English translation. *From the Soil: The Foundations of Chinese Society*. Berkeley, CA: University of California Press.

Fernandez, Roberto, and Nancy Weinberg. 1997. "Sifting and Sorting: Personal Contacts and Hiring in a Retail Bank." *American Sociological Review* 62: 883–902.

Ferrary, Michel. 2003. "The Gift Exchange in the Social Networks of Silicon Valley." *California Management Review* 45: 120–38.

Fisman, Raymond, Jing Shi, Yongxiang Wang, and Rong Xu. 2018. "Social Ties and Favoritism in Chinese Science." *Journal of Political Economy* 126: 1134–71.

Fligstein, Neil, and Jianjun Zhang. 2011. "A New Agenda for Research on the Trajectory of Chinese Capitalism." *Management and Organization Review* 7: 39–62.

Foucault, Michel. 1983. "The Subject and Power." Pp. 208–26 in *Beyond Structuralism and Hermeneutics*, edited by Hubert Dreyfus and Paul Rainbow. Chicago, IL: University of Chicago Press.

Fried, Morton. 1953 original/1969 reprint. *Fabric of Chinese Society: A Study of the Social Life in a Chinese County Seat*. New York, NY: Octagon Books.

Fu, Pingping, Anne Tsui, and Gregory Dess. 2006. "The Dynamics of *Guanxi* in Chinese Hightech Firms: Implications for Knowledge Management and Decision Making." *Management International Review* 46: 277–305.

Fu, Yang-chih. 2005. "Measuring Personal Networks with Daily Contacts: A Single-item Survey Question and the Contact Diary." *Social Networks* 27: 169–86.

Fu, Yang-chih. 2009. "Immediate Returns on Time Investment in Network Overlapping: Evidence from Contact Diaries." Pp. 327–47 in *Contexts of Social Capital: Social Networks in Markets, Communities, and Families*, edited by Ray-May Hsung, Ronald Brieger, and Nan Lin. London: Routledge.

Fu, Yang-chih, Hwai-Chung Ho, and Hsiu-Man Chen. 2013. "Weak Ties and Contact Initiation in Everyday Life: Exploring Contextual Variations from Contact Diaries." *Social Networks* 35: 279–87.

Geertz, Clifford. 1983 *Local Knowledge: Further Essays in Interpretive Anthropology*. New York, NY: Basic Books.

Giddens, Anthony. 2001. "Elites and Power." Pp. 212–15 in *Social Stratification: Class, Race, and Gender in Sociological Perspective* (2nd edition), edited by David B. Grusky. Boulder, CO: Westview Press.

Gold, Thomas. 1985. "After Comradeship: Personal Relations in China Since the Cultural Revolution." *The China Quarterly* 104: 657–75.

Gold, Thomas. 1990. "Urban Private Business and Social Change." Pp. 157–80 in *Chinese Society on the Eve of Tiananman: The Impact of Reform*, edited by Deborah Davis and Ezra Vogel. Cambridge, MA: Harvard University Press.

Gold, Thomas, Doug Guthrie, and David Wank. 2002. *Social Connections in China: Institutions, Culture, and the Changing Nature of Guanxi.* New York, NY: Cambridge University Press.

Gomez-Arias, Tomas. 1998. "A Relationship Marketing Approach to Guanxi." *European Journal of Marketing* 32: 145–56.

Goodman, David. 2014. *Class in Contemporary China.* Cambridge: Polity.

Granovetter, Mark. 1973. "The Strength of Weak Ties." *American Journal of Sociology* 78: 1360–80.

Granovetter, Mark. 1974. *Getting a Job: A Study of Contacts and Careers.* Cambridge, MA: Harvard University Press.

Granovetter, Mark. 1981. "Toward a Sociological Theory of Income Differences." Pp. 11–48 in *Sociological Perspectives on Labor Markets*, edited by Ivar Berg. New York, NY: Academic Press.

Granovetter, Mark. 1985. "Economic Action and Social Structure: The Problem of Embeddedness." *American Journal of Sociology* 91: 481–510.

Granovetter, Mark. 1995. "Afterword." Pp. 139–82 in *Getting a Job: A Study of Contacts and Careers* (2nd edition). Chicago, IL: University of Chicago Press.

Granovetter, Mark. 2007. "The Social Construction of Corruption." Pp. 152–72 in *On Capitalism*, edited by Victor Nee and Richard Swedberg. Stanford, CA: Stanford University Press.

Gregory, Neil, Stoyan Tenev, and Dileep Wagle. 2000. *China's Emerging Private Enterprises: Prospects for the New Century.* Washington, DC: World Bank.

Guo, Chun, and Jane Miller. 2010. "Guanxi Dynamics and Entrepreneurial Firm Creation and Development in China." *Management and Organization Review* 6: 267–91.

Guo, Xuezhi. 2001. "Dimensions of Guanxi in Chinese Elite Politics." *The China Journal* 46: 69–90.

Guthrie, Doug. 1998. "The Declining Significance of Guanxi in China's Economic Transition." *The China Quarterly* 154: 254–82.

Guthrie, Doug. 1999. *Dragon in a Three-Piece Suit: The Emergence of Capitalism in China.* Princeton, NJ: Princeton University Press.

Guthrie, Doug. 2002. "Information Symmetries and the Problem of Perception: The Significance of Structural Position in Accessing the Importance of Guanxi in China." Pp. 37–56 in *Social Connections in China: Institutions, Culture, and the Changing Nature of Guanxi*, edited by Thomas Gold, Doug Guthrie, and David Wank. New York, NY: Cambridge University Press.

Hague, Rod, and Martin Harrop. 2013. *Comparative Government and Politics: An Introduction*. New York, NY: Palgrave Macmillan.

Hanser, Amy. 2002. "Youth Job Searches in Urban China: The Use of Social Connections in a Changing Labor Market." Pp. 137–61 in *Social Connections in China: Institutions, Culture, and the Changing Nature of Guanxi*, edited by Thomas Gold, Doug Guthrie, and David Wank. New York, NY: Cambridge University Press.

Haveman, Heather, Nan Jia, Jing Shi, and Yongxiang Wnag. 2017. "The Dynamics of Political Embeddedness in China." *Administrative Science Quarterly* 62: 67–104.

He, Xin. 2016. "Double Whammy: Lay Assessors as Lackeys in Chinese Courts." *Law & Society Review* 50: 733–65.

He, Xin, and Kwai Hang Ng. 2018. "'It Must Be Rock Strong!' Guanxi's Impact on Judicial Decision-Making in China." *American Journal of Comparative Law* 65: 841–71.

Hershkovitz, Linda. 1985. "The Fruits of Ambivalence: China's Urban Individual Economy." *Pacific Affairs* 58: 427–50.

Hewstone, Miles, Mark Rubin, and Hazel Willis. 2002. "Intergroup Bias." *Annual Review of Psychology* 53: 575–604.

Ho, Samuel P. S. 1994. *Rural China in Transition: Non-Agricultural Development in Rural Jiangsu, 1978–1990*. Oxford: Clarendon Press.

Hu, Hsien Chin. 1944. "The Chinese Concepts of 'Face.'" *American Anthropologist* 46: 45–64.

Huang, Xianbi. 2008. "*Guanxi* Networks and Job Searches in China's Emerging Labour Market: A Qualitative Investigation." *Work, Employment and Society* 22: 467–84.

Huang, Xianbi, and Yanjie Bian. 2015. "Job-Search Networks and Wage Attainment in China: A Comparison of Job Changers and Non-Changers." *International Journal of Japanese Sociology* 24: 5–19.

Hwang, Kwang-kuo. 1987. "Face and Favor: The Chinese Power Game." *American Journal of Sociology* 92: 944–74.

Jacobs, Bruce. 1979. "A Preliminary Model of Particularistic Ties in Chinese Political Alliances: Kan-ch'ing and Kuan-hsi in a Rural Taiwanese Township." *The China Quarterly* 78: 237–73.

Jovanovic, Boyan. 1979. "Job Matching and the Theory of Turnover." *Journal of Political Economy* 87: 972–90.

Kalleberg, Arne. 2007. *The Mismatched Worker*. New York, NY: Norton.

Keister, Lisa. 1998. "Engineering Growth: Business Group Structure and Firm Performance in China's Transition Economy." *American Journal of Sociology* 104: 404–40.

Keister, Lisa. 2000. *Chinese Business Groups: The Structure and Impact of Interfirm Relations during Economic Development*. New York, NY: Oxford University Press.

Keister, Lisa. 2001. "Exchange Structures in Transition: Lending and Trade Relations in Chinese Business Groups." *American Sociological Review* 66: 336–60.

King, Ambrose Yeo-chi. 1985. "The Individual and Group in Confucianism: A Relational Perspective." Pp. 57–70 in *Individualism and Holism: Studies in Confucian and Taoist Values*, edited by Donald Munro. Ann Arbor, MI: Center for Chinese Studies, University of Michigan.

King, Ambrose Yeo-chi. 1991. "*Kuan-hsi* and Network Building: A Sociological Interpretation." *Daedalus* 120: 63–84.

Kipnis, Andrew. 1997. *Producing Guanxi: Sentiment, Self, and Subculture in a North China Village*. Durham, NC: Duke University Press.

Knight, Frank. 1921. *Risk, Uncertainty and Profit*. New York, NY: Hart, Schaffner and Marx.

Kornai, Janos. 1986. "The Soft Budget Constraint." *Kyklos* 39: 3–30.

Kraatz, Matthew. 1998. "Learning by Association? Interorganizational Networks and Adaptation to Environmental Change." *Academy of Management Journal* 41: 621–43.

Kraus, Willy. 1991. *Private Business in China: Revival between Ideology and Pragmatism*. Honolulu, HI: University of Hawaii Press.

Kung, James. 1999. "The Evolution of Property Rights in Village Enterprises: The Case of Wuxi County." Pp. 95–120 in *Property Rights and Economic Reform in China*, edited by Jean Oi and Andrew Walder. Stanford, CA: Stanford University Press.

Law, Kenneth, Chi-Sum Wong, Duanxu Wang, and Lihua Wang. 2000. "Effect of Supervisor–Subordinate *Guanxi* on Supervisory Decisions in China: An Empirical Investigation." *International Journal of Human Resource Management* 11: 751–65.

LeVine, Robert, and Donald Campbell. 1972. *Ethnocentrism: Theories of Conflict, Ethnic Attitudes and Group Behavior*. New York, NY: Wiley.

Lévi-Strauss, Claude. 1949 French original/1969 English translation. *The Elementary Structures of Kinship*, translated and edited by J. H. Bell, J. R. von Sturmer, and Rodney Needham. London: Traviston.

Li, Bobai, and Andrew G. Walder. 2001. "Career Advancement as Party Patronage: Sponsored Mobility into the Chinese Administrative Elite." *American Journal of Sociology* 106: 1371–1408.

Li, Cheng. 1994. "University Networks and the Rise of Qinghua Graduates in China's Leadership." *The Australian Journal of Chinese Affairs* 32: 1–30.

Li, Ling. 2011. "Performing Bribery in China: *Guanxi*-Practice, Corruption with a Human Face." *Journal of Contemporary China* 20: 1–20.

Li, Shi, and Chuliang Luo. 2012. "Changes in Household Income Inequality in China: Short-Term Variation and Long-Term Trend." *Comparative Economic & Social Systems* 162: 186–94.

Li, Stan Xiao, Xiaotao Yao, Christina Sue-Chan, and Youmin Xi. 2011. "Where Do Social Ties Come From: Institutional Framework and Governmental Tie Distribution among Chinese Managers." *Management and Organization Review* 7: 97–124.

Lin, Nan. 1982. "Social Resources and Instrumental Action." Pp. 131–47 in *Social Structure and Network Analysis*, edited by Peter Marsden and Nan Lin. Beverly Hills, CA: Sage.

Lin, Nan. 1995. "Local Market Socialism: Rural Reform in China." *Theory and Society* 24: 301–54.

Lin, Nan. 1999. "Social Networks and Status Attainment." *Annual Review of Sociology* 25: 467–88.

Lin, Nan. 2001a. "*Guanxi*: A Conceptual Analysis." Pp. 153–66 in *The Chinese Triangle of Mainland, Taiwan, and Hong Kong: Comparative Institutional Analysis*, edited by Alvin So, Nan Lin, and Dudley Poston. Westport, CT: Greenwood.

Lin, Nan. 2001b. *Social Capital: A Theory of Social Structure and Action*. Cambridge: Cambridge University Press.

Lin, Nan. 2011. "Capitalism in China: A Centrally Managed Capitalism (CMC) and Its Future." *Management and Organization Review* 7: 63–96.

Lin, Nan. 2017. "*Guanxi*: Sentiment-Based Social Exchange." Paper presented at the Sunbelt Conference on Social Network Analysis, Beijing, May 30–June 3.

Lin, Nan, and Dan Ao. 2008. "The Invisible Hand of Social Capital." Pp. 107–32 in *Social Capital: An International Research Program*, edited by Nan Lin and Bonnie Erickson. Oxford: Oxford University Press.

Lin, Nan, Dan Ao, and Lijun Song. 2009. "Production and Return of Social Capital in Urban China." Pp. 107–32 in *Contexts of Social Capital: Social Networks in Communities, Markets, and Organizations*, edited by Ray-May Hsung, Nan Lin, and Ronald Breiger. London: Routledge.

Lin, Nan, and Yanjie Bian. 1991. "Getting Ahead in Urban China." *American Journal of Sociology* 97: 657–88.

Lin, Nan, Yang-chih Fu, and C. Jay Chen (eds.). 2014. *Social Capital and Its Institutional Contingency: A Study of the United States, China and Taiwan.* London: Routledge.

Lin, Nan, and Mary Dumin. 1986. "Access to Occupations Through Social Ties." *Social Networks* 8: 365–85.

Lin, Nan, and Wen Xie. 1988. "Occupational Prestige in Urban China." *American Journal of Sociology* 93: 793–832.

Lin, Yimin. 2001. *Between Politics and Markets: Firms, Competition, and Institutional Change in Post-Mao China.* Cambridge: Cambridge University Press.

Lin, Yimin, and Zhanxin Zhang. 1999. "Backyard Profit Centers: The Private Assets of Public Agencies." Pp. 203–25 in *Property Rights and Economic Reform in China*, edited by Jane Oi and Andrew Walder. Stanford, CA: Stanford University Press.

Liu, Sida, and Terence Halliday. 2011. "Political Liberalism and Political Embeddedness: Understanding Politics in the Work of Chinese Criminal Defense Lawyers." *Law & Society Review* 45: 831–66.

Liu, Yaling. 1992. "Reform from Below: The Private Economy and Local Politics in the Rural Industrialization of Wenzhou." *The China Quarterly* 130: 293–316.

Lo, Ming-Cheng, and Eileen Otis. 2003. "*Guanxi* Civility: Processes, Potentials, and Contingencies." *Politics & Society* 31: 131–62.

Logan, John, and Yanjie Bian. 1993. "Inequalities in Access to Community Resources in a Chinese City." *Social Forces* 72: 555–76.

Lovett, Steve, Lee Simmons, and Raja Kali. 1999. "*Guanxi* Versus the Market: Ethics and Efficiency." *Journal of International Business Studies* 30: 231–47.

Luo, Jar-Der. 2011. "*Guanxi* Revisited: An Exploratory Study of Familiar Ties in a Chinese Workplace." *Management and Organizational Review* 7: 329–51.

Luo, Jar-Der, and Meng-Yu Cheng. 2015. "*Guanxi* Circles' Effect on Organizational Trust: Bringing Power and Vertical Social Exchanges into Intraorganizational Network Analysis." *American Behavioral Scientist* 59: 1024–37.

Luo, Jar-Der, Meng-Yu Cheng, and Tian Zhang. 2016. "*Guanxi* Circle and Organizational Citizenship Behavior: Context of a Chinese Workplace." *Asia Pacific Journal of Management* 33: 649–71.

Luo, Yadong. 2008. "The Changing Chinese Culture and Business Behavior: The Perspective of Intertwinement between *Guanxi* and Corruption." *International Business Review* 17: 188–93.

Luo, Yadong, and Min Chen. 1997. "Does *Guanxi* Influence Firm Performance?" *Asia Pacific Journal of Management* 14: 1–16.

Luo, Yadong, Ying Huang, and Stephanie Lu Wang. 2011. "*Guanxi* and Organizational Performance: A Meta-Analysis." *Management and Organization Review* 8: 139–72.

Macaulay, Stewart. 1963. "Non-Contractual Relations in Business: A Preliminary Study." *American Sociological Review* 28: 55–67.

Marsden, Peter, and Karen Campbell. 1984. "Measuring Tie Strength." *Social Forces* 63: 482–501.

Maurer, Indre, and Mark Ebers. 2006. "Dynamics of Social Capital and Their Performance Implications: Lessons from Biotechnology Start-Ups." *Administrative Science Quarterly* 51: 262–92.

Mauss, Marcel. 1967. *The Gift*. New York, NY, and London: Norton.

McDonald, Steve. 2015. "Network Effects across the Earnings Distribution: Payoffs to Visible and Invisible Job Finding Assistance." *Social Science Research* 49: 299–313.

McKenzie, Robert B., and Gordon Tullock. 1989. *The Best of the New World of Eocnomics*. Homewood, IL: Irwin.

Michelson, Ethan. 2007a. "Climbing the Dispute Pagoda: Grievances and Appeals to the Official Justice System in Rural China." *American Sociological Review* 72: 459–85.

Michelson, Ethan. 2007b. "Lawyers, Political Embeddedness, and Institutional Continuity in China's Transition from Socialism." *American Journal of Sociology* 113: 352–414.

Mitchell, James. 1969. "The Concept and Use of Social Networks." Pp. 1–50 in *Social Networks in Urban Situations*, edited by James Mitchell. New York, NY: Humanities Press.

Mizruchi, Mark, and Joseph Galaskiewicz. 1993. "Networks of Interorganizational Relations." *Sociological Methods & Research* 22: 46–70.

Morita, Ken, and Kazuo Zaiki. 1998. "A Comparative Analysis of Privatization: A Chinese Way and a Polish Way." Pp. 97–106 in *Eastern Europe and the World Economy*, edited by Iliana Zlock-Christy. Northampton, MA: Edward Elgar.

Mouw, Ted. 2003. "Social Capital and Finding a Job: Do Contacts Matter?" *American Sociological Review* 68: 868–98.

Mulvenon, James. 2006. "So Crooked They Have to Screw Their Pants On: New Trends in Chinese Military Corruption." *China Leadership Monitor* 19: 1–8.

Mulvenon, James. 2015. "So Crooked They Have to Screw Their Pants On: Part 3. The Guo Boxiong Edition." *China Leadership Monitor* 48: 1–5.

Nakane, Chie. 1970. *Japanese Society*. Berkeley, CA: University of California Press.

Nash, Rob, Alan Hudson, and Cecilia Luttrell. 2006. *Mapping Political Context: A Toolkit for Civil Society Organisations.* London: Overseas Development Institute.

Naughton, Barry. 2007. *The Chinese Economy: Transitions and Growth.* Cambridge, MA: MIT Press.

Nee, Victor. 1989. "A Theory of Market Transition: From Redistribution to Markets in State Socialism." *American Sociological Review* 54: 663–81.

Nee, Victor. 1992. "Organizational Dynamics of Market Transition: Hybrid Forms, Property Rights, and Mixed Economy in China." *Administrative Science Quarterly* 37: 1–27.

Nee, Victor, and Rebecca Matthews. 1996. "Market Transition and Societal Transformation in Reforming State Socialism." *Annual Review of Sociology* 22: 401–35.

Nee, Victor, and Sonja Opper. 2010. "Political Capital in a Market Economy." *Social Forces* 88: 2105–32.

Nee, Victor, and Sonja Opper. 2012. *Capitalism from Below: Markets and Institutional Change in China.* Cambridge, MA: Harvard University Press.

Newman, Mark, Albert-Laszlo Barabási, and Duncan Watts. 2006. *The Structure and Dynamics of Networks.* Princeton, NJ: Princeton University Press.

Nolan, Jane. 2011. "Good *Guanxi* and Bad *Guanxi*: Western Bankers and the Role of Network Practices in Institutional Change in China." *The International Journal of Human Resource Management* 22: 3357–72.

North, Douglass. 1990. *Institutions, Institutional Change and Economic Performance.* Cambridge: Cambridge University Press.

Obukhova, Elena. 2012. "Motivation vs. Relevance: Using Strong Ties to Find a Job in Urban China." *Social Science Research* 41: 570–80.

Obukhova, Elena, and George Lan. 2013. "Do Job Seekers Benefit from Contacts? A Direct Test with Contemporaneous Searches." *Management Science* 59: 2204–16.

Oi, Jean. 1992. "Fiscal Reform and the Economic Foundations of Local State Corporatism in China." *World Politics* 45: 99–126.

Oi, Jean. 1998. "The Evolution of Local State Corporatism." Pp. 35–61 in *Zouping in Transition: The Process of Reform in Rural North China,* edited by Andrew G. Walder. Cambridge, MA: Harvard University Press.

Oi, Jean. 1999. *Rural China Takes Off: Incentives for Industrialization.* Berkeley and Los Angeles, CA: University of California Press.

Oleinik, Anton. 2004. "A Model of Network Capitalism: Basic Ideas and Post-Soviet Evidence." *Journal of Economic Issues* 38: 85–111.

Parish, William. 1984. "Destratification in China." Pp. 84–120 in *Class and Social Stratification in Post-Revolution China,* edited by James Watson. Cambridge: Cambridge University Press.

Parnell, Michael. 2005. "Chinese Business Guanxi: An Organization or Non-Organization?" *Journal of Organizational Transformation and Social Change* 2: 29–47.

Parsons, Talcott. 1937/1949. *The Structure of Social Action*. New York, NY: Free Press.

Parsons, Talcott, and Edward Shils. 1951. *Toward a General Theory of Action*. Cambridge, MA: Harvard University Press.

Paulson, Henry M. 2015. *Dealing with China*. New York, NY: Twelve.

Pearce II, John, and Richard Robinson Jr. 2000. "Cultivating *Guanxi* as a Foreign Investor Strategy." *Business Horizons* 43: 31–8.

Peng, Yusheng. 2004. "Kingship Networks and Entrepreneurship in China's Transitional Economy." *American Journal of Sociology* 109: 1045–74.

Pfeffer, Jeffrey. 1997. *New Directions for Organization Theory: Problems and Prospects*. New York, NY: Oxford University Press.

Pfeffer, Jeffrey, and Gerald Salancik. 2003. *The External Control of Organizations: A Resource Dependence Perspective*. Stanford, CA: Stanford University Press.

Podolny, Joel. 2005. *Status Signals: A Sociological Study of Market Competition*. Princeton, NJ: Princeton University Press.

Podolny, Joel, and James Baron. 1997. "Resources and Relationships: Social Networks and Mobility in the Workplace." *American Sociological Review* 62: 673–93.

Podolny, Joel, and Karen Page. 1998. "Network Forms of Organization." *Annual Review of Sociology* 24: 57–76.

Portes, Alejandro. 1998. "Social Capital: Its Origins and Applications in Modern Sociology." *Annual Review of Sociology* 24: 1–24.

Powell, Walter. 1990. "Neither Market Nor Hierarchy: Network Forms of Organization." *Research in Organizational Behavior* 12: 295–336.

Prendergast, Canice, and Robert Topel. 1996. "Favoritism in Organizations." *Journal of Political Economy* 104: 958–78.

Putnam, Robert. 2000. *Bowling Alone: The Collapse and Revival of American Community*. New York, NY: Simon & Schuster.

Pye, Lucian. 1992. *The Spirit of Chinese Politics*. Cambridge, MA: Harvard University Press.

Pye, Lucian. 1995. "Factions and the Politics of *Guanxi*: Paradoxes in Chinese Administrative and Political Behaviour." *The China Journal* 34: 35–53.

Redding, Gordon. 1990. *The Spirit of Chinese Capitalism*. Berlin: Walter de Gruyter.

Rees, Albert. 1966. "Information Networks in Labor Markets." *The American Economic Review* 56: 559–66.

Ring, Peter Smith, and Andrew Van de Ven. 1992. "Structuring Cooperative Relationships between Organizations." *Strategic Management Journal* 13: 483–498.

Rosenbaum, Paul, and Donald Rubin. 1983. "The Central Role of the Propensity Score in Observational Studies for Causal Effects." *Biometrika* 70: 41–55.

Ruan, Danching. 1998. "The Content of the GSS Discussion Networks: An Exploration of GSS Discussion Name Generator in a Chinese Context." *Social Networks* 20: 247–64.

Ruan, Danching, and Shu Zhu. 2015. "Birds of a Feather: A Case Study of Friendship Networks of Mainland Chinese College Students in Hong Kong." *American Behavioral Scientist* 59: 1100–14.

Sabin, Lora. 1994. "New Bosses in the Workers' State: The Growth of Non-State Sector Employment in China." *The China Quarterly* 140: 944–70.

Sahlins, Marshall. 1965/1972. "On the Sociology of Primitive Exchange." Pp. 139–236 in *The Relevance of Models for Social Anthropology*, edited by Michael Banton. London: Tavistock.

Saloner, Garth. 1985. "Old Boy Networks as Screening Mechanisms." *Journal of Labor Economics* 3: 255–67.

Scandura, Terri, and George Graen. 1984. "Moderating Effects of Initial Leader–Member Exchange Status on the Effects of a Leadership Intervention." *Journal of Applied Psychology* 69: 428–36.

Schmidt, D. A. 2008. "Internal and External Logics of Abstract Interpretations." *International Conference on Verification Proceedings* 16: 263–78.

Scott, Richard. 2005. "Institutional Theory: Contributing to a Theoretical Research Program." Pp. 460–84 in *Great Minds in Management: The Process of Theory Development*, edited by Kenneth Smith and Michael Hitt. New York, NY: Oxford University Press.

Seidel, Marc-David, Jeffrey Polzer, and Katherine Stewart. 2000. "Friends in High Places: The Effects of Social Networks on Discrimination in Salary Negotiations." *Administrative Science Quarterly* 45: 1–24.

Shi, Yigong, and Yi Rao. 2010. "China's Research Culture." *Science* 329: 1128.

Shirk, Susan. 1993. *The Political Logic of Economic Reform in China*. Berkeley, CA: University of California Press.

Shirk, Susan. 2007. *China: Fragile Superpower*. Berkeley, CA: University of California Press.

Smart, Alan. 1993. "Gifts, Bribes, and *Guanxi*: A Reconsideration of Bourdieu's Social Capital." *Cultural Anthropology* 8: 388–408.

Snell, Robin, and Choo Sin Tseng. 2002. "Moral Atmosphere and Moral Influence under China's Network Capitalism." *Organization Studies* 23: 449–78.

So, Alvin. 2003. "The Changing Patterns of Classes and Class Conflict in China." *Journal of Contemporary Asia* 33: 363–76.

Son, Joonmo, and Nan Lin. 2012. "Network Diversity, Contact Diversity, and Status Attainment." *Social Networks* 34: 601–13.

Sorensen, Aage B. 2001. "The Basic Concepts of Stratification Research." Pp. 287–300 in *Social Stratification: Class, Race, and Gender in Sociological Perspective* (2nd edition), edited by David B. Grusky. Boulder, CO: Westview Press.

Suchman, Mark, and Lauren Edelman. 1996. "Legal Rational Myths: The New Institutionalism and the Law and Society Tradition." *Law & Social Inquiry* 21: 903–41.

Tian, Felicia, and Nan Lin. 2016. "Weak Ties, Strong Ties, and Job Mobility in Urban China: 1978–2008." *Social Networks* 44: 117–29.

Tönnies, Ferdinand. 1887 original/1957 English translation. *Community and Society*. East Lansing, MI: Michigan State University Press.

Tsui, Anne, Yanjie Bian, and Leonard Cheng. 2006. *China's Domestic Private Firms: Multidisciplinary Perspectives on Management and Performance*. New York, NY: M. E. Sharpe.

Tsui, Anne, and Chung-Ming Lau. 2002. "Research on the Management of Enterprises in the People's Republic of China: Current Status and Future Directions." Pp. 1–27 in *The Management of Enterprises in the People's Republic of China*, edited by Anne Tsui and Chung-Ming Lau. Boston, MA: Kluwer Academic.

Tu, I. C. 1991. "Family Enterprises in Taiwan." Pp. 114–25 in *Business Networks and Economic Development in Southeast Asia*, edited by George Hamilton. Hong Kong: University of Hong Kong, Centre of Asian Studies.

Tu, Weiming. 1993. *Way, Learning, and Politics: Essays on the Confucian Intellectual*. Albany, NY: State University of New York Press.

Tu, Weiming (ed.). 1994. *The Living Tree: The Changing Meaning of Being Chinese Today*. Stanford, CA: Stanford University Press.

Tung, Rosalie, and Verner Worm. 2001. "Network Capitalism: The Role of Human Resources in Penetrating the China Market." *The International Journal of Human Resource Management* 12: 517–34.

Verbrugge, Lois. 1979. "Multiplexity in Adult Friendships." *Social Forces* 57: 1286–1309.

Vogel, Ezra. 1965. "From Friendship to Comradeship: The Change in Personal Relations in Communist China." *The China Quarterly* 22: 46–60.

Vogel, Ezra. 1990. *One Step Ahead in China: Guangdong Under Reform*. Cambridge, MA: Harvard University Press.

Walder, Andrew. 1986. *Communist Neo-Traditionalism: Work and Authority in Chinese Industry*. Berkeley, CA: University of California Press.

Walder, Andrew. 1992. "Property Rights and Stratification in Socialist Redistributive Economies." *American Sociological Review* 57: 524–39.

Walder, Andrew. 1995. "Career Mobility and the Communist Political Order." *American Sociological Review* 60: 309–28.

Walder, Andrew, and Jean Oi. 1999. "Property Rights in the Chinese Economy: Contours of the Process of Change Property Rights and Economic Reform in China." Pp. 1–24 in *Property Rights in Transitional Economies: Insights from Research on China*, edited by Jean Oi and Andrew Walder. Stanford, CA: Stanford University Press.

Wang, Barbara X., and Chris Rowley. 2016. "Business Networks and the Emergence of *Guanxi* Capitalism in China: The Role of the 'Invisible Hand.'" Pp. 93–118 in *Business Networks in East Asian Capitalisms*, edited by Jane Nolan, Chris Rowley, and Malcolm Warner. London: Chandos.

Wang, Peng. 2016. "Military Corruption in China: The Role of *Guanxi* in the Buying and Selling of Military Positions." *The China Quarterly* 228: 970–91.

Wank, David. 1995. "Bureaucratic Patronage and Private Business: Changing Networks of Power in Urban China." Pp. 153–83 in *The Waning of the Communist State: Economic Origins of Political Decline in China and Hungary*, edited by Andrew G. Walder. Berkeley, CA: University of California Press.

Wank, David. 1996. "The Institutional Process of Market Clientelism: *Guanxi* and Private Business in a South China City." *China Quarterly* 147: 820–38.

Wank, David. 1999. *Commodifying Communism: Business, Trust, and Politics in a Chinese City*. New York, NY: Cambridge University Press.

Warner, Malcolm. 2010. "In Search of Confucian HRM: Theory and Practice in Greater China and Beyond." *International Journal of Human Resource Management* 21: 2053–78.

Warner, Malcolm. 2014. *Understanding Chinese Management: Past, Present, and Future*. London and New York, NY: Routledge.

Wellman, Barry. 1988. "Structural Analysis: From Method and Metaphor to Theory and Substance." Pp. 19–61 in *Social Structures: A Network Approach*, edited by Barry Wellman and S. D. Berkowitz. Cambridge: Cambridge University Press.

Wellman, Barry. 2001. "Computer Networks as Social Networks." *Science* 293: 2031–4.

Wellman, Barry, Wenhong Chen, and Weizhen Dong. 2002. "Networking *Guanxi*." Pp. 221–42 in *Social Connections in China: Institutions, Culture, and the Changing Nature of Guanxi*, edited by Thomas Gold, Doug Guthrie, and David Wank. New York, NY: Cambridge University Press.

Whyte, Martin King. 1995. "The Social Roots of China's Economic Development." *The China Quarterly* 144: 999–1019.

Whyte, Martin King. 1996. "The Chinese Family and Economic Development: Obstacle or Engine?" *Economic Development & Cultural Change* 45: 1–30.

Whyte, Martin King, and William Parish. 1984. *Urban Life in Contemporary China*. Chicago, IL: University of Chicago Press.

Williamson, Oliver. 1981. "The Economics of Organization: The Transaction Cost Approach." *American Journal of Sociology* 87: 548–77.

Wong, Yui-Tim, Shiu-Ho Wong, and Yui-Woon Wong. 2010. "A Study of Subordinate–Supervisor *Guanxi* in Chinese Joint Ventures." *International Journal of Human Resource Management* 21: 2142–55.

Wu, Jieh-min. 1998. *Local Property Rights Regime in Socialist Reform: A Case Study of China's Informal Privatization*. Doctoral thesis, Department of Political Science, Columbia University.

Xiao, Zhixing, and Anne Tsui. 2007. "When Brokers May Not Work: The Cultural Contingency of Social Capital in Chinese High-Tech Firms." *Administrative Science Quarterly* 52: 1–31.

Xin, Katherine, and Jone Pearce. 1996. "*Guanxi*: Connections as Substitutes for Formal Institutional Support." *Academy of Management Journal* 39: 1641–58.

Yan, Yunxiang. 1996. *The Flow of Gifts Reciprocity and Social Networks in a Chinese Village*. Stanford, CA: Stanford University Press.

Yang, Ching-Kun. 1959 original/1965 2nd edition. *The Chinese Family in the Communist Revolution*. Cambridge, MA: Harvard University Press.

Yang, Dali. 2004. *Remaking the Chinese Leviathan: Market Transition and the Politics of Governance in China*. Stanford, CA: Stanford University Press.

Yang, Mayfair Mei-hui. 1994. *Gifts, Favors, and Banquets: The Art of Social Relationships in China*. Ithaca, NY: Cornell University Press.

Yang, Mayfair Mei-hui. 2002. "The Resilience of *Guanxi* and Its New Deployments: A Critique of Some New *Guanxi* Scholarship." *The China Quarterly* 170: 459–76.

Yen, Dorothy, Bradley Barnes, and Chenglu Wang. 2011. "The Measurement of *Guanxi*: Introducing the GRX Scale." *Industrial Marketing Management* 40: 97–108.

Young, Susan. 1995. *Private Business and Economic Reform in China*. Armonk, NY: M. E. Sharpe.

Zang, Xiaowei. 2001. "University Education, Party Seniority, and Elite Recruitment in China." *Social Science Research* 30: 62–75.

Zhang, Lei. 2016. *Business Performance of Chinese Enterprises in a Relational Perspective*, Doctoral thesis, Department of Sociology, University of Minnesota.

Zhao, Wei. 2013. "Social Networks, Job Search and Income Disparity in a Transitional Economy: An Institutional Embeddedness Argument." *Research in the Sociology of Work* 24: 103–32.

Zhou, Xueguang, Qiang Li, Wei Zhao, and He Cai. 2003. "Embeddedness and Contractual Relationships in China's Transition Economy." *American Sociological Review* 68: 75–102.

Zhou, Xueguang, Nancy Tuma, and Phyllis Moen. 1996. "Stratification Dynamics Under State Socialism: The Case of Urban China, 1949–1993." *Social Forces* 74: 759–96.

Zhou, Xueguang, Nancy Tuma, and Phyllis Moen. 1997. "Institutional Change and Job-Shift Patterns in Urban China, 1949 to 1994." *American Sociological Review* 62: 339–65.

Zhu, Ying, Malcolm Warner, and Chris Rowley. 2007. "Human Resource Management with 'Asian' Characteristics: A Hybrid People-Management System in East Asia." *The International Journal of Human Resource Management* 18: 745–68.

Chinese-Language References

Albrow, Martin. 2017. "Pragmatic Universalism and Change of the Global Age." Review of *Social Sciences in China* 1: 5–8. 马丁.阿尔布劳，"实用普遍主义与全球时代的变迁"《中国社会科学评价》2017年1期，第5–8页。

Bian, Yanjie. 2010. "Relational Sociology and Its Academic Significance." *Journal of Xi'an Jiaotong University (Social Sciences)* 30 (May): 1–6. 边燕杰，"关系社会学及其学科地位"，《西安交通大学学报》（社会科学版）2017年第3期，第1–6页。

Bian, Yanjie, and Xiaoxian Guo. 2015. "Social Eating and Drinking Networks and Their Social Exchange Functions: A Comparative Analysis of China, Japan, and Korea." *Academic Exchange* 251: 152–9. 边燕杰、郭小弦，"餐饮网社交功能的中日韩比较"，《学术交流》，2015年第2期，第152–9页。

Bian, Yanjie, and Ming Lei. 2017. "Between Virtual and Actual: The Generation of Social Capital from Cyberspace." *Jilin University Journal of Social Science* 57: 81–91. 边燕杰、雷鸣，"虚实之间：社会资本从虚拟空间到实体空间的转换"，《吉林大学学报》（社会科学），2017年第3期，第81–91页。

Bian, Yanjie, and Haixiong Qiu. 2000. "Social Capital of the Firm and Its Significance." *Chinese Social Sciences* 2 (March): 87–99. 边燕杰、丘海雄，"企业的社会资本及其功效"《中国社会科学》2000年第2期，第87–99页。

Bian, Yanjie, Wenhong Zhang, and Cheng Cheng. 2012. "A Social Network Model of Job-Search Processes: Testing the *Guanxi* Effect Hypothesis." *Chinese Journal of Sociology* 3: 24–7. 边燕杰、张文宏、程诚，2012年，"求职过程的社会网络模型：检验关系效应假设"《社会》第3期，第24–7页。

Bian, Yanjie, and Li Zong (eds.). 2016. *Western China in Transition: Development and Social Governance*. Beijing: Social Science Press. 边燕杰、宗力主编，2016，《转型中的西部中国：发展现状与社会治理》。北京：社会科学出版社。

CCPCC (Chinese Communist Party Central Committee). 2014. *Regulations on the Selection and Appointment of Party and Administrative Officials*. Beijing: CCPCC Documents Press. 中共中央，2014，《党政领导干部选拔任用工作条例》。北京：中央文献出版社。

Chen, Junjie, and Zhen Chen. 1998. "Rethinking the Mode of Differential Asso-ciations." *Social Science Frontline* 1: 197–204. 陈俊杰、陈震，"'差序格局'再思考"《社会科学战线》1998年第5期，第197–204页。

Chinese Academy of Social Sciences. 2017. *Urban Bluebook: China's Urban Development Report No. 10*. Beijing: Social Science Academics Press. 中国社会科学院，2017年，《城市蓝皮书：中国城市发展报告No. 10》。北京：社会科学文献出版社。

Feng, Junqi. 2010. *Cadre in Central County*. Doctoral thesis, Department of Sociology, Peking University. 冯军旗，《中县干部》，北京大学社会学系博士论文，2010年。

Fushi. 2006. *Celadon*. Changsha: Hunan Wenyi Press. 浮石，《青瓷》，长沙：湖南文艺出版社，2006年。

Geng, Biao. 2009. *Geng Biao Memoirs*. Beijing: China Book Company. 耿飚，《耿飚回忆录》，北京：中华书局出版社，2009年。

Hao, Mingsong. 2016. *The Social-Network Effect and Its Limit: A Study on Job-Worker Matching*. Doctoral thesis, Department of Sociology, Xi'an Jiaotong University. 郝明松，《社会网络的作用及其边界：基于人职匹配视角的研究》，西安交通大学社会学系博士论文，2016年。

He, Xuefeng. 2007. "The Mode of Differential Associations and Regional Differences in Governance of Village Community." *Journal of Jianghai* 4: 114–17. 何贺峰，"差序格局与乡村治理的区域差异"《江海学刊》2007年第4期，第114–17页。

Lei, Ming. 2018. *Guanxi-Sponsored Mobility Inside Work Organizations*. Department of Sociology, Xi'an Jiaotong University. 雷鸣，《工作组织中的关系庇护性流动研究》，西安交通大学社会学系博士论文，2018年。

Li, Qiang. 2005. "On Western Theories of Middle Class and the Status Quo of China's Middle Class Today." *Chinese Journal of Sociology* 1: 28–42. 李强"西方中产阶级理论与中国阶级现状"《社会》2005年第1期第28–42页。

Liang, Shuming. 1949 original/1986 reprint. *The Essential Meanings of Chinese Culture*. Hong Kong: Zheng Zhong Press. 梁漱溟，《中国文化要义》，香港：正中出版社，1949年；1986年再版。

Lin, Nan, Chih-jou Jay Chen, and Yang-chih Fu. 2010. "Types and Effects of Social Relationship in a Three-Way Comparison: Taiwan, the United States, and Chinese Mainland." *Taiwanese Journal of Sociology* 45: 117–62. 林南、陳志柔、傅仰止，"社會關係的類型與效應：台灣、美國、中國大陸的三地比較"《台灣社會學刊》第45卷第117–62頁。

Liu, Weifeng, Yunsong Chen, and Yanjie Bian. 2016. "Occupational Interaction and Income: A Social Capital Study Using the First-Order Difference Analysis." *Journal of Sociological Studies* 182: 34–56. 刘伟峰、陈云松、边燕杰，

"中国人的职场交往与收入：基于差分方法的社会资本分析"《社会学研究》总182期第34–56页。

Nie, Rongzhen. 2007. *Memoirs of Nie Rongzhen*. Beijing: PLA Publishing House. 聂荣臻，《聂荣臻回忆录》，北京：解放军出版社，2007年。

Pan, Guangdan. 1993. *Collection of Essays by Pan Guangdan*. Beijing: Peking University Press. 潘光旦，《潘光旦全集》，北京：北京大学出版社，1993年。

Shi, Xianmin. 1993. *The Breakthrough of the System*. Beijing: Chinese Social Science Press. 时宪民，《体制的突破》，北京：中国社会科学出版社，1993年。

Sun, Liping. 1996. "*Guanxi*, Social Relations, and Social Structure." *Journal of Sociological Research* 5: 20–30. 孙立平，"'关系'、社会关系与社会结构"《社会学研究》1996年第5期，第20–30页。

Wu, Jinglian. 2003. *Economic Reforms in Contemporary China*. Shanghai: Shanghai Yuan Dong Press. 吴敬琏，《当代中国经济改革》，上海：上海远东出版社，2003年。

Wu, Si. 2009. *Hidden Rules of Officialdom in Ancient China*. Shanghai: Fudan University Press. 吴思，《潜规则》，复旦大学出版社，2009年。

Xi, Jinping. 2018. *Secure a Decisive Victory in Building a Moderately Prosperous Society in All Respects and Strive for the Great Success of Socialism with Chinese Characteristics for a New Era: Delivered at the 19th National Congress of the Communist Party of China*. Beijing: People's Press. 习近平，2018，《决胜全面建成小康社会夺取新时代中国特色社会主义伟大胜利——在中国共产党第十九次全国代表大会上的报告》（2017年10月18日）。

Xiao, Ying. 2014. "The Mode of Differential Associations and the Transition of Chinese Society toward Modernity". *Exploration and Contention* 6: 48–54. 肖瑛，"差序格局与中国社会的现代转型"，《探索与争鸣》第6期第48–54页。

Yan, Yunxiang. 2006. "The Mode of Differential Associations and the Status Perception in Chinese Culture." *Journal of Sociological Research* 4: 201–45. 阎云翔，"差序格局与中国文化的等级观"《社会学研究》2006年第4期，第201–45页。

Zhang, Guotao. 1980. *My Memories*. Beijing: People's Publishing House. 张国焘，《我的回忆》，北京：人民出版社，1980年。

Zhang, Houyi. 1999. *Report on the Development of Chinese Private Enterprises*. 张厚义，《中国私营企业发展报告》，中国社会科学文献出版社，1999年。

Zhang, Houyi, et al. 2015. "Private Businesses and Employment Relations in China: A Research Report of 2015." 张厚义等，《中国个体私营经济与就业关系研究报告》2015年，http://news.hexun.com/2015-10-30/180239926.html.

Zhang, Wenhong. 2011a. "A 30-Year Research in Social Network and Social Capital in China (Part 1)." *Jianghai Academic Journal* 1: 104–12. 张文宏，"中国社会网络与社会资本研究30年(上)"《江海学刊》2011年第1期第104–12页。

Zhang, Wenhong. 2011b. "A 30-Year Research in Social Network and Social Capital in China (Part 2)." *Jianghai Academic Journal* 2: 96–106. 张文宏，"中国社会网络与社会资本研究30年(下)"《江海学刊》2011年第2期第96–106页。

Zhou, Feizhou. 2017. "Ethical Behavior and Guanxi Society: The Chinese Path to Sociology." *Journal of Sociological Research* 1: 41–62. 周飞舟，"行动伦理与"关系社会"—社会学中国化的路径"，《社会学研究》2017年第1期第41–62页。

Zhou, Xueguang. 2017. *The Institutional Logic of State Governance in China.* Beijing: Sanlian Books. 周雪光，《中国国家治理的制度逻辑》，北京：生活·读书·新知三联书店。

Index